T

DISCOURSE AND IDEOLOGY
IN NABOKOV'S PROSE

"The book will be highly controversial and widely read. I admire its audacity. It may well inaugurate a new era in Nabokov Studies ... The field needs this book and the arguments it will provoke."

Eric Naiman, *University of California, Berkeley*

"These essays finally quash the naive view that Nabokov's writings – especially *Lolita*, *Pale Fire* and the bewitching short stories – are free ideological zones, neutral and vacant. Students of the Nabokovian text, as well as Russian literature in the twentieth century, will want to consult this anthology before they ponder their next Nabokovian tactic."

George Sebastian Rousseau, Oxford, England

The prose writings of Vladimir Nabokov form one of the most intriguing oeuvres of the twentieth century. His novels, which include *Despair*, *Lolita* and *Pale Fire*, have been celebrated for their stylistic artistry, their formal complexity, and their unique treatment of themes of memory, exile, loss, and desire.

This collection of essays offers readings of several novels as well as discussions of Nabokov's exchange of views about literature with Edmund Wilson, and his place in 1960s and contemporary popular culture.

The volume brings together a diverse group of Nabokovian readers, of widely divergent scholarly backgrounds, interests, and approaches. Together they shift the focus from the manipulative games of author and text to the restless and sometimes resistant reader, and suggest new ways of enjoying these endlessly fascinating texts.

David H. J. Larmour is Professor of Classics and Comparative Literature at Texas Tech University. He co-edited *Russian Literature and the Classics* (1996) and since 1997 has been one of the editors of the journal *INTER-TEXTS*.

STUDIES IN RUSSIAN AND EUROPEAN LITERATURE

ROUTLEDGE HARWOOD

A series edited by

Peter I. Barta
University of Surrey
and
David Shepherd
University of Sheffield

DISCOURSE AND IDEOLOGY IN NABOKOV'S PROSE

Edited by

David H. J. Larmour

London and New York

First published 2002
by Routledge
11 New Fetter Lane, London EC4P 4EE

Simultaneously published in the USA and Canada
by Routledge
29 West 35th Street, New York, NY 10001

Routledge is an imprint of the Taylor & Francis Group

Typeset in Sabon by Wearset Ltd, Boldon, Tyne and Wear
Printed and bound in Great Britain by MPG Books Ltd, Bodmin

British Library Cataloguing in Publication Data
A catalogue record for this book is available from the British Library

Library of Congress Cataloging in Publication Data
A catalog record for this book has been requested

ISBN 0-415-28658-1

CONTENTS

CONTENTS

CONTRIBUTORS

Galya Diment is Professor in the Department of Slavic Languages and Literatures, University of Washington. She is the author of *The Autobiographical Novel of Co-consciousness: Goncharov, Woolf and Joyce* (Florida 1994) and *Pniniad: Vladimir Nabokov and Marc Szeftel* (Washington 1997) and edited *Between Heaven and Hell: The Myth of Siberia in Russian Culture* (with Yuri Slezkine) (St. Martin's 1993) and *Goncharov's Oblomov: A Critical Companion* (Northwestern 1998). She has also written numerous articles, many on Nabokov. She is currently president of the International Vladimir Nabokov Society and co-editor of NABOKV-L, the Nabokov e-mail discussion forum.

D. Barton Johnson is Professor Emeritus of Russian at the University of California at Santa Barbara. Twice president of the International Vladimir Nabokov Society, he is the founding editor of the journal *Nabokov Studies* and NABOKV-L. The Russian translation of his 1985 *Worlds in Regression* will soon appear as part of a new series of classic Nabokov monographs.

David H. J. Larmour is Professor of Classics and Comparative Literature at Texas Tech University. He is the author of *Lucian's Science Fiction Novel: True Histories* (Brill 1998) and *Stage and Stadium: Drama and Athletics in Ancient Greece* (Weidmann 1999), and co-editor of *Russian Literature and the Classics* (Harwood 1996) and *Rethinking Sexuality: Foucault and the Ancient World* (Princeton 1998). He has written articles on *Lolita, Bend Sinister, The Return of Chorb*, and Nabokov's "Ovidian Metamorphoses." He is one of the editors of *Intertexts*, a journal of Comparative Literature and theoretical reflection.

Paul Allen Miller is Director of Comparative Literature and Associate Professor of Classics at the University of South Carolina. He is the author of *Lyric Texts and Lyric Consciousness* (Routledge 1994) and co-editor of *Bahktin and Ancient Studies* (Arethusa 1993), *Rethinking Sexuality: Foucault and the Ancient World* (Princeton 1998) as well as of *Carnivalizing Difference: Bakhtin and the Other* (Routledge 2001). His *Latin Erotic Elegy: An Anthology and Reader* will be published by Routledge in 2002.

Tony Moore is a Lecturer in modern drama, contemporary drama, and twentieth-century American poetry at Boston University. He was educated at the University of London (BA, MA) and Boston University (PhD). He is completing a reappraisal of Robert Lowell and some contemporaries which defines poetic revision as a positive principle of creativity. Before concentrating on academic work, he spent thirty-five years in commerce and was CEO of international food companies based in Britain.

Elizabeth Patnoe is an adjunct Professor in the Department of English at Ohio Wesleyan University and an R.N., now practicing as a neuropsychiatric nurse. Her major work-in-progress, *Dying for the End: Fiction, Reality, and Female Suicide*, explores the relationships between real and fictional suicide.

Galina Rylkova is Assistant Professor of Russian Studies at the University of Florida. Her publications include articles on Tolstoy, Nabokov, Pil'niak, Viktor Erofeev and cultural memory of the Russian Silver Age.

Suellen Stringer-Hye is a digital librarian at the Jean and Alexander Heard Library, Vanderbilt University. She has written "Nabokov and Popular Culture," "Nabokov and Melville," as well as articles on *Ada*. She is also the creator and compiler of VNCollations, a regular column on NABOKV-L of references to Nabokov from popular online and print sources. Additionally, she edits the CoLOlations web page for the premier Nabokov website, Zembla. She interviewed Stephen Schiff, screenwriter of Adrian Lyne's film adaptation of *Lolita* as well as Stacy Schiff, author of the Pulitzer Prize-winning biography of Vera Nabokov, *Zembla*.

Brian D. Walter teaches English and Film Studies at Washington University. His work has previously appeared in *Boulevard*, *Nabokov Studies*, and *American Studies International*.

ACKNOWLEDGMENTS

At the annual meeting of the American Association for the Advancement of Slavic Studies in Honolulu in 1994, I participated in a panel on Nabokov. After the discussion at the end of the presentations, I decided it was time for a conference which would focus on the ideological underpinnings of the Nabokovian text and authorized modes of interpretation. On-the-spot encouragement came from one of my fellow-panelists, Galya Diment, and from Peter I. Barta, who was then my colleague and Director of Russian Language and Area Studies at Texas Tech University. I am grateful to both of them for their enthusiastic support of this undertaking.

In 1995 a conference on Discourse and Ideology in Nabokov's Prose took place at Texas Tech University. Several of my colleagues in the Department of Classical and Modern Languages and Literatures – Paul Allen Miller, Sharon Nell, Susan Stein, and Lewis Tracy – provided invaluable assistance throughout the event, as did a number of undergraduates studying Russian. In planning the conference, I received helpful advice from Donald Barton Johnson, who continued to give me the benefit of his knowledge in later years as I prepared the papers for publication. To all of these individuals, I would like to express my most sincere gratitude.

I thank the editors of the series *Studies in Russian and European Literature*, Peter I. Barta, now at the University of Surrey, and David Shepherd, at the University of Sheffield, for inviting me to publish *Discourse and Ideology in Nabokov's Prose*. Thanks are due also to those who read and evaluated the manuscript along the way: Stephen Hutchings, Eric Naiman, David Rampton, and George Rousseau. Michael Wells helped me compile the index. At Routledge, I have been ably assisted by Liz Thompson.

Last but not least, now that this volume is finally emerging, I wish to thank all the contributors for their co-operation and, especially, their patience. It has been a pleasure to work with such a diverse and interesting group of scholars, each with a unique perspective on Nabokov's oeuvre.

INTRODUCTION
Collusion and collision

David H. J. Larmour

This volume arises from a conference held at Texas Tech University in 1995 on the topic of "Discourse and Ideology in Vladimir Nabokov's Prose." That event was motivated by a belief that the ideological underpinnings of Nabokov's novels are a suitable area of investigation from a perspective which holds that all such texts both embody and promulgate a certain view of the world and how we organize our understanding of it.[1] The theme of the conference was underpinned by two interpretative positions: first, that ideology is a web of discursive effects in the real world of the reader's lived experience, and second, that these effects are brought about by the operations of power. Discourse and ideology are linked here through the phenomenon of power, but not without an awareness of the complex nature of the interaction between the two terms. The complexity arises in part from the definitional fluidity of each, charted in recent studies by Sara Mills (1997) in the case of discourse and by Terry Eagleton (1991) for ideology. Significantly, both Chapter 2 of Mills's study and Chapter 7 of Eagleton's are entitled "Discourse and Ideology," a conjunction which bears eloquent testimony to the close association between the two terms and the interpretive strategies they have engendered. Nonetheless, such combinations remain problematic. For some practitioners and theorists of discourse analysis, for instance, discourse and discursively-based criticism are to be differentiated from ideology and ideologically-based methodologies by styling ideology as essentially a matter of "false consciousness," that is to say, false ideas which strive to legitimize the interests of a dominant social class or political power structure. Thus, it is possible for Roger Fowler to describe discourse as "speech or writing seen from the point of view of the beliefs, values and categories which it embodies; these beliefs etc. constitute a way of looking at the world, an organization or presentation of experience – 'ideology' in the *neutral, non-pejorative sense*" (Fowler 1990, 54; Hawthorn 1992, 48; emphasis added). Such a definition of discourse relies heavily on several elements that are

1

integral to some of the more nuanced understandings of ideology in contemporary theory, but then seeks to distance itself by reducing ideology to the basic Marxist formulation of false consciousness. Mills works within a broadly similar paradigm, as we can see from her discussion of the differences between ideological critics and discourse theorists in their approaches to sexism in language:

> within an ideological view, sexism would be seen as a form of false consciousness, a way that subjects were, in Althusserian terms, interpellated, that is called upon to recognise themselves as certain types of gendered subjects ... whilst this is a useful first stage in analysing sexism, one which enables us to recognise the process whereby sexism comes to feel "natural" or dominant within a culture, it does not allow us any real sense of how it would be possible to intervene and change that process.
>
> (Mills 1997, 44–45)

The key to such intervention and change, she suggests, lies in the recognition, predicated upon Foucault's rejection of the "repressive hypothesis," that power is not simply an infringement of the rights of one individual or group by another, but something which is to be held or taken away, fought for or relinquished, struggled against or submitted to. If we conceive of discourse in this Foucauldian mode, the analysis of discursive practices is inevitably an act of contestation because, as Foucault puts it:

> Discourses are not once and for all subservient to power or raised up against it, any more than silences are. We must make allowances for the complex and unstable process whereby discourse can be both an instrument and an effect of power, but also a hindrance, a stumbling block, a point of resistance and a starting point for an opposing strategy. Discourse transmits and produces power; it reinforces it, but also undermines it and exposes it, renders it fragile and makes it possible to thwart it.
>
> (Foucault 1978, 100–101; Mills 1997, 42–45)

And yet, it is difficult to insist that ideologically-based criticism cannot be as effectively interventionist or challenging as that which arises from discourse analysis, especially if we consider ideology as a fundamentally discursive phenomenon. This is the point of Eagleton's proposition that ideology may be viewed "less as a particular set of discourses, than as a particular set of effects *within* discourses" (Eagleton 1991, 194) and that it "represents the points where power impacts upon certain utterances and inscribes itself tacitly within them" (p. 223). In seeking to analyze discourse and ideology in Nabokov's prose, then, this volume posits an encounter between the reader and a set of ideological structures which are manifest in the discursive utterances and practices in and around the novels and short stories under discussion. The purpose is not to offer an exhaustive examination of Nabokovian Discourse or Nabokovian Ideology – which would, of course, have to be situated within their larger cultural contexts in order to be properly delineated and understood – but rather to suggest some lines of enquiry by which their exclusionary, naturalizing, and manipulative devices may be comprehended.

The title, *Discourse and Ideology in Nabokov's Prose* draws attention to the system of power relations in which the author, text, and reader are enmeshed, and to its constitution as an arena of negotiation and contestation. It also seeks to shift the emphasis away from author-based criticism to a form of critical practice in which the author is no longer – either explicitly or implicitly – the validator of meaning in the text, but is instead an author-function, a "principle of grouping of discourses, conceived as the unity and origin of their meaning" (Foucault 1981, 58; cf. Barthes 1986). It may be difficult for some to accept, in Barthes's terms, the death of an author as determinedly present as Nabokov has proved to be, but this would seem to be a necessary first step if as readers we are to liberate ourselves from discursive constraints and the threatened imposition of ideological unities. Nabokovian discourse needs to be understood in this context not only as the aggregate of statements or individualizable groups of statements in the texts arranged around the author-function, but also as the regulated practices that account for a number of statements, both in these texts and in the commentaries written upon them by Nabokovian critics and scholars.[2]

The call for papers for this conference was an attempt to solicit readings which would discuss and expose the operations of Nabokovian discourse and its ideological resonances, with special reference to gender and sexuality, politics and history, and social and cultural structures. The fact that Nabokov's novels have generally been treated as works of self-conscious artifice which are somehow ideologically neutral makes the case for such readings even more compelling. For many readers, it is clear that terms like "smokescreen" and "distortion" are just as meaningful as the talismans of traditional Nabokov criticism, "play" and "artifice." Such reactions are symptomatic of the broader issue of how to map the operations of Nabokovian discourse and, in particular, its representation of men and women, socio-economic classes, nationalities (especially Russian, German, and American), sexualities, and political views (those either congenial or inimical to those of the authorial organizing consciousness). The task necessitates a shift of emphasis from language as signification and play to the scrutiny of the inscription of ideological and discursive strategies in language, in other words from a reading position of collusion with the text to one of collision.

The Latin verb *colludo* (*cum* + *ludo*) means to "play with" and "have a secret understanding with (often to the detriment of a third party)," giving us our English "collude"; the similar sounding verb *collido* (*cum* + *lido*) means to "strike against" or "bring into conflict with."[3] Both words have judicial overtones: they are connected with the discovery of truth, who did what to whom, where, when, and why. The Roman rhetorician Quintilian remarks in his *Institutes of Oratory* that there is often a collision between written testimony (*testatio*) and that of witnesses actually present (*testes*): *saepe inter se collidi solent inde testatio, hic testes* (5.7.32); the former is liable to be perceived as clever manipulation of the facts, while the word of the latter can be questioned on several grounds. In the act of reading, there is a similar encounter, between the text's testimony about the world and the reader's own witnessing of experience. We read with a mixture of collusion and collision with the ideology of any text: if the reader were to collude all the time, reading would be a self-satisfying, but presumably unstimulating, way of spending time; if the reader were to collide all the time, reading, for all the enlightenment it might produce, would become an exhausting and ultimately unpleasant activity.

Collusion-based and collision-based readings are of course productive of different types of scholarship and interpretation. The dominant discourse of the Nabokovian text clearly invites collusion rather than collision, created as it is by one of the master game-players of our era. There is a widespread interpretative tendency, grounded partly in the author's own prescriptions about art, life, and literary criticism, to regard Nabokov's novels as self-reflexive linguistic games, which have only a tangential or nebulous association with the phenomenal world.[4] This leads us to chase down allusions, follow up references, and celebrate the jouissance of a supposedly pure artifice. The pleasure afforded by these pursuits has produced a whole troop of Enchanted Hunters, who have demonstrated not only Nabokov's but also their own considerable learning and detective powers.[5] And there is no doubt that the Nabokovian text works very hard to ensure that the reader "plays the game," guided more often than not by an authorial – and "authorizing" – Introduction.

What exactly is a game, however? A game depends on rules and conventions, established by an authority, which the players consent to follow. A game can also be an exercise in dominating or defeating an opponent.[6] Nancy Morrow demonstrates that the nineteenth-century realist novel is a genre which emphasizes the games of characters (i.e. plot games) and suppresses two other games: those between the reader and the text and between the narrator and the characters (Morrow 1988, 22). Nabokov, in common with other twentieth-century writers like Borges and Joyce, does not suppress these latter two forms of the game, but actually flaunts them.[7] The result of this, however, is not only that the games of the characters are correspondingly "played down"; the effect is also to conceal something about the text itself: its ideological assumptions and discursive operations. Thus, when David Rampton distinguishes between criticism which "ranges over" Nabokov's writing and that which attempts to "pierce" it, he asks the following questions about these texts: "What kind of reality do they depict? What kind of meaning do they posit? What kind of truth do they tell about Nabokov and the world?" (Rampton 1984, Pref. vii). A critical approach which centers upon discourse and ideology will seek to question the unquestionable, and to say the unsayable, by interrogating the naturalization of the discursive structures within which these texts speak and are spoken about. Rather than focussing on words and sentences in isolation, and assuming that these have stable meanings by themselves, it will examine them from a relational perspective, and, in particular, in relation to the larger discursive structures, or framing discourses, within which we interpret these texts.

When we talk about ideology and discourse, we are inevitably also talking about the conditions of material existence beyond the text.[8] The recognition that literature is a form of social discourse makes it impossible to divorce texts from social forces, institutions and practices, and from the dialectic interactions of history. Moreover, the varieties of language we encounter in literary texts, as in other forms of discourse, both embody and engender different interpretations of the world, a world in which all readers must function.[9] Given the intense interest shown by scholars and critics in Nabokov's linguistic pyrotechnics, his oeuvre is ripe for discourse analysis of the kind described by Roger Fowler, M. K. Halliday and others.[10] This might concentrate on the formal and stylistic structure of the Nabokovian text,[11] or the ideological structures which are also encoded in its linguistic patterns. The latter offers a particular challenge in the case of Nabokov. If we really want to get to grips with the ideological matrices which uphold the Nabokovian narrative, it is necessary to refuse to "play the game," at least according to the rules presented to the reader. When the Nabokovian novel makes aggressive claims that it is fictional not factual, it is just as aggressively seeking to veil its connections with the real world. For some readers in particular, this veil is all too transparent. If we assert the right of the reader to object to, and engage with, the ideological discourse of texts which seek to marginalize or trivialize her or his experiences and anxieties, we should also examine, or at least speculate upon, the concretization of, say, *Mary* or *King, Queen, Knave* by women readers; of *Lolita* by victims of childhood or spousal abuse; of *Pale Fire* by gay and lesbian readers; and of *Bend Sinister* by political and social dissidents in various eras and systems. We might term such readings oppositional, in that they often collide rather than collude with the dominant belief-system the texts purport to uphold. But this collision is productive rather than destructive. It can open up new dimensions of polyphony and reveal inner tensions and contradictions which not only promote multifarious readings, but also expand our understanding of the dialectical relationship between communication and society. Such collisions are, then, an alternative way of celebrating these endlessly fascinating texts.

This volume brings together a varied set of encounters with Nabokov's prose, under the broad concerns of discourse and ideology in and around Nabokovian narrative. The contributors are all, to varying degrees, players of the game, but here they have been invited to use their skills to examine the connections between the Nabokovian text and the extra-textual reality of the world of actual experience. Using a variety of critical methods, and treating several different texts, some scrutinize ideological polarities and hierarchies (including those implied by the claim "art for art's sake"), revealing their fundamental instability; others focus on variant readings of, and competing discourses within, novels like *Lolita*, *Pale Fire* and *Bend Sinister*; while others link Nabokov and his oeuvre with issues and changes in surrounding cultural structures, including the 1960s in America. As the chapters in this volume show, readers can and do move freely along the continuum between collusion and collision as they encounter Nabokov's novels and short stories. The collection presents a dynamic struggle over meaning, in which dialogism displaces monologism, and there is a healthy incredulity towards all meta- and master-narratives. Paradoxically almost, the linguistic facility which makes Nabokov such an excellent game-player also encourages these readers, through its defamiliarizing effects, to think anew about artistry and reality, subjectivity and alterity, authority and autonomy.

Galya Diment's article "The Nabokov–Wilson Debate: Art versus Social and Moral Responsibility" examines the fraught relationship between Nabokov and Edmund Wilson, and between their perceived critical positions, and, in the process, deconstructs some cherished oppositions and hierarchies. While granting that Wilson has not fared well in Nabokov criticism, Diment argues that there may be another side to the story, and begins by rejecting the facile notion that Wilson was simply envious of Nabokov's success and talent. She proposes that we evaluate their divergent political and artistic ideologies by contrasting Nabokov's "ultimate Russianness" and Wilson's "ultimate Americanness." Rorty's antithesis of Nabokov and Orwell is refined by positioning Wilson in the middle ground, between the broadly termed camps of "art for art's sake" and "social intent." She engages with those Nabokovian critics who blithely put Wilson into the social intent camp and suggests that Nabokov is actually the more limited critic of the two. The chapter concludes with the famous debate over *Eugene Onegin* and Wilson's likening of Nabokov to Marx, suggesting that the distinction between Marxists and anti-Marxists threatens to dissolve, if both parties are absolutists.

Any claim for the non-referential, ideologically neutral, nature of the

Nabokovian text, or for its essentially apolitical import, is always going to be at least partially vitiated by the existence of *Bend Sinister*, often described as the author's only political, or overtly political, novel. Brian Walter's "Two Organ-Grinders: Duality and Discontent in *Bend Sinister*" examines this anomalous document which interrupts Nabokov's supposedly apolitical corpus. The Introduction, with its admission of the historical references of the novel which follows, ironically fulfills the responsibility of the Marxist critic, while the distancing of the author from the story results in a narrative counterpart of Brecht's alienation effect. Walter detects a distinct personal animus on the part of the author towards Paduk and a corresponding sympathy for Krug, as well as a general distancing of characters from the reader which alienates the story itself from its audience. Following on Frank Kermode's observation that Nabokov is fundamentally hostile to readers, he argues that there are nonetheless some rewards for those who are patient enough to persevere. As with the Afterword to *Lolita*, the Introduction to *Bend Sinister* attempts to shield the text from misreadings and from itself.

The role of the Introduction is also a major concern in David H. J. Larmour's "Getting One Past the Goalkeeper: Sports and Games in *Glory*," which discusses the implications of Nabokovian discourse about men and women, and the nature of Martin Edelweiss's fractured and fragile identity. The article focusses on three sporting scenes in the novel as pivotal moments in the hero's quest for self-definition. The text associates Martin's quest for glory on the sports field with his attempts to construct a sexual, social, and political identity for himself. Departing from the authorized interpretation suggested by the Introduction, Larmour offers a reading of Martin's interaction with the female and male characters around him informed by Freudian analysis of male identity and Eve Kosofsky Sedgwick's neo-Girardian paradigm of homosocial bonding between men. He suggests that Martin's "heroic" identity is fragile and contradictory, and that the tensions can only be resolved by a return to a simpler time and self: the maternal homeland. This chronotope, however, is no longer available, leaving only death at the end of the winding path which disappears into the dark forest.

Galina Rylkova discusses another of Nabokov's early novels with homoerotic themes, *The Eye*, in "Okrylonnyy *Soglydatay* – The Winged Eavesdropper: Nabokov and Kuzmin." Examining possible sources of *The Eye* first, she posits Kuzmin's *Wings* as one of the texts which influenced Nabokov. Following up on references to Kuzmin in the short story "Lips to Lips" pointed out by Barnstead, Rylkova turns to *The Eye*, whose protagonist Smurov and his beloved Vanya take their names from the Vanya Smurov of *Wings*. Kuzmin's novel was influenced by Symbolist notions of spiritual rebirth through homoerotic love; Nabokov's Smurov also seeks a rebirth, but one devoid of philosophical and symbolic implications.

Rylkova discusses Plato's dialogue on the soul, *Phaedrus*, as an intertextual document with reference to the relationship of Smurov and Kashmarin, the latter being a parody of the Platonic lover, like Kuzmin's Stroop. The narrator of *The Eye* is seen as narcissistically in love with Smurov. Nabokov's discourse of alienation is informed, Rylkova suggests, by contemporary scientific discourses on narcissism. Nabokov's émigré and Kuzmin's homosexual are thereby linked through their common societal alienation.

Concerns about gender and sexuality are combined with close examination of structuring polarities and hierarchies in Paul Allen Miller's "The Crewcut as Homoerotic Discourse in Nabokov's *Pale Fire*." He treats the description of Kinbote's young lover Bob as a semiological intersection of some of the novel's most important structuring oppositions: homosexuality versus heterosexuality, the effeminate versus the virile, European versus American, refined intricacy versus naive simplicity, and aristocratic culture versus lower-class barbarism. Miller proceeds to demonstrate that the vertical relations between these sets of oppositions are radically unstable, with the homosexual versus heterosexual opposition threatening to undermine the whole system. Bob's crewcut – intriguingly linked with the close-cropped appearance of the Oklahoma City bomber, Timothy McVeigh – Kinbote's windbreaker, and a pair of trousers purchased in Cannes are all treated to Miller's penetrating scrutiny. As the oppositions implode, we are left with a new awareness of how a fragile subjectivity drives our desire for the despised Other.

The next two articles deal with *Lolita* and how the reader interacts with this provocative text. The mini-debate between the perspectives of Moore and Patnoe can be seen as part of the long-standing critical argument over *Lolita*: does it privilege Humbert's solipsistic aestheticism or undermine it, or even both?[12]

Tony Moore's "Seeing through Humbert: Focussing on the Feminist Sympathy in *Lolita*" picks up on competing discourses in the text and discerns in one a feminist voice. He argues that as a postmodern text, requiring continual "focal adjustment," the novel subverts the conventions of male ownership in Humbert's memoir and allows Dolores to break free from his rhetoric. This masculine rhetoric, in fact, imprisons Humbert himself. For Moore, some of Camille Paglia's ideas find echoes in Nabokov's novel and he suggests that Humbert experiences Lolita as a Paglian daemonic archetype. Linda Kauffman's approach, on the other hand, he finds to be an instance of the "critical perversity that *Lolita* still attracts."[13] Charting Lolita's escape from Humbert's solipsism as the story progresses, the chapter contends that the text's criticism of the narrator becomes gradually more apparent. This is best understood when we reread the book. Even if it is true that this novel has no clear answers to the problems of incest and spousal abuse, Moore points out, "that does not prove it is unaware of them."[14]

These pressing social problems occupy a central position in Elizabeth Patnoe's "Discourse, Ideology, and Hegemony: The Double Dramas in and around *Lolita*." This investigates the Lolita Myth, which perpetuates the figure of Lolita as a seductive adolescent girl, not a molested and raped one. Exposing the complicity of Nabokovian critics and particularly male readers in this process, she argues that those who have been excluded from hegemonic readings of this text should, far from simply rejecting it, reclaim the book and the textual Lolita, counter the co-opted mythical Lolita, and resist the cultural appropriation of female sexuality which this episode so clearly exemplifies. The famous "seduction scene" in the Enchanted Hunters episode must be read for what it is: a rape. Readers who are seduced by the book's form trivialize Lolita's experience and fail to take adequate account of the trauma many other readers are likely to experience. This has direct pedagogical implications, as we confront the personal and cultural implications of *Lolita*.

The last two chapters in the volume connect Nabokov as author and icon with the literary and cultural conditions surrounding the publication of his most successful writings. They also explore the complex relationship between the author's personal perspective on political events and social conditions around him, and the effect his work had on these same phenomena. D. Barton Johnson's article "Nabokov and the Sixties" traces the impact of *Lolita* and *Pale Fire* upon the cultural world of the 1960s in America, attempts to place Nabokov among his mainstream, Beat, and postmodernist coevals, and speculates on the writer's reaction to the political and social changes which marked this decade. His name was everywhere and became associated with the liberation of the arts from censorship, yet, as Johnson points out, Nabokov was an absent presence, a king across the water in Montreux. For Johnson, Nabokov is also already absent from those literary trends, particularly postmodernism, on which he nevertheless left an indelible imprint. Nabokov's extraterritorial existence may indicate a disaffection from the political and social disruption he saw in his adopted country. Scarcely apolitical for all his protestations (endorsing the Vietnam war was not an apolitical stance), he may have interpreted the disorder through the mirror of his memories of Russia and Germany in the earlier part of the century. Paradoxically, *Lolita* was part of this disorder, in the literary and, more broadly, the cultural arena. It is a text which breaks all sorts of barriers and taboos, and because of the time of its publication and its reception by the readers of the sixties, cannot but be associated with the physical manifestations of liberation from authoritarian control which are familiar to us all through video retrospectives.

Suellen Stringer-Hye's "Vladimir Nabokov and Popular Culture" takes us beyond the sixties and into the nineties. It considers the iconography of the author in written sources and on the Internet, where *Lolita* is the object of a cyberpunk parody by Chuck Hammell, rescued from its ephemeral existence for us by Stringer-Hye. She goes on to associate *Lolita* with the Beats, through its status as a road novel. Ranging over the iconic field from Charlie Chaplin to Hitchcock, and from Kurt Cobain to Joey Buttafuoco, lover of the "Long Island Lolita" Amy Fisher, the survey establishes the continuing cult status of both text and author, and raises again the question of their relationship to actual events with real political and social consequences. What do we make now, for instance, of the Lolita Society? Or of Humbert's abusive treatment of Lolita, which Elizabeth Patnoe tackles head-on in her article? The ambiguous status of the icon remains highly problematic.

Notes

1 I would like to express my gratitude to Peter I. Barta, Paul Allen Miller, Sharon D. Nell and Susan Isabel Stein for their intellectual support of this project, their helpful observations on Nabokov's writing, and their suggestions for critical and theoretical approaches to these texts.
2 Here I am following the range of meanings attributed to discourse by Foucault (1978, 80): "sometimes as the general domain of all statements, sometimes as an individualizable group of statements, and sometimes as a regulated practice that accounts for a number of statements."
3 *Colludo*: Cicero, *Verrine Oration* 2.58 (*nisi tecum tum collusisset*); Seneca, *Controversiae* 9.4.5 (*ne nos colludere tyrannus intellegat*); cf. *collusio*: Seneca, *Contr.* 2.3.22 (*suspicionem ... inter raptae patrem et raptorem collusionis*). *Collido*: Petronius, *Satyricon* 10.5 (*mille causae quotidie inter nos collident*); Quintilian, *Institutes of Oratory*, 7.7.2; 9.4.37.
4 Hutchinson (1983) counts Nabokov, with Joyce, among authors with an especially intense instinct for gaming (p. 15) and discusses *Pale Fire* as an example of "complex games" (pp. 38–40). See also Lilly (1979), Packman (1982, Chapter 1, "A Problem of Reading," 1–22); Motte (1995, especially Chapter 1, "Reading Games," 3–27; Chapter 4, "Authoritarian Nabokov," 71–90; and the good bibliography, 215–229).
5 For examples of the kind of criticism which enters willingly into the spirit of Nabokov's games, see Appel (1970); Proffer (1978); Johnson (1985); Barabtarlo (1989).
6 For discussions of play and games in culture generally and also in literature, see Huizinga (1955); Miller (1970); Irwin (1976); Hamburger (1979); Hans (1981); Morrow (1988).
7 Merivale (1967); Bader (1972).
8 See, for example, the discussion of discourse and ideology in Hampton (1990) and Eagleton (1991), 193–220.
9 Bakhtin (1981, especially 291–292).
10 Halliday (1978); Fowler (1981).
11 For examples of these methods at work, see Carter and Simpson (1989).
12 Readers may find that several of the issues raised – doubling, paedophilia and collusion – are interestingly refracted in the recent reading of Virginia Blum in her "Nabokov's Lolita/Lacan's Mirror" (Blum 1995), which compares Nabokovian and Lacanian narcissism.

13 Kauffman (1989); Paglia (1991).
14 Cf. Pifer (1980), who suggests that self-conscious artifice does not eliminate reality from Nabokov's novels, but "reveals it in new ways" (p. 47); Schneiderman (1985); Edelstein (1996) comments (p. 49) that "many contemporary works (e.g. *Lolita*, *Beloved*) raise ethical questions, even if they don't provide definitive answers, and encouraging readers to ponder ethical issues can itself have an ethical effect."

Part I

THE ARTIST AND IDEOLOGY

1

THE NABOKOV–WILSON DEBATE

Art versus social and moral responsibility

Galya Diment

It is well known that Wilson did not like *Lolita*, of which he informed Nabokov in his characteristically blunt fashion: "I like [*Lolita*] less than anything else of yours I have read" (Nabokov and Wilson 1980, 288–289). Nabokov was quite at a loss to explain why Wilson did not care for the novel, which he himself thought was his best and artistically purest creation. To change Wilson's mind, Nabokov, who would later state with so much firmness that "Lolita has no moral in tow" (Nabokov 1966a, 286), even assured Wilson, somewhat tongue-in-cheek, that "Lolita ... is a highly moral affair and does not portray American kulaks" (Nabokov and Wilson 1980, 298). What Nabokov was alluding to in this comment was his and Wilson's long-standing disagreement on the nature of art, and as to whether "good" art and social and moral issues were at all compatible.

Edmund Wilson has not fared well in Nabokov criticism, which tends to be rather partisan on the issue of the two men's differences. It is a commonplace in Nabokov scholarship, for example, to assume that Wilson envied Nabokov his success and his talent, and that his envy somehow poisoned his reaction to Nabokov and his works. This view is very prominent in Brian Boyd's biography, and a recent book by Gene Barabtarlo strengthens it even further. "It seems quite likely," writes Barabtarlo, "that an ulcerous trace of Wilson's spite toward Nabokov became noticeable by the mid-forties, worsened over the years, and turned especially acute after *Lolita* ... because [Wilson] thought that Nabokov succeeded commercially where he [himself] ... had failed" (Barabtarlo 1993, 274).

Yet anyone who is familiar with Wilson's journals and letters, as well as with other writers' reminiscences about him, will find this interpretation of Wilson's reaction to another writer quite out of character. Wilson could be cruelly blunt and overbearing but to his contemporaries he was much more known for celebrating other writers' talents, rather than begrudging them their successes. Pritchett, who knew Wilson personally and who admired Nabokov as a writer, was one of many who was quite convinced that envy had nothing to do with Wilson's evaluation of *Lolita*: "Some have thought that Wilson's distaste for *Lolita* sprang from his envy of the success of Nabokov's book, but Wilson was the least envious, most generous of men, as generous as the forthright Dr. Johnson, more particularly the Johnson of *Lives of the Poets*" (in Groth 1989, 183). Wilson's reaction to *Lolita* was probably more "territorial" than anything else. He appears to have been irked by Nabokov's assumption that he knew things American to the same extent that Nabokov was often irked by Wilson's assumption that he knew things Russian.

"It is difficult to imagine a close friendship between two people with such different political and aesthetic views," John Kopper writes about Wilson and Nabokov in the recent *Garland Companion to Vladimir Nabokov* (Alexandrov 1995, 57). Nabokov himself characterized his relationship with Wilson to Andrew Field as one where there was "hardly a moment when the tension between two highly dissimilar minds, attitudes and educations is slackened" (Boyd 1991, 494). And yet, throughout the 1940s, their relationship was relatively uncomplicated. For Edmund Wilson, Nabokov represented the culture and literature which had always fascinated him. For Vladimir Nabokov, Wilson, an accomplished man of letters, served as a gateway to American culture and the literary establishment. Their early letters to each other were full of appreciation and even tenderness. "Dear Vladimir: How are you?" read a typical letter from 1942, "I've been reading more Pushkin with great enthusiasm, and wish you were around to talk to" (Nabokov and Wilson 1980, 67). "Dear Edmund," Nabokov would write after a visit to Massachusetts to see Wilson and his wife at the time, Mary McCarthy. "Those 24 hours were lovely. We shall be very disappointed ... if we do not see you on Sunday" (Nabokov and Wilson 1980, 61).

And then something went terribly wrong, and seemingly irreconcilable differences, rather than appreciation or mutual tolerance, took over. There are various ways to account for these differences, of course. There are issues of personal temperaments involved, and those of professional inclinations. As one Wilson scholar pointed out recently, Nabokov was, after all, "quintessentially an artist and Wilson ... quintessentially a critic" (Groth 1989, 199), and artists and critics often view things differently. Yet, it seems to me, it was precisely what had attracted them to each other in the first place that would split them apart later on, for it was Nabokov's ultimate Russianness and Wilson's ultimate Americanness that may best account for most of their disagreements.

As Rosalind Baker Wilson puts it, her father always had an unmistakable longing for "a very American frame of reference" (1989, 223). While he envied Europe its culture and its writers, he, unlike other American-born writers such as Ezra Pound or T. S. Eliot, always believed in the

American potential to develop an interesting cultural and literary scene of its own. He took personal and professional pride in the appearance of talented local writers, in particular his friend Scott Fitzgerald, whom he often tried to shape and guide. Thus he wanted Fitzgerald to get the best of what Europe could offer: "Learn French," he admonished Fitzgerald in 1921, "and apply a little French leisure and measure to that restless and nervous system. It would be service to American letters: your novels would never be the same afterwards" (Wilson 1977, 64). "American letters" appeared to be what concerned Wilson most, for when, several years later, Fitzgerald decided to stay in Europe for a lengthy period of time, Wilson's admonition changed to: "I . . . wish you didn't insist upon living abroad, which I'm convinced is a great mistake for American writers, hard as America can be to live in" (Wilson 1977, 202).

Wilson as an author, critic, and journalist is also "quintessentially American." In an article appropriately entitled "The American Edmund Wilson," Robert Alter aptly captures Wilson's intellectual hunger: "He was . . . the least bored of modern intellectuals, constantly finding new materials to read and new scenes to explore that powerfully engaged his attention, excited him to further inquiry" (Alter 1984, 171). Wilson's is the hunger and the restlessness of the New Intellectual World, it is the burning and driving desire to uncover, rediscover, and reinvent what the Old World, the world most familiar to Nabokov, may have known for ages, and may have got tired of. In his political development, Wilson was equally "American," and that, too, set him very much apart from Nabokov. Like many intellectuals of his generation, Wilson contemplated Marxism in the 1930s and, for a while, was even duped into believing that the Soviet model of development contained some hope for mankind. By the time he met Nabokov, in 1940, both his Marxism and his very brief love affair with Soviet Russia were largely behind him, but to the end of his days he, unlike someone like Dos Passos or Steinbeck, remained a staunch liberal. Throughout his life, he protested inequalities in the position of American Indians and blacks, and he also publicly condemned the Vietnam War.

On many of those issues, Nabokov often appeared to be on the opposite side. He was understandably anti-Communist and anti-Marxist, but in the early 1950s, in the midst of the worst "purges" of the liberal intelligentsia, Nabokov's colleagues at Cornell were quite astonished by the seemingly callous and dangerous remarks he made about some people's allegedly "pro-Soviet" inclinations. During the Vietnam War, Nabokov left no doubt that he had nothing but contempt for the protesters. Thus when he translated *The Waltz Invention* into English in 1966, he wrote in the Foreword that he would not have even attempted to write the play "lest any part of me, even my shadow, even one shoulder of my shadow, might seem thereby to join in those 'peace' demonstrations conducted by

old knaves and young fools, the only result of which is to give the necessary peace of mind to ruthless schemers in Tomsk or Atomsk" (Nabokov
1966b, 4). Needless to say, some of those "old knaves" were Wilson's
friends, several of whom frequently marched and were at times arrested.
What is interesting in Nabokov's statement – beyond its obvious anti-
peacenik rhetoric – is his allusion to "Atomsk" and "Tomsk." Unlike
Wilson, with his "very American frame of reference" which translated into
his concern over what the war was doing to the American society, its
youth, and its morale, the émigré Nabokov's frame of reference obviously
omits the United States and focusses on the hateful regime he left back in
Russia, and the benefits that regime can draw from the anti-war demonstrations in this country.

Given these stark differences between the two men, it should obviously
not come as a surprise that Wilson and Nabokov disagreed, among other
things, on the role that moral and social concerns should play in art in
general, and in literature in particular. What should come as a surprise,
however, is that, upon close inspection, the debate was not – or should
not have been – as extreme as it often sounds or is being portrayed. For,
while Nabokov's views on art were definitely absolutist, Wilson's were
not.

It was not an accident, therefore, that when Richard Rorty wanted to
find a perfect antithesis to Nabokov's views on art he settled on Orwell,
rather than Wilson, who to many would have seemed a more natural
choice. Orwell and Nabokov allowed Rorty to set up a perfect paradigm. On the one hand, there was the author of *1984* whose article
"The Frontiers of Art and Propaganda" was often used as a manifesto
against the art-for-art's-sake doctrine, and, on the other, there was
Nabokov who liked to state, unequivocally, that "nothing bore[d him]
more than political novels and the literature of social intent" (Nabokov
1973, 3).

Orwell's and Nabokov's statements contrast quite nicely. "You cannot
take a purely aesthetic interest in a disease you are dying from," Orwell
wrote in "The Frontiers," "you cannot feel dispassionately about a man
who is about to cut your throat." Orwell also went on to state that the
strongly politicized late 1930s and 1940s "did a great service to literary
criticism, because it destroyed the illusion of pure aestheticism.... It
debunked art for art's sake" (Rorty 1989, 145). Vladimir Nabokov, who
was quite active during the period Orwell is describing, obviously did not
share that view. The example of Nabokov's approach that Rorty gives is
quite telling. Rorty draws on Nabokov's lecture on *Bleak House* where he
analyzes the narrative lamentation which follows the death of the boy Jo:
"Dead, your majesty! Dead my lords and gentlemen!... And dying around
us every day" (Nabokov 1980, 94). "This," says Rorty, "is a call to public
action if anything in Dickens is. But Nabokov tells us that the chapter is 'a

18

lesson in style, not in participative emotion'." "Notice," Rorty continues, "that if Nabokov had said 'as well as' instead of 'not,' nobody would have disagreed. By saying 'not' he maintains his stance as someone who is concerned with nothing *but* 'aesthetic bliss'." "Both Nabokov and Orwell," concludes Rorty, "unfortunately got enmeshed in attempts to excommunicate people with talents and interests different from their own" (Rorty 1989, 145–147).

Wilson's attitude toward the art versus moral and social responsibility question fitted in between Nabokov's and Orwell's. He did believe in a social mission for intellectuals and artists. "We are under a certain obligation not to let this sick society down," he wrote to Louise Bogan, a poet, in 1931. "We have to take life – society and human relations – more or less as we find them – and there is no doubt that they leave much to be desired. The only thing that we can really make is our work. And deliberate work of the mind, imagination, and hand ... in the long run remakes the world" (Wilson 1977, 206). But Wilson also habitually upheld one's absolute right to be a "pure artist" if the artist's talents and inclinations directed him or her that way. Wilson was, after all, an early popularizer of sophisticated literary perfectionists like Joyce and Proust, and he always appreciated them precisely for what they were, not for what they were not. While he may not have been particularly strong as a critic when it came to close artistic analyses (in which Nabokov was often superb), Wilson's sense of literature as a constantly evolving whole may actually have been more acute and more comprehensive than Nabokov's. We should remember, for example, that Wilson was among the first literary scholars not only to link Modernism to Romanticism, through the Subjective Impulse, but also to separate the two because, according to Wilson, unlike Romanticism, Modernism, thrived on "ugly" as well as "beautiful" and on "profane" as well as "sacred."

Nabokov and Wilson's numerous debates on the appropriateness of moral and social issues for art are well known. Faced with Nabokov's outright rejection of anything that was not, in Nabokov's mind, "pure" literature, Wilson often lost his cool and could sound more extreme than he actually was. "I have never been able to understand," wrote an exasperated Wilson to Nabokov in 1948, "how you manage, on the one hand, to study butterflies from the point of view of their habitat and, on the other, to pretend that it is possible to write about human beings and leave out of account all questions of society and environment. I have come to the conclusion that you simply took over in your youth the ... Art for Art's sake slogan and have never thought it out" (Nabokov and Wilson 1980, 211). Nabokov was equally adamant in his response: "I do not give a hoot whether a writer is writing about China or Egypt, or either of the two Georgias – what interests me is his book" (Nabokov and Wilson 1980, 212).

The publication of Nabokov's own uncharacteristically "political" novel, *Bend Sinister*, presented an apparent paradox in their ongoing debate. Contrary to what one may expect of a critic who was overall *not* bored by "political novels and the literature of social intent," Wilson was actually displeased with the novel. "You aren't good at this kind of subject which involves questions of politics and social change," he wrote to Nabokov in 1947, "because you are totally uninterested in these matters and have never taken the trouble to understand them.... Now don't tell me that the real artist has nothing to do with the issues of politics. An artist may not take politics seriously but if he deals with such matters at all he ought to know what it is all about" (Nabokov and Wilson 1980, 182–183). Wilson expressed similar objections about Nabokov's "political" play, *The Waltz Invention*.

Nabokov critics often dismiss Wilson's reaction – as well as his subsequent refusal to review the novel – as a pre-*Lolita* case of envy. It is impossible to say how Nabokov himself interpreted it privately, but publicly he attributed Wilson's low estimate of *Bend Sinister* to his friend's dogmatism: "In historical and political matters you are partisan of a certain interpretation which you regard as absolute..." (Nabokov and Wilson 1980, 185). And yet Wilson was neither envious nor dogmatic. He was simply stating his life-long held belief – and he was stating it with his typical bluntness – that different writers have different strengths, and they should avoid the risk of being undercut by something they were not good at.

Wilson may have liked writers like Anatole France or Malraux, whom Nabokov could not stand, but it did not mean that he wanted everyone to write "political novels." On the contrary, with Scott Fitzgerald – as with Nabokov later – Wilson definitely felt that his friend could be a better writer if he left political and social concerns alone, because he was not good at expressing them. "It would all be better if you would tighten up your artistic consciousness and pay a little more attention to form," Wilson wrote to Fitzgerald in 1919. He also told him to learn from Joyce because of his "rigorous form . . . and polished style" (1977, 46).

Since Nabokov critics like to present Wilson as someone belonging primarily to the "social intent" camp, the fact that Wilson often fought against the extremes of this doctrine is largely overlooked. But in 1950 Wilson vigorously attacked *The Saturday Review of Literature* precisely because it published an editorial which called for "The Destruction of Art for Art's Sake," the editorial's actual title. Wilson condemned *The Saturday Review*'s view as ignorant, simplistic, and extremely irresponsible for a journal devoted to literature (1977, 484). And even in the intense heat of Wilson's argument with Nabokov over Nabokov's translation of *Eugene Onegin*, the critic took some time off criticizing Nabokov to criticize those who comb ... literature for masked symbols and significant images [representing] ideas, philosophical, theological and political, which can never have entered the author's head [while] show[ing] remarkably little sensitivity to the texture and rhythm of writing, to the skill in manipulating language, for the rendering of varied effects.

(Wilson 1972, 228)

Wilson himself did sometimes sin on the side of placing too much emphasis on literature as a social document but, when Nabokov confronted him with his objections, it was Nabokov, rather than Wilson, who ended up sounding the more inflexible of the two. Typical in this respect is Nabokov's 1956 response to Wilson's preface to the translated works of Chekhov:

You can well imagine how strongly I disapprove of your preface. Do you really think that Chehov is Chehov because he wrote about "social phenomena," "kulaks," and "rising serfs" (which sounds like the seas)?... I think that at a time when American readers are taught from high school on to seek in books "general ideas," a critic's duty should be to draw their attention to the specific detail, to the unique image, without which ... there can be no art, no genius.

(Nabokov and Wilson 1980, 298)

The truth is, Wilson does talk in this preface almost exclusively about what he calls "an anatomy of Russian society" as found in Chekhov's late stories, which Wilson selected with that particular purpose in mind. He does mention "kulaks" and "rising serfs," and he also alludes to "the difficult readjustments of a new industrial middle class" (Wilson 1956, viii, ix). But, characteristically, as in the analysis of Dickens which Rorty cites, Nabokov does not suggest that Wilson should have focussed on the artistic details and images *in addition to* possible "social phenomena" – which are actually quite obvious in Chekhov's stories of that period; he wants Wilson to concentrate on details and images *instead of* it.

It is easy to account for Nabokov's distaste for *any* present or perceived "social intent" in literature. Those went against the grain of two sensibilities which were strongly developed in him – that of a modernist and that of an anti-Chernyshevsky and anti-socialist-realism Russian intellectual. If he sometimes exaggerated the danger of any discussion of moral or political content in literature, he was in good company, and yet we should not overlook the fact that it often made him a rather limited critic. As I mentioned earlier, while Nabokov's literary tastes and sensibilities were more refined than Wilson's, and his insights into the creative process invaluable,

21

it was Wilson, rather than Nabokov, who attempted to look at literature in a more comprehensive and wholesome fashion. Wilson came quite close to what Rorty, for one, considers an ideal critic, someone who understands that

> [t]he pursuit of private perfection is a perfectly reasonable aim for some writers – ...like Plato ... Proust, and Nabokov, who share certain talents. Serving human liberty is a perfectly reasonable aim for other writers – ... like Dickens ... Orwell..., who share others. There is no point in trying to grade these different pursuits on a single scale ... nor is there any point in trying to synthesize them.
>
> (Rorty 1989, 145–146)

As Rorty points out, Nabokov, on the other hand, frequently and summarily excommunicated many writers who were different from himself, dismissing them with devastating one-liners – like branding T. S. Eliot or Dostoevsky as third-rate artists. What is even more remarkable, though, in my opinion, is how Nabokov made other writers, whom he generally admired, look like his own artistic clones by virtually ignoring or underestimating their possible or even clearly-expressed social or moral concerns. Dickens and Chekhov are but the two examples here, while the most dramatic case in point is probably that of late Tolstoy, whose heavy moralistic side Nabokov conveniently tossed off as a minor annoyance not worthy of serious consideration.

Finally a few thoughts on how the last Nabokov–Wilson debate, that on *Eugene Onegin*, reflected on their previous arguments over the issues of art and "social intent." I am not aware that anyone has made the point yet, but this last debate can be seen, in some ways, as an ironic reversal of the roles that Wilson and Nabokov had played before. Whereas in his early letters to Nabokov, like the one cited in the beginning of this chapter, Wilson complained that while Nabokov was interested in the "habitat" of butterflies, he left out "all questions of [human] society and environment," in "The Strange Case of Pushkin and Nabokov," Wilson actually lamented that there was too little "artistry" in Nabokov's translation of Pushkin, and too much information on the "physical" world. "[W]e are almost surprised," Wilson sarcastically states at one point, "not to be given the zoological data on the bear in Tatyana's dream" (Wilson 1972, 222).

Long tired of Nabokov's suggestions that, while no longer a Marxist in his politics, Wilson might have been still a Marxist in his approach to art, Wilson also turned the tables on Nabokov by likening *him* to Marx. Nabokov's review of Walter Arndt's translation of *Eugene Onegin*, Wilson pointed out, "sounded like nothing so much as one of Marx's niggling and nagging attacks on someone who had had the temerity to write about economics and to hold different views from Marx's" (Wilson 1972, 209). That was undoubtedly the most insulting comparison that Wilson could ever have drawn. While he did it mainly to tease Nabokov and probably to hurt him, Wilson was also suggesting that there was little distinction between Marxists and anti-Marxists if the parties involved happen to be absolutists. Nabokov obviously disagreed – but then, he and Wilson disagreed about almost everything else, especially towards the sad end of their strange and tumultuous relationship.

2

TWO ORGAN-GRINDERS

Duality and discontent in *Bend Sinister*

Brian D. Walter

In the middle of *Bend Sinister*'s seventh chapter, a watchful Adam Krug fatefully interrupts Ember, just as his friend attempts to proceed with their conversation on the problems of translating Shakespeare. In this novel of interruptions, Krug's silencing of his friend clearly presages the rupture which is momentarily to follow – Hustav's and Linda Bachofen's invasion of Ember's home to arrest the harmless scholar:

> [Krug] had become aware of the yard. Two organ-grinders were standing there, a few paces from each other, neither of them playing – in fact, both looked depressed and self-conscious. Several heavy-chinned urchins with zigzag profiles (one little chap holding a toy cart by a string) gaped at them quietly.
> "Never in my life," said Krug, "have I seen *two* organ-grinders in the same back yard at the same time."
> "Nor have I," admitted Ember. "I shall now proceed to show you–"
> "I wonder what has happened?" said Krug. "They look most uncomfortable, and they do not, or cannot play."
> "Perhaps one of them butted into the other's beat," suggested Ember, sorting out a set of fresh papers.
> "Perhaps," said Krug.
> "And perhaps each is afraid that the other will plunge into some competitive music as soon as one of them starts to play."
> "Perhaps," said Krug. "All the same – it is a very singular picture. An organ-grinder is the very emblem of oneness. But here we have an absurd duality."
>
> (p. 121)

In their ominous duality, it is the organ-grinders who introduce the first minor chord into Krug's and Ember's composition, a theme that the forthcoming arrest will develop in full to drown out what had been the schol-ars' private duet.

This scene, like the chapter in which it is set, serves as an emblem for the novel, in which Krug's life is repeatedly and ruinously interrupted by the intrusions of Paduk's Ekwilist minions. At a still further remove, the two organ-grinders also reify the generally-accepted status of *Bend Sinister* within its author's corpus as the political novel that interrupts Nabokov's aggressively apolitical program. Nabokov's first novel written in America seems to stick out at odd angles from the body of his work. His novels prefer to offer an artist dressed up in the tall hat and long tails of the magi-cian, conjuring the pleasant surprise of his audience with unexpectedly embellished parlor tricks, polysyllables like colorful flowers pulled tri-umphantly from the hat, metaphors blooming like mischievous rabbits from the tip of the cane – the artist as giddy verbal showman. In a famous statement in "On a Book Entitled *Lolita*," he describes the goal of his work as the generation of "aesthetic bliss, that is a sense of being somehow, somewhere connected with other states of being where art (curiosity, tenderness, kindness, ecstasy) is the norm" (Nabokov 1989a, 314) – the reader's blissful, even transcendent, experience finally confirm-ing the author's. But aesthetic bliss plays no part in Nabokov's description of *Bend Sinister* to a potential publisher, which instead underlines its unorthodoxy, at least with respect to the author's customary goals:

> I propose to portray in this book certain subtle achievements of the mind in modern times against a dull-red background of night-mare oppression and persecution. The scholar, the poet, the scientist and the child – these are the victims and witnesses of a world that goes wrong in spite of its being graced with scholars, poets, scientists, and children.... Although I do not believe in message of hope books whose intention is to solve the more or less transient problems of mankind, I do think that a certain very special quality of this book is in itself a kind of justification and redemption, at least in the case of my likes.
>
> (Nabokov 1989b, 48–49)

Although tentative and highly qualified, Nabokov's acknowledgment of the novel's historical underpinnings would seem to consign *Bend Sinister* to a category the author never fails to scorn: the "Literature of Ideas." Nabokov's description of the novel in fact allows it to be understood as an example of the "political novel," a work, in Irving Howe's terms, of "internal tensions" produced by a confrontation between "experience in its immediacy" and "general and inclusive" ideology (Howe 1992, 20). To call any of Nabokov's works a political novel suggests immediately that it represents some compromise on the author's part, not only because of his theoretical statements on the incompatibility of art and politics, but also because of his personal alienation from the subject. Nabokov knew from early experiences that political topics did not focus his talents well, as they had for his diplomat and jurist father, and that his own attempts at political speech thus rang false. In an interview, he refers to his political disinterest as his "second favorite fact" about himself:

> [S]ince my youth – I was 19 when I left Russia – my political creed has remained as bleak and changeless as an old grey rock. It is classical to the point of triteness. Freedom of speech, freedom of thought, freedom of art. The social or economic structure of the ideal state is of little concern to me. My desires are modest. Portraits of the head of government should not exceed a postage stamp in size. No torture and no executions. No music, except coming through earphones, or played in theaters.
>
> (Nabokov 1990b, 34–35)

Given this limited ideological "commitment" in the author, *Bend Sinister* represents an apparently unwilling political novel, one that admits the conflict between specific experience and general ideology only grudgingly.

Even as an unwilling political novel, however, *Bend Sinister* would fail one of Nabokov's primary tests of art by acknowledging and – much worse – actually depending on the existence of so conventional a notion as the persecution of the "mind in modern times." Not surprisingly then, the author uses his introduction to shield *Bend Sinister* from such readings. But Nabokov's protective scorn for the villains of history finally only emphasizes their pertinence to the novel's project:

> [T]he influence of my epoch on my present book is as negligible as the influence of my books, or this book, on my epoch. There can be distinguished, no doubt, certain reflections in the glass directly caused by the idiotic and despicable regimes that we all know and that have brushed against me in the course of my life: worlds of tyranny and torture, of Fascists and Bolshevists, of Philistine thinkers and jack-booted baboons. No doubt, too, without those infamous models before me I could not have interlarded this fantasy with bits of Lenin's speeches, and a chunk of the Soviet constitution, and gobs of Nazi pseudo-efficiency.
>
> (Nabokov 1990a, xii–xiii)

By his own description, then, the showman who usually takes unmistakable pleasure in conceiving and directing his own program has, in choosing *Bend Sinister*'s topic, limited himself to the part of a relatively detached player. Like his characters – "victims and witnesses," as he calls them –

Nabokov's relation to his fictional history remains (for him) surprisingly and painfully passive, dictated by the goal of testifying to a world gone wrong.

It is telling that Nabokov's grudging acknowledgment of his novel's historical reflections adapts easily to theories of the innate sociality of literary production. In fact, Nabokov's acknowledgment ironically executes the Marxist critic's responsibility, as defined by Fredric Jameson:

> These [past literary] matters can recover their original urgency for us only if they are retold within the unity of a single great collective story; only if, in however disguised and symbolic a form, they are seen as sharing a single fundamental theme – for Marxism, the collective struggle to wrest a realm of Freedom from a realm of Necessity; only if they are grasped as vital episodes in a single vast unfinished plot.... It is in detecting the traces of that uninterrupted narrative, in restoring to the surface of the text the repressed and buried reality of this fundamental history, that the doctrine of a political unconscious finds its function and its necessity.
>
> (Jameson 1981, 19–20)

By his acknowledgment, Nabokov restores to the surface the traces of history for which the Marxist critic is responsible. The author's attempt to undercut the ideological character of his material – to write it off as "reflections" and borrowings – also could suggest the inescapability of his social and historical moorings.

The impression of Nabokov's unhappy compulsion leaves *Bend Sinister* susceptible to Virginia Woolf's criticism of work born of clear social and political motivation – that it frequently suffers from the author's own unhappiness with the compulsion of his topic. Much of *Bend Sinister* betrays precisely this sullenness in its author. Despite its intended philanthropy, the novel conveys an equally strong impression of the author's horror and hatred, featuring images of brutality and violence – including the arrests of Krug's friends, the dismemberment of his eight-year-old son (which is filmed for the father's anguished audience), and the rape of the child's former nursemaid by forty soldiers – that cannot help undercutting the novel's "message of hope." Nabokov's transparent concern to expose and implicate the criminals responsible for Krug's world gone wrong counters his straightforwardly noble intentions for the novel.

The narrator's frequent intrusions upon the story – usually a favorite device of Nabokov's for emphasizing his role as the creator of the fiction – further register the author's discomfort with his delimited role here. The intrusions in *Bend Sinister* lack the playfulness, the self-pleasure, that mark their use in other novels, resulting in what Brian Boyd has described as the novel's coldness toward the reader, its "refusal to satisfy the ordinary interests of readers" (Boyd 1991, 106). What *Bend Sinister* ultimately reveals is the author's strenuous and not altogether successful effort to compose a "political novel" that would belie generic convention, in which conventional tyranny is exposed for its conventional suppression of the conventionally anomalous individual. Unsure in his attempts to parody this formula, Nabokov ultimately produces a novel that strives to fend off the reader's conventional interests even as it finds itself forced to court them. Lucy Maddox has touched on this point in the connection she draws between *Bend Sinister*'s "self-consciously artificial" nature and its "indictment of the common impulse Nabokov saw behind both political totalitarianism and the misguided tendency of writers or readers to inflict 'general ideas' on works of art" (Maddox 1983, 53). My aim here is to draw out, in much greater detail than either she or Boyd has, the results of this forbidding narrative artifice within the novel's highly ambivalent and unusually domineering relationship with its readers.

The distancing of the author from his story, so foreign to Nabokov's preferences, results in a narrative counterpart of Brecht's alienation effect, whereby the actor self-consciously detaches himself from his part to make the "spectator adopt an attitude of inquiry and criticism" to the events depicted (Brecht 1964, 136). Tellingly, the ultimate benefit of the alienation effect is social, to set up a dialogue between spectator and play (or author and audience) about social conditions, "prompt[ing] the spectator to justify or abolish these conditions according to what class he belongs to" (p. 139). The discussion of social conditions prompted by the alienation effect parallels, in Marxist idiom, Nabokov's reference to *Bend Sinister*'s designs on a "message of hope."

By finding an analogue for Brecht's alienation effect in *Bend Sinister*, my argument in effect suggests that the author of *The Gift* and *Lolita* has also authored a political satire of fundamental internal tensions, uncomfortable as it is with the ways in which it makes itself available to generic classification as satire. "Satire is a lesson, parody a game," the author once proclaimed in documenting his preference – on principle – for the latter (Nabokov 1990b, 75), providing at the same time an apt description of *Bend Sinister* as an example of the former in its dutiful assertion of a "message of hope." Satire is a lesson, moreover, that brings out in its author, as Italo Calvino has argued, the "moralist [who] thinks he is better than others ... [who] believes that things are simpler than they appear to be to others ... [but who] is prevented by repulsion from gaining a better knowledge of the world he is attracted to, [even as] he is forced by attraction to concern himself with the world that repels him" (Calvino 1986, 62–63). For Calvino, satire remains fundamentally uncongenial to comedy, and Nabokov, to judge from his distinction between necessarily didactic satire and his preferred parody, agrees. So, no matter how successful or appropriate its work as satire, *Bend Sinister* would seem at least partially to fail one of its own author's key tests of artistic achievement, betraying as it does precisely the kind of love–hate relationship between the author and the fictional world he has constructed that Calvino imputes to satire.

In its uneasy political satire, *Bend Sinister* betrays too a fundamental uneasiness in its relations with its audience. While Nabokov's work on the whole evinces a preference for guiding and often even controlling its reader's response, in the case of this novel, the authorial need for control takes on revealing urgency. The novel's relationship with the reader in fact closely resembles Peter I. Barta's description of the author–reader dynamic in Nabokov's short story "The Visit to the Museum," in which "the narrative does not seem to invite the reader's full experience of these texts to create meaning. Rather, Nabokov leads an implied reader in accordance with his intention" (Barta 1995, 227). But, just as Barta shows is the case with "The Visit to the Museum," if *Bend Sinister* transparently under-mines Nabokov's claim that he "abhors didacticism," showing how he "manipulates his reader into patterning the diverse elements in the story into the meaningful scheme he has in mind" so that the reader is allowed "no alternative ways of making sense of the past," the book also under-mines its own satiric intentions, limited as they are by the author's distaste for the genre's moralistic traits, so that finally, the "didactic intention invites ... ironically enough, 'misreadings' which question [the work's] silent affirmations and open up the text to the making of alternative mean-ings" (Barta 1995, 234).

Hence, the troubled applicability of both the generic label *satire* and Brecht's alienation effect serves to make of *Bend Sinister* a highly instruc-tive, if oblique, lesson in Nabokov's preferred relations with his reader, for both satire as a genre and the alienation effect as Brecht describes it com-prise "the exact opposite of that which aims at empathy" (Brecht 1964, 136). The generation of Nabokov's aesthetic bliss – sensations of curiosity, tenderness, kindness, and ecstasy – depends, in direct contrast, on an *empathic* relationship between the writer and the reader. Despite their well-known structural complexity and frequently forbidding appearance, Nabokov's works prefer to offer the reader an embrace, provided that the reader demonstrates the faculties of comprehension and of sympathy that permit entrance into the author's private world:

> Up a trackless slope climbs the master artist, and at the top, on a windy ridge, whom do you think he meets? The panting and happy reader, and there they spontaneously embrace and are linked forever if the book lasts forever.
>
> (Nabokov 1980, 2)

In *Bend Sinister*, however, Nabokov finds that the slope of political purpose he has chosen to scale is not trackless, that no matter how artfully he diverts his course, others have been there before him. Not surprisingly, then, he cannot find it in himself simply to open his arms to the reader of this novel. The union that finally does take place is awkwardly self-conscious, with the reader kept at a cautious arm's-length; the author's distrust of his project being transformed into an uneasy relationship with his audience. Far from "welcom[ing] the risk of a novel that will appeal to a very few" in *Bend Sinister*, as Boyd suggests, Nabokov rather, in my view, accepts this risk as the best and only possible compromise between his preferred aims for unengaged art and the unusually domineering political project in this novel. His unmistakable ambivalence toward the novel emphasizes how little he, in fact, welcomes the prospect of alienating his audience.

Nabokov vs. the characters of *Bend Sinister*

The clearest sign of Nabokov's unease with the project of *Bend Sinister* is his unmistakable animosity for the characters he must call upon to depict its world gone wrong. The spite he shows in characterizing the soldiers and agents tormenting Krug represents a significant departure from his preferred indifference toward his characters. When asked in an interview whether he has shared other writers' experience of a character "taking hold" of them to "dictate the course of the action," Nabokov can only respond in horror, emphasizing instead the "perfect dictator[ship]" he maintains in his fictional worlds, the indifference he maintains toward his characters. *Bend Sinister*, however, lacks this authorial indifference. Nabokov clearly exaggerates the stupidity and the ugliness of the state functionaries responsible for Krug's tragedy, endowing them with the most repulsive mental and physical characteristics. Conversely, Nabokov's protection of Krug betrays an attachment that none of his other creations – not even the protagonists of his other novels – enjoys. An obvious emotional involvement with the characters punctures Nabokov's perfect dictatorship in *Bend Sinister*, with an important consequence for the reader: the only responses allowed are a similar disgust for the villains and a similar affection for Krug, with the author driving all characterizations toward this dual goal.

Evidence of the author's personal animus litters the novel, clearly directing, for instance, the characterization of his dictator, Paduk. Nicknamed the Toad as a schoolboy, the eventual head of the Party of the Average Man distinguishes himself only by being "dull, commonplace, and insufferably mean" (Nabokov 1990a, 68). When Krug encounters the adult Paduk, now the dictator, the philosopher learns that maturation has not improved the Toad, whose physical ugliness is still so severe and parodied that even the narrator doubts his description:

Physically the Toad had hardly changed except that every particle of his visible organism had been expanded and roughened. On the top of his bumpy, bluish, shaven head a patch of hair was neatly brushed and parted. His blotched complexion was worse than ever, and one wondered what tremendous will power a man must possess to refrain from squeezing out the blackheads that clogged the coarse pores on and near the wings of his fattish nose.... In a word, he was a little too repulsive to be credible...

(p. 143)

The narrative magnifying glass here, trained on the ugliness of human skin, resembles Gulliver's perspective in Brobdingnag, whose inhabitants' gigantic features reveal to him only their imperfections. Like Swift, Nabokov clearly intends to arouse disgust in his reader for the viewed object. The blotchy complexion is, in fact, one of the distinguishing characteristics of the Ekwilist; Nabokov fastens on the "repulsive patches of unshaven skin and pustules" that mark David's abductors (p. 198).

The same desire to alienate the reader guides the characterization of Paduk's schoolboy followers, the forebears of the Ekwilist soldiers and agents who torture the adult Krug. An unlikely and unlovely inventory of disabilities distinguishes the young Paduk's entourage:

Every one of [Paduk's] followers had some little defect or "background of insecurity" as an educationist after a fruit cocktail might put it: one boy suffered from permanent boils, another was morbidly shy, a third had by accident beheaded his baby sister, a fourth stuttered so badly that you could go out and buy yourself a chocolate bar while he was wrestling with an initial p or b: he would never try to by-pass the obstacle by switching to a synonym, and when finally the explosion did occur, it convulsed his whole frame and sprayed his interlocutor with triumphant saliva.... Protection was provided by a truculent simian youth who at seventeen could not memorize the multiplication tables but was able to hold up a chair majestically occupied by yet another disciple, the fattest boy in school.

(p. 74)

Although Nabokov's narrators consistently train their gaze on outward features to suggest personality traits, in none of his other novels does this strategy function so ruthlessly or reductively. In his critical statements, Nabokov frequently advocates the power of the odd or seemingly irrelevant detail, the sign of uniqueness that the artist alone is sensitive to. He criticizes Dostoyevsky, for instance, for not "seeing" his characters, for offering in them "mere ideas in the likeness of people" (Nabokov 1981,

31

130); but clearly, his own attention to physical detail in describing Paduk's followers leaves him open to an even worse charge – that he clothes repulsive ideological defects in the physical likeness of people. Servicing the author's personal anger, this emphasis on physical detail turns nasty, discerning only the ugly trait.

The prospect of drawing a politically-motivated character clearly brings out the bitterness in Nabokov. The novel offers two types of this character, both the simpleton who is merely attracted to the immediate power of a uniform and a rifle, as well as the less obviously but more truly dangerous dupe who seeks to justify the violence of the state by spouting the party line. Nabokov introduces both the soldier and the self-blinded ideologue in an early chapter of *Bend Sinister*. Returning from the hospital where his wife has just died and contemplating the unwelcome prospect of relating this news to their son, Krug is forced to pass back and forth across a bridge by the heedless but authoritarian guards of the new regime who ignore his pass, consigning him to the company of an enthusiastic convert to Ekwilism. The differences in Krug's responses to his tormentors reflect the differences in the author's attitude toward the two types. Krug condescends openly to the guards, the mere automatons of officiousness and potential violence, scarcely acknowledging their existence, much less their importance; when his glasses are broken in an excess of official paranoia, Krug laments openly, "[N]ow there is not much to choose between my physical illiteracy and your mental one" (p. 10). Despite their weapons, these soldiers clearly offend Krug far less than the Ekwilist mouthpiece who accompanies him on the bridge. Arendt has described the appearance of this figure – the willing dupe of propaganda – in post-World War I Germany, noting the crucial function of this "mass man's" rationalizations in leading to Hitler's eventual dictatorship:

> The peculiar selflessness of the mass man appeared here as a yearning for anonymity, for being just a number and functioning only as a cog, for every transformation, in brief, which would wipe out the spurious identifications with specific types or predetermined functions within society. War had been experienced as that "mightiest of all mass actions" which obliterated individual differences so that even suffering, which traditionally had marked off individuals through unique unexchangable destinies, could now be interpreted as "an instrument of historical progress."
>
> (Arendt 1979, 329)

The Ekwilist proselyte who accompanies Krug corresponds closely to Arendt's "mass man," an eager social iconoclast who freely condones murder in the name of the State, deepening absurdity into obscenity. Confronted by this voluble ideologue, Nabokov's philosopher remains mute. The son and brother who so blithely replaces filial affection with membership in the Ekwilist party contrasts strongly with the grieving husband and father in this key early passage. Nabokov refers to the ideologue as Krug's "delightful companion" – delightful not because the author in any way condones his willful moral blindness, but because this character offers a sarcastic means of magnifying the apathy, even the antipathy, of the Ekwilist toward the plight of the grieving individual.

Krug has precipitated the bridge scene with a fateful declaration, "I am not interested in politics" (p. 6), a stance that reflects the author's preference as well, but clearly not one that he or his protagonist finds it easy to maintain in this novel. The best Nabokov can do to satisfy both his specific goals for *Bend Sinister* and his professed scorn for politics is to emphasize the mental and spiritual repugnance of the politically-interested character. This strategy of compromise clearly dooms even the young Krug's headmaster, who merely insists on developing general political interest in his students. A hatefully one-dimensional caricature, the anonymous headmaster serves as a simple embodiment of class theory and a contrived target for the author's lavish, scornful wit:

> [The new headmaster] saw the world as a lurid interplay of class passions amid a landscape of conventional gauntness, with Wealth and Work emitting Wagnerian thunder in their predetermined parts; a refusal to act in the show appeared to him as a vicious insult to his dynamic myth as well as to the Trade Union to which the actors belonged.
>
> (p. 73)

The contrivance of this stooge becomes particularly clear when his characterization in the novel is compared with the actual figure upon whom the author drew for the characterization, a headmaster of Tenishev school in St. Petersburg, which numbered the adolescent Nabokov among its students in the last few years before the revolution. Nabokov's memories of this figure, described affectionately in his autobiography, *Speak, Memory*, as the "kindest and most well-meaning among [his] teachers" (Nabokov 1989c, 186), deviate sharply from the fictional version imposed on Krug. For the sake of his political message of hope, Nabokov has stripped this comparatively kind, well-meaning character of all sympathetic possibilities, consigning him to the role of a hateful pedagogical tyrant.

In its relentlessly degrading characterization of the Party of the Average Man, *Bend Sinister* finally conveys an unmistakable sense of personal injury – the author's personal injury. Nabokov's need to spite Krug's tormentors is painfully clear in a passage from the introduction:

33

> Is there any judgement on my part carried out, any sentence pro-
> nounced, any satisfaction given to the moral sense? If imbeciles
> and brutes can punish other brutes and imbeciles, if crime still
> retains an objective meaning in the meaningless world of Paduk
> (all of which is doubtful), we may affirm that crime is punished at
> the end of the book when the uniformed waxworks are really
> hurt, and the dummies are at last in quite dreadful pain, and
> pretty Mariette gently bleeds, staked and torn by the lust of forty
> soldiers.
>
> (Nabokov 1990a, xiv)

The most jarring element in this passage is Nabokov's apparently unknow-
ing imitation of his sordid, dim-brained dictator, Paduk, who hopes to
assuage Krug's grief by parading before the philosopher the brutal punish-
ments of those responsible for David's death (p. 228). As an unmistakable
register of his alienation from Ekwilist "justice," Krug is entirely immune
to such vengeful "pleasures," making Nabokov's offer to his reader of
similar "consolation" all the more revealing, an unlikely and unacceptable
endorsement of this often unpleasant book's most brutal images. The
author's need to stoop to such "moral satisfaction" betrays the depth of
his hatred both for his own characters as well as for the political ideologies
he disagrees with.

The counterpart of Nabokov's cruelty toward Krug's tormentors is his
unprecedented (and, in subsequent works, unmatched) sympathy for Krug
himself. Nabokov's description of his role as Krug's savior, the benevolent
intruder who pulls the maddened philosopher from the narrative just
before Paduk's henchmen finally shoot him, reveals how strongly the
author recoils from the power which Paduk's dictatorship must be given
over his protagonist:

> It was at that moment, just after Krug had fallen through the
> bottom of a confused dream and sat up on the straw with a gasp –
> and just before his reality, his remembered hideous misfortune
> could pounce upon him – it was then that I felt a pang of pity for
> Adam and slid towards him along an inclined beam of pale light –
> causing instantaneous madness, but at least saving him from the
> senseless agony of his logical fate.
>
> (p. 233)

Nabokov's novels feature numerous other victims of a senseless and agonizing fate, but no narrative deity intrudes to save Cincinnatus from Pierre
or Lolita from Humbert or John Shade from Gradus. Unlike these other
characters, Krug is the victim of the simplified stooges of a hateful and
simplified ideology, the character Nabokov has condemned to protago-

nist's status within his most politically-committed work. As such, this Adam enjoys special pity from his author.

Nabokov's intervention on Krug's behalf suggests a deeper subversion of his customary authorial dictatorship: the indifference of the new Ekwilist State to his philosopher's private tragedy has replaced Nabokov's usual indifference. William Gass has described the typical form of this authorial indifference:

> [Nabokov's] characters are his clowns. They blunder comically about. Clubbed by coincidence, they trip when most passionate. With rouge on their pates and wigs on their features, their fundaments honk and trousers tear. Brought eagerly, naively near, beauty in a boutonnière pees on their faces. Like the other clowns, how we laugh at that. Pieces in the play, they live, unaware, in the world of Descartes' evil demon, that relentless deceiver whose deceptions do not qualify, but constitute, his nature.
>
> (Gass 1989, 116)

The description applies most usefully to Krug, however, only when Paduk and his minions substitute for Nabokov, villains composed of equal parts of impertinence and incompetence, bursting in on the idyllic scholarly conversation to arrest his friend Ember, or kidnapping Krug's son just as the philosopher has discovered new inspiration for his work.

The kidnapping scene in particular demonstrates the most monstrous form of Ekwilist indifference to Krug's special plight: the complete incomprehension of the parent's endangered and finally severed bond with his child. Restrained by the burly Mac from defending his son, Krug appeals in vain to David's nursemaid, causing the narration to shift – in an apparent sign of authorial sympathy – from third person to first: " 'Mariette, do me a favour': he frantically signaled to her to run, to run to the nursery and see that my child, my child, my child–" (Nabokov 1990a, 200). When Krug, still restrained, a moment later repeats his appeal, a confused Mariette responds with atrocious callousness – " 'Does anybody know what he wants of me?' " – and proceeds (humming, we are told), with the task of making up her lips (p. 201). Still more repulsive, however, is his indifference to Krug's paternal desperation is Kolokololiteischikov, the excruciatingly unimaginative Ekwilist functionary in charge of Krug's arrest. Technically a father himself, Kolokololiteischikov had been rehearsing – with his own children – the "moans of artificial pain" with which Krug was to be tortured into capitulation (pp. 212–213), a jarring illustration of the brutality to which even the most traditional filial ties are callously subjected under Ekwilism. John Burt Foster persuasively suggests that David Krug's death recalls *Macbeth* and the "obliteration of MacDuff's family in 'one fell swoop' " (Foster 1995, 29), but the other Shakespearean sub-text here is clearly *King Lear*, whose main character, like Krug heedlessly ignoring the attempts of the resistance movement to help him escape, insists on a ruinous strategy that leads ultimately to the death of his child. In final compensation to his protagonist, then, for subjecting him to the monstrous indifference of Mariette, Kol, and the murderous experimenters at the Institute for Abnormal Children, Nabokov withdraws Krug in the middle of the final scene, rescuing his philosopher just before the deadliest boutonnière discharges in his face.

The most subtle consequence of Nabokov's antipathy for Krug's tormentors and his special pity for Krug occurs in the novel's relations with its reader. Gass points out that Nabokov typically exploits his characters for the sake of the overall comic effect, with the reader allowed, in some capacity, to be entertained by the spectacle of their predicaments, so far beyond their control – "like the other clowns how we laugh at that." But in *Bend Sinister*, Nabokov clearly extends much greater control over his reader's response: only hatred is allowed for Krug's tormentors, and only sympathy for Krug. The measures Nabokov takes to ensure this response reveal his fear in this novel – that the reader will not respond properly to Krug's plight, that the image of his protagonist's personal grief will not dominate the reader's final impression. This fear drives Nabokov to unprecedented cruelty toward the novel's villains, and unequalled kindness toward their victim. Rescuing Krug from Paduk's marksmen, Nabokov also rescues him from any unsympathetic reader.

Nabokov vs. the plot of *Bend Sinister*

Nabokov's decision to distance his characters from the reader participates in a larger strategy to alienate the story itself from its audience. The message of hope in *Bend Sinister*, such as it is, is clearly conveyed not through any triumph Krug wins over Paduk's dictatorship, but through the ultimate impression of the absurdity, even the unreality, of the brutal rule of the Party of the Average Man. Making this impression all the harder to achieve, Nabokov has indulged a higher degree of verisimilitude – manifested in the circulars and speeches clearly borrowed from Soviet and Nazi models – than in any of his other works. Thus, in an attempt to achieve the right mixture of realism and farce, Nabokov constantly undercuts his storyline by intruding self-consciously upon the narrative, repeatedly reminding the reader that his imagination still guides the fiction. But as Laurie Clancy has noted, the interruptions here seem to signal "Nabokov's own instinctive dissatisfaction with the novel, a feeling of impatience" with the needs of his topic (1984, 98). The final impression is thus one of the author's own disbelief, as if he himself cannot accept the situations imposed upon him by the design of depicting a world gone politically wrong.

The well-known "*Hamlet* chapter" of the novel manifests this authorial dissatisfaction clearly. Nabokov substitutes stage directions for actual description during Krug and Ember's dialogue, underlining his sense of the scene's contrivance, forcing himself to "[r]elate the horror of those rehearsals" (p. 106). This last phrase suggests the author's horror at the requirements of this passage – a rehearsal, the prelude to another appearance by Paduk's henchmen. Ember's impending arrest pressurizes this scene; the author soon warns himself, "Last chance to describe the bedroom," followed immediately by the declaration, "Too late" (p. 107). These stage directions manifest the pattern that informs the plot as a whole – Nabokov slipping in the private moments of Krug's life before the exigencies of his political horror story intrude in the form of Paduk or his representatives.

The odd and highly self-conscious restraint of the arrest itself represents Nabokov's attempt to deflect, or at least manage, the brutality of the scene. Instead of stormtroopers, Nabokov sends Linda Bachofen and Hustav, a "handsome lady in a dove-grey tailor-made suit and a gentleman with a glossy red tulip in the buttonhole of cutaway coat" to take Ember; Hustav even offers Krug his card (p. 122). Pleased with the arrest's clever orchestration, Hustav interrupts his flirtation with Linda long enough to instruct Krug in the unwarranted artistry of an encounter that might easily – and perhaps should – devolve into physical violence:

> "Oh, I know what you [Krug] are going to say" – purred Hustav; "this element of gracious living strikes you as queer, does it not? One is accustomed to consider such things in terms of sordid brutality and gloom, rifle butts, rough soldiers, muddy boots – *und so weiter*. But headquarters knew that Mr. Ember was an artist, a poet, a sensitive soul, and it was thought that something a little dainty and uncommon in the way of arrests, an atmosphere of high life, flowers, the perfume of feminine beauty, might sweeten the ordeal. Please, notice that I am wearing civilian clothes.
>
> (p. 123)

Hustav's terms also apply to the novel as a whole. With self-conscious deviations from generic convention, Nabokov seeks to distinguish himself as still an artist, a poet, a sensitive soul, imploring the reader to notice that his political novel comes dressed in civilian clothing. He must find some way to sweeten his own ordeal as the author of Krug's tragedy.

But the despairing tone of these devices betrays the futility of an attempt to rescue the work from convention. The first interview between Paduk and Krug further manifests the author's alienation from his story. Nabokov offers two versions of this key exchange, the first farcical, the second almost corrective, a more "realistic" version. In the first version,

Krug chats familiarly with his former schoolmate, requiting Paduk's habit of scrambling personal names into anagrams with his own mockery of the contrived interview. The patter continues light and fast with Paduk's functionaries interrupting constantly to scold Krug for impoliteness to the dictator. But then Nabokov himself interrupts with, "No, it [the conversation] did not go on quite like that" (p. 147), and proceeds to describe an awkward, often silent meeting between Paduk and the philosopher, alternately amused and bemused by the terms of the dictator's demand for his endorsement. As if bored by this second version, Nabokov calls attention to its banality:

> Which, of course, terminated the interview. Thus? Or perhaps in some other way? Did Krug really glance at the prepared speech? And if he did, was it really as silly as all that? He did, it was. The seedy tyrant or the president of the State, or the dictator, or whoever he was – the man Paduk in word, the Toad in another – did hand my favourite character a mysterious batch of neatly typed pages.
>
> (p. 151)

Nabokov here describes his own unhappy capitulation. "He did, it was" signals the author's acquiescence to the external needs for such a scene – the discomfitingly political needs of his design.

The clear narrative discomfort of such passages betrays Nabokov's difficulty in attempting to turn his sensibilities and talents to the task of *Bend Sinister*. When Ember reads from "The Real Plot of *Hamlet*," an essay that explains the proper Ekwilist staging of Shakespeare's tragedy, he not only describes a painfully polemicized view of the play, but also suggests a reading of *Bend Sinister* as the politically determined interpretation of what would otherwise present itself as the product of a free artistic conception. Nabokov's impulse is to write moody, politically impotent Krug's story, to insult historical determinism and ideological common sense by refusing to subject his bereaved philosopher to the revolutionary success of the Ekwilist dictator – intellectually and spiritually quite incidental, no matter how physically dangerous. But Nabokov has set out to compose a message of political hope, and, fundamentally alien though that design may be, he pursues it doggedly, embodying what this design has boded. The constant undercutting of the narrative represents his only means of rebellion against the unwonted compulsion of his design.

This pervasive narrative slipperiness ultimately functions to destabilize the act of reading *Bend Sinister*. Nabokov never allows the reader any sure grasp on the narrative, defamiliarizing or even snatching away a scene immediately upon describing it. The reader is never to become comfortable with the story of Krug's grief – or at least no more comfortable with it than the author finds himself to be. This discomfiting quality of *Bend Sin-*

ister differs fundamentally from the playful elusiveness that characterizes most of Nabokov's work. His novels love to play cat-and-mouse, challenging the reader to a chase through a hedge of allusions, complex syntax, and various structural tricks to get at the often rather simple story. But in *Bend Sinister*, the hedge is replaced by a thicket of angry narrative self-consciousness, the overgrowth of the author's own distaste for his rather simple political story – a barrier imposed before the reader as well.

Nabokov vs. the reader of *Bend Sinister*?

Near the end of his foreword to *Bend Sinister*, appended to explanations of several of the novel's innumerable allusions, Nabokov sets the reader's likely perception of the book directly against his own. The passage manifests not only Nabokov's much-discussed concern with the sanctity of the artist's vision, but also his crucial concern with the reader's understanding of his work:

> Most people will not even mind having missed all this [the allusions]; well-wishers will bring their own symbols and mobiles, and portable radios, to my little party; ironists will point out the fatal fatuity of my explications in this foreword and advise me to have footnotes next time.... In the long run, however, it is only the author's private satisfaction that counts. I reread my books rarely, and then only for the utilitarian purpose of controlling a translation or checking a new edition; but when I do go through them again, what pleases me most is the wayside murmur of this or that hidden theme.
>
> (p. xviii)

Written in 1963, sixteen years after the novel's first American publication, but only a year after the publication of *Pale Fire* had cemented the popularity Nabokov first enjoyed with *Lolita*, this author's introduction hopes to guide the reader to appreciate the same "hidden" themes in *Bend Sinister*. It represents Nabokov's transparent attempt to control not a new translation, but his reader. Failing of such control, Nabokov resorts to designating his readers the novel's "well-wishers," harmless spectators of his Krug's nightmare – a gesture of protection to precede the narrative itself.

The internal tension of *Bend Sinister*, its discomfort with itself, finally grows from this latent tension between Nabokov and his reader. In his review of the novel, Frank Kermode (1962) in fact argued that its author betrays hostility toward his reader, and, further, that this hostility is a fundamental problem in Nabokov's work. Kermode's point is well-taken in the case of *Bend Sinister*. Concerned to deliver his message in highly personalized terms, Nabokov simply will not allow the reader to participate in this story, to share his relations with Krug, in the way that he admits entrance into, for instance, *Invitation to a Beheading*. On the surface, at least, Cincinnatus's plight is as horrible as Krug's, but his story of imprisonment and execution is still made available to the reader in a way that the tale of Krug's losses is not. Nabokov seems, as Kermode suggests, to feel his intelligence insulted by the project of *Bend Sinister*, and thus redirects the insult toward his reader in the form of a painful, distancing lesson in the horrors of the totalitarian state.

Fortunately for Nabokov, it certainly overstates the case to impute this scorn for the reader to all his work. His novels may not trust their readers, testing their motivation for reading, for instance, by warning from the outset that the protagonist will finally, inescapably, be sacrificed before their eyes. But for the readers who pass this and similar tests, for those who latch onto the hidden murmurs and wayside themes the author has planned as their lead attractions, the novels harbor only affection and gratitude. The great possibility in Nabokov's work for affection between the author and his reader is often missed by his critics. Nabokov's work only asks its reader to play his game to receive its various and abundant rewards. Even in *Bend Sinister*, with as dour an impression as it tends to make, Nabokov plans rewards for the patient reader. The list of the author's favorite themes in the foreword serves a dual purpose: as a shield against historical and political readings but also as a guide to the novel's bright spots, a preview of coming attractions.

The urgency of this dual purpose informs the entire author's introduction to *Bend Sinister* – easily the longest Nabokov has attached to any of his novels. Boyd has characterized the prefaces to the novels as "part of the irascible and arrogant Nabokov persona, in part a game, a parody, a running joke" (Boyd 1991, 477) – playful protective devices designed to put off any reader so inclined. But the notable length of *Bend Sinister*'s preamble, coupled with the pains – unusual even for Nabokov – taken to ensure the reader's "proper" appreciation of this book, together suggest both a greater urgency to, and deeper concern for, its project. The introduction to *Bend Sinister* stands with the author's afterword to *Lolita* as Nabokov's most extensive comment on his own work, a telling link. Just as Nabokov feels compelled to defend at considerable length his most controversial novel from the charge of pornography, he cannot release *Bend Sinister* to the reader without shielding it – at least partially – from itself, from its highly-complicated designs on a message of hope.

The reader thus falls in line behind the artist, the poet, the scientist, and the child on the list of the victims and witnesses of Krug's world gone wrong. Much as the prospect of the competing organ-grinders leaves especially the onlooking children confused and disappointed, the daunting duality of *Bend Sinister* leaves the reader in a state of perplexity – engaged, perhaps, but not enthralled by the work of the author's discontent.

Part II

DISCOURSES OF GENDER AND SEXUALITY

3

OKRYLYONNYY *SOGLYADATAY* – THE WINGED EAVESDROPPER

Nabokov and Kuzmin

Galina Rylkova

Вздохнуть поглубже и, до плеч
в крылья вдев расправленные руки,
с подоконника на воздух лечь
и лететь, наперекор науке [...]
    Боюсь, не вынесу полета ...
Нет, вынес. На полу сижу впотьмах,
и в глазах пестро, и шум в ушах,
и блаженная в плечах ломота.[1]

(Nabokov [1929] 1979, 225)

To Alfred Appel's question – "In which of your early works do you think you first begin to face the possibilities that ... reach an apotheosis in the 'inviolate abode' of *Pale Fire*?" – Vladimir Nabokov gave the least expected answer, "Possibly in *The Eye*..." (Nabokov 1973, 74). Up to now, scholars have usually evoked this famous reply in the concluding portions of their studies on *Soglyadatay* [*The Eye*] (1930), to justify a preoccupation and fascination with this lesser known novel by Nabokov. However, there is still much more to be said about this underrated work which indeed marks a turning-point in Nabokov's writing and provides an insight into the makings of his Weltanschauung, which was shaped at the time when this novel was in gestation.

In the late 1920s and early 1930s, although steadily turning into one of the most prominent (and certainly one of the most publishable) Russian émigré writers, Nabokov was nevertheless subjected to severe criticism. Uncertain how to classify his works, critics labeled them poor imitations of French and German originals. Sirin-Nabokov rapidly gained the reputation of a trickster, seeking cheap success with his readers. Georgiy Ivanov, whose review of Sirin's *King, Queen, Knave, The Defense*, and

The Return of Chorb appeared in the first issue of the Parisian *Chisla*, described his works as "trite, banal, not lacking in virtuosity, however," and lamented about "our wretched critics" and "undemanding reading public" who contributed to the success of the "Sirins" of this world (Ivanov 1994, 524–525). Ivanov portrayed Nabokov as "an impostor" and an outcast, who could not possibly belong to the great Russian tradition.[2]

If in the earlier years of his career, suffering from the imposed loss of his motherland and the tragic death of his beloved father, Nabokov found refuge in writing patently imitative works of poetry (Bethea 1995), in his maturity he claimed decidedly unconventional sources of inspiration. Thus in *Dar* [*The Gift*] (1938) Nabokov's alter ego, Fedor Godunov-Cherdyntsev, insists on "borrow[ing his] wings" of artistic inspiration "from conversations with [his] father, from daydreams in his absence, from the neighborhood of thousands of books full of drawings of animals, from the precious shimmer of the collections, from the maps [and] from all the heraldry of nature and the cabbalism of Latin names..." (Nabokov 1991, 115). Notwithstanding these claims, one should not ignore another possible supplier of Nabokov's "wings," namely the famous *fin-de-siècle* writer and poet Mikhail Kuzmin (1872–1936), whose novel *Kryl'ya* [*Wings*] was successfully appropriated by Nabokov in *The Eye*. It is the purpose of this chapter to offer explanations for Nabokov's interest in Kuzmin's "legacy" in the early 1930s. I will show how different thematic blocks, collisions, and motivations for the actions of the characters in *Wings* were melted down by Nabokov into *The Eye*. Moreover, I will demonstrate how his literary "affair" with Kuzmin gave birth to Nabokov's archetypal character – an ambivalent, sexually inverted, émigré loner – whose strivings and misfortunes became the main focus of most of his subsequent works.

Why Kuzmin?

When Kuzmin's novel appeared in literary *Vesy* in 1906, it brought its author "instant fame and notoriety" (Malmstad 1977, 99). This was not fortuitous. In his work Kuzmin not only failed to portray homosexuals as doomed and tragically misunderstood (as would have been expected), but came up with a picture of a homoerotic paradise, readily accessible to those who so desired. Having gone through a number of trials and tribulations, the young homosexual Vanya Smurov is gradually led to understand that there is nothing unnatural or perverse in any activity in itself: "[w]hat is important in every action is one's attitude toward it, its aim and also the reasons behind it; actions in themselves are merely the mechanical movements of our bodies and cannot offend anyone, much less the Good Lord" (p. 107).[3] Smurov's maturation is presented as a spiritual journey, by the end of which he comes to appreciate love and beauty (Shmakov 1972; Harer 1992).

The publication of *Wings* became a significant event in the cultural life of Russia in the 1900s, giving rise to various debates and discussions. The impact of the novel on the reading public was equivalent to that of Chernyshevsky's *What is to Be Done?* (Blok 1931, 135). Thus, upon his return to Russia from France, the artist Aleksandr Benua attributed the disturbing changes that he found in his friends – they were no longer concealing their homosexuality – primarily to the influence of "new young people" like Kuzmin (Benua 1990, 477).

However, despite his popularity – often scandalous – Kuzmin was largely misunderstood by his contemporaries; because of the deceptive "lightness" (or as Markov puts it, "non-vodka-like quality" [1977, 409]) of his poetry and works of prose, he was often assessed as a second-rate author, whose works belong to the literary salons. For many of his readers, Kuzmin became the symbol of "art for art's sake" – an unrewarding position within the literary tradition, the main virtue of which has been seen as that of educating and guiding its readers, rather than of entertaining and amusing them. Interestingly, the husks of these accusations were articulated twenty years later by the very same Georgiy Ivanov who criticized Nabokov, in the section of his pseudo-autobiographical *Peterburgskie zimy* [*Petersburg Winters*] devoted to Kuzmin. This collection of feuilletons was published in Paris in 1928 and it is very likely that Nabokov was familiar with it. Kuzmin is presented as a light-weight author whose talent came in handy when the "progressive" reading public got weary after the outburst of Russian Symbolism and demanded simplicity. Ivanov's Kuzmin is more concerned with his wardrobe than with what to write or how to write; he writes effortlessly and mindlessly and sends his works off to the publisher immediately – "why bother rewriting them – my handwriting is impeccable," he confides in Ivanov (Ivanov 1994, 98–108).

Ivanov's critique of Kuzmin was part of a larger campaign against the cultural legacy of the Russian Silver Age (1890–1917) and everything it stood for (unprecedented diversity in themes and approaches, individualism, and the decisive lack of traditional moralizing) launched by Vladislav Khodasevich and carried on by the younger literati Yuri Terapiano and Nikolay Otsup. If Khodasevich in his 1928 article "The End of Renata" attested soberly to the ultimate failure of the Symbolist "life-creating" project (1996, 19–29), then Otsup and especially Terapiano were even more aggressive in their advocacy of simplicity and paucity both in lifestyle and as an aesthetic principle. In his article "A Man of the 1930s" Terapiano propped up his denunciation of the cultural legacy of his immediate predecessors in favor of Lev Tolstoy by the all too familiar notion of one's duty to adhere to the "truth" both in life and in art, arguing that a man of the thirties "has learnt to distrust himself [and therefore] demands telling the truth about himself, [being always] severe and earnest [with himself]" (1933, 211).

In such an austere environment, openly hostile to any artistic activity that was not pursuing indentifiable ideological purposes, the "light-weight" Kuzmin (with his legendary inability and unwillingness to adhere to any particular school or movement) should have appeared a perfect father-figure to a seemingly fatherless and rootless aesthete like Nabokov.[4]

Nabokov and Kuzmin were first paired by Andrew Field (1963) and later by Gennadiy Shmakov (1982) and Vladimir Markov (1984). The similarities adduced to bring these two authors together are, however, very general in nature. Kuzmin and Nabokov are matched either because of their shared disregard for the didactic, ideological function of literature or because of stylistic innovations which they appear to have had in common. Nabokov himself never made any open statements of his attitude to Kuzmin's oeuvre. Kuzmin's name is not listed in the indices of books written by or about Nabokov. The links between Nabokov and Kuzmin are, however, much closer than would appear at first sight.

John Barnstead (1986) has exposed a complicated system of references to Kuzmin's various works in Nabokov's short story "Lips to Lips" (1929/1931). In a footnote to his paper he also mentions that the name of the protagonist in Kuzmin's *Wings*, Vanya Smurov, reappears in Nabokov's *The Eye*, but is split between two characters: Smurov, the protagonist, and the girl he loves, who bears the nickname Vanya (Barnstead 1986, 59n). In fact, the last name of Kuzmin's protagonist comes from Dostoevsky's *The Brothers Karamazov*: Smurov is a little left-handed boy befriended by Alyosha.[5] His first name is never revealed to the reader, so the combination "Vanya Smurov" is unmistakably Kuzminian. Nabokov cunningly preserves references to both literary sources: his Smurov is described by one of the characters as a "sexual lefty" [seksual'nyy levsha] (p. 85).[6]

Allusions to Kuzmin in *The Eye* can be discerned, but they are camou-flaged, which probably explains why Kuzmin's name, apart from the foot-note in Barnstead's article, has not been mentioned in connection with this novel. In giving the name "Vanya" to the object of Smurov's unrequited love, Nabokov provides it with an etymological explanation. The girl is reported to be nicknamed "Vanya" as a result of her "demand[ing] to be called 'Mona Vanna' (after the heroine of some play or other)" (p. 37). Another allusion that is intentionally left open to different interpretations occurs when Smurov's mistress, Matilda, invites him home to borrow the book, *Arianne, Jeune Fille Russe* [o kakoy-to russkoy devitse Ariadne] (p. 15). This has been identified by Barton Johnson as the novel written by Jean Schopfer, but in Johnson's words, "does not seem to have thematic implications for *The Eye* as a whole" (1985, 399–400). The pairing of Matilda and Ariadne, though, brings to mind Kuzmin's *Tikhiy strazh* [*The*

Gentle Knight], written in 1915 and reprinted by "Petropolis" in 1924.[7] In this work, the longing of a dying Matilda Petrovna for her son is mockingly compared to the suffering of the mythological Ariadne, deserted by Theseus (Kuzmin 1994, 397).[8] Each of the three opening paragraphs of *The Gentle Knight* starts with the name Matilda, which is rare to a Russian ear. This section tells of Matilda's burdensome love for her son. Nabokov evokes the general mood of Kuzmin's original in the following passage that comes near the beginning of *The Eye*:

> Matilda, who would inquire coyly if I wrote poetry; Matilda, who on the stairs or at the door would artfully incite me to kiss her, only for the opportunity to give a sham shiver and passionately whisper, "You insane boy...."; Matilda, of course, did not count.
>
> (pp. 17–18)[9]

Nabokov's depiction of the relationship between Smurov, Matilda, and her husband Kashmarin (which frames the "main" story) also sets *The Eye* in an unmistakably Kuzminian context. Here is the gist of what happens. Having learnt of Matilda's infidelity, Kashmarin loses control and beats Smurov up. Humiliated, Smurov attempts suicide. Kashmarin, however, finds out that Smurov was not his wife's first – or even last – lover, divorces her, and puts his energy into looking for his former rival. Not only does he succeed in locating Smurov, he also offers him his guidance and protection with the possibility of future trips to Italy. Smurov accepts Kashmarin's proposal with gratitude. A situation similar to this one is described by Kuzmin in his novel *Plavayushchie-puteshestvuyushchie* [*Travelers by Land and Sea*] (1915),[10] in which the two former contestants for the attention of a woman finally see through to her "shallowness" and develop a special relationship between themselves. In Kuzmin's fictional world, a conventional love-triangle (two men competing for one woman) is turned upside down, and it is usually a man and a woman who both fancy one man.[11] Similar love-triangles are outlined in *Wings*. Vanya has to compete for Stroop's attention, first, with the "absolutely revolting" Nata, and then with the more sophisticated Ida Goldberg.

One of the striking things about *The Eye* is the photographic quality of its fictional world. The characters are either shown as if posing for the taking of a picture or are perceived by the narrator as static photographic images. In *The Eye* the world of the photograph takes precedence over "real" life. It is not the photograph which reflects everyday life but vice versa. For example, Smurov breaks into Vanya's apartment in order to see whether she still cherished the picture that showed him and her together. He starts suspecting that his love is unrequited not because his common sense tells him so, but because he finds himself missing from that picture – Vanya has carefully cut him out. Incidentally, Georgiy Ivanov remarked in

1928 that Kuzmin's "treacherous 'beautiful clarity' [prekrasnaya yasnos] was responsible for imparting a lifeless-photographic quality to the meaningless 'jabber' of his uninteresting characters..." (Ivanov 1994, 101–102).

As this brief analysis shows, the Kuzminian subtext in Nabokov's *The Eye*, although obscured, is, nevertheless, recoverable. Although Nabokov was most unlikely to have been aware of this, the title of his novel, *Soglyadatay* (translated by Nabokov himself as *The Eye*), comes from Kuzminian vocabulary. In May 1906 – a few months prior to the publication of his *Wings* – Kuzmin wrote in his diary about one of the soirées at Vyacheslav Ivanov's:

> Мне стало вдруг скучно, что я никого здесь не люблю (так особенно, не влюблен) и, главное, меня никто не любит и что я какой-то лишний соглядатай.
>
> (Kuzmin 1986, 417)

> I suddenly felt weary of not loving anyone here (not really being in love) and, most importantly, of nobody loving me, and of my being a sort of unwanted eavesdropper.

Nabokov's Smurov combines the distinctive characteristics of both writers. Like Nabokov he is a Russian émigré and works as a tutor for a Russian family in Berlin. Like Kuzmin he is endowed with an effeminate appearance. "[H]is frailness, his decadence, his mincing gestures, his fondness for Eau de Cologne, and, in particular, those furtive, passionate glances" that he allegedly directs at men, convince one of the characters that Smurov is a homosexual (p. 85).

Both Kuzmin and Nabokov contributed – not without the help of others – to the creation of the myth about their *Doppelgänger* personalities.[12] Kuzmin, for instance, claimed that his "I" comprised three different personae (Bogomolov and Malmstad 1996, 96–97). With Nabokov's Smurov, the myth of the elusive soul reaches its apogée; there are as many different Smurovs as there are different people who come into contact with him. Each of the passers-by goes away with his own unique image of Smurov. Nabokov's *Bildungsroman* tells of Smurov's learning to cope with his scattered personality.

The *Bildungsroman*

Like *Wings*,[13] *The Eye* belongs to the genre of the *Bildungsroman*. A typical *Bildungsroman* recounts the story of the moral development of an initially unsophisticated protagonist – often an orphan – who eventually finds his place in life. Following the literary canon, both Smurovs unexpectedly find themselves in an unknown, even hostile, environment. The mother of Vanya Smurov in *Wings* dies suddenly, and he is looked after, first by his mediocre relatives from St. Petersburg, next by some Old Believers, then by a teacher of Greek, and, finally, he is left under the protection and guidance of the Russified Englishman, Stroop. Nabokov's Smurov not only loses all of his relatives, but is forced to emigrate, and – on the one hand – to live among indifferent Germans, and – on the other – to be in touch with equally detached and suspicious compatriots.

Kuzmin's *Bildungsroman* was written in the heyday of the Symbolist movement and was informed by the conception, popular among Russian Symbolists, that the ultimate goal of enlightened men and women should be not procreation but continuous striving towards spiritual rebirth or resurrection. In this context, homoerotic love (as a form which denied procreation) was seen as an effective vehicle in the process of accelerating this rebirth (Matich 1994, 24–50). In agreement with this theory, Vanya's advancement in life is shown metaphorically as the development of a fetus within the mother's womb. The novel opens with Vanya's traveling from the province to St. Petersburg in a train car with "misted windows" and concludes with his famous opening of the window in Canon Mori's house. The open window shows the reader that Vanya is reborn as a "completely transformed being," who accepts the role of Stroop's companion and beloved one. In the greater portion of the book, however, Vanya sits snugly in rooms with windows closed or even moves into the dark cellar with the Old Believers. This, apparently, stems from Vanya's unwillingness to part company with the comfortable protection of the womb; the second birth – admission of one's homosexuality – is not all roses.

At one point in the story, Nabokov's Smurov also feels the need to return and hide himself in a well-sheltered space. Having been severely beaten by Kashmarin, Smurov decides to take his own life. He delays his decision, however, and resolves "for five minutes at least, to sit in safety," and goes "to his former address" [tuda, gde zhil ran'she] (p. 25). Smurov's desire to return to the place where he lived previously, together with the description of "the familiar room" cluttered with various vessels that the landlady keeps filling up with water for no particular reason, is suggestive of his craving to re-enter his mother's womb.

Nabokov's Smurov commits suicide in the outer darkness, and the last thing that he remembers is "a delightful vibrating sound ... It was immediately replaced by the warble of water, a throaty gushing noise. I inhaled, and choked on liquidity; everything within me and around me was aflow and astir" (p. 28). The flowing water is reminiscent of the breaking of uterine water. Subsequent mention of Smurov's "incomprehensible sensation of tight bandages" and the fact that he finds himself surrounded by neighbors ("mummies like [himself]") bring to mind not only "the semblance of a hospital" but, more precisely, that of a maternity ward (p. 29). Nabokov, however, stages the "resurrection" of his Smurov in the first, and not in the final chapter, as might have been expected. By doing this he strips this act of its symbolic and philosophical implications. The second birth is presented not as a desired culmination – the outcome of the character's moral revival – but only as a motivation of the plot.

The platonic theme

As Donald Gillis has shown (1978), Kuzmin's discourse on homoerotic love echoes the second speech of Socrates in Plato's *Phaedrus* about the nature of the relationship between the "lover" and his "beloved." For the sake of "simplification," Socrates describes the soul of the lover as a charioteer in charge of two horses. One horse is beautiful in appearance and is always obedient: "it is a lover of honor ... It needs no whip but is driven simply by a word or command" (*Phaedrus* 253D). The other – the epitome of lust – is, therefore, "crooked in conformation ... deaf and barely responds to a combination of whip and goad" (253E). When the lover first sees the beloved, he is overcome with lust and the charioteer has a difficult task taming his obstinate horse. Gradually, however, the lover learns to rid himself of his unbecoming, base emotions, and his efforts are amply rewarded. The lover is allowed to take "care of all his darling's needs and treats him like an equal of gods ... and the darling himself naturally becomes a friend to the one who cares for him" (255A).

Socrates speaks mainly about the actions of the lover, who first starts growing wings himself – as a result of contemplating the beauty of his darling – and then returns "the stream of beauty" to the beloved, thereby helping his soul to regain its wings too (255C–D). In *Wings* Kuzmin chose to elaborate on the story of the beloved, which is only briefly outlined by Socrates. In Socrates' speech, we learn that the beloved was initially convinced by his friends that it is shameful to be associated with his lover. Similarly, Vanya Smurov also has to see through all the "false" accusations against Stroop (for instance, Stroop's alleged responsibility for Ida Goldberg's suicide), "and as time goes along destiny and increasing maturing lead him to accept" Stroop as his lover (*Phaedrus* 255A).

The relationship between Smurov and Kashmarin in Nabokov's story has all of the necessary platonic ingredients. Kashmarin at first is described as "savagely jealous" and as a likely owner of rolling eyes, who "gnash[es] his teeth and breath[es] heavily through the nose" (p. 16). His portrait evokes the description of Plato's "bad" horse with "bloodshot eyes." Smurov's only recollection of their first encounter was Kashmarin's "heavy bright-knobbed cane with which he would tap on the floor" (p. 14). When they meet for the second time, Kashmarin allows his emotions to overtake him, he refuses to shake hands with Smurov and beats him up instead. Kashmarin's repeated thrusting of a "thick black cane" at Smurov in the presence of the two boys, eagerly condoning his violence – "[t]here he was, teeth bared, cane upraised, and behind him, on either side of the door, stood the boys" – is suggestive of a gang-rape, with the stick as a phallic instrument (p. 23).

In the last scene, however, we are introduced to a totally different Kashmarin. Not only has he parted company with his gruesome stick, but he humbly begs Smurov for his forgiveness: "I'm trying to apologize for my vile temper. I couldn't live at peace with myself after our – uh – heated discussion. I felt horrible about it" (p. 101). Encouraged by the silent approval of Smurov, who blushes like a boarding-school girl, hiding his face in a bunch of flowers, Kashmarin invites Smurov to see him the next day at the Hotel Monopole[14] to discuss their future arrangements. This episode is almost an exact replica of a similar scene between Stroop and Vanya in the concluding portion of *Wings*. The "lovers" express their gratitude to their "beloved ones" in almost identical words: "I am so grateful that you agreed to come," says Stroop ... (p. 107); Kashmarin exclaims, "I'm so glad, so very glad I ran into you" (p. 102). Both Stroop and Kashmarin urge their "beloved ones" to give them definite answers by the next afternoon and morning, respectively; and while Stroop and Vanya are already living in Italy – a Mecca for Russian homosexuals – Kashmarin reassures Smurov that "trips to the Riviera and to Italy are not to be ruled out" (p. 102).

Kashmarin – despite all the evidence of his spiritual growth – is, however, nothing but a parody of a genuine platonic lover like Stroop. He appears briefly only at the very beginning and the very end of the novel and, in Smurov's words, is important only as a bearer of "yet another image" of himself (p. 102). One-third of the way through *The Eye*, however, we learn from the narrator that he is seriously engaged in spying on Smurov. He sits back in the same room as Smurov and eyes him shamelessly. Smurov produces a strong and lasting impression on the narrator:

> He was not very tall, but well proportioned and dapper. His plain black suit and black bow tie seemed to intimate, in a reserved way, some secret mourning. His pale, thin face was youthful, but the perceptive observer could distinguish in it the traces of sorrow and experience. His manners were excellent. A quiet, somewhat melancholy smile lingered on his lips. He spoke little, but everything he said was intelligent and appropriate, and his infrequent jokes, while too subtle to arouse roars of laughter, seemed to unlock a concealed door in the conversation, letting in an unexpected freshness.
>
> (p. 40)

The enchanted narrator resolves to continue spying on Smurov and his eyes tell him that Smurov was "obviously a person who, behind his unpretentiousness and quietness, concealed a fiery spirit" (p. 43).

The statements of the "observing" narrator betray at first that he is not totally indifferent to Smurov – "I definitely liked him" (p. 44) – then, that he becomes addicted to his "espionage" to the point of admitting that he has been experiencing "an excitement new [to him]" (p. 59). The narrator creeps behind Smurov like a shadow. He peeps at him in the bookstore, "I see him ... behind the counter in his neat black suit, hair combed smooth, with his clean-cut, pale face" (p. 49); then he listens to Smurov's breathtaking adventures in the Crimea. Even after learning of Smurov's deficiencies – Smurov is a proven liar – he cannot stop regarding him with affection.

The bizarre behavior of Nabokov's narrator is explicable in the light of the same theory that informed the behavior of Kuzmin's characters; that is, Plato's theory of love. Contemplation of any form of beauty – particularly that of a beloved one[15] – is an essential means of achieving immortality in Plato's myth of the winged soul, "for sight is the keenest of the sensations coming to us through the body" (*Phaedrus* 250D). At the sight of his beloved, the lover

> is awestruck, as though he were gazing upon a god [...] He is warmed by the effluence of beauty he receives through his eyes, which naturally moistens the wing-feathers. As he grows warmer, the follicles, which had earlier hardened and closed so that the feathers could not sprout are softened; and as the nourishing moisture flows over them, the shafts of the feathers swell and begin to grow from their roots over the entire form of the soul, which was feathered all over before [...] The soul of the one who is beginning to sprout feathers itches and is irritated and excited as it grows its wings.
>
> (251A–C)

It does not take too long for the reader to realize that Smurov and the narrator are, in fact, one person.

Smurov–Narcissus

The narrator's love for Smurov is called narcissism. As Irina Paperno shows, the story of the fair-haired Greek youth Narcissus – who fell in love with his own reflection – was extremely popular with Kuzmin (1989, 60). At the beginning of *Wings*, Vanya's behavior is clearly reminiscent of that of Narcissus. Twice he is shown absorbed in examining his own reflection in the looking-glass and each time it coincides with someone's mentioning the name of his future lover, Stroop, who at this point remains a complete stranger to Vanya. Later, with the development of their mutual attachment and attraction to each other, he stops looking in the actual mirror, and relies on Stroop to provide him with the needed reflection, for, in Plato's words, the beloved "is seeing himself in his lover as in a mirror" (*Phaedrus* 255D).[16] Psychoanalysts would describe Vanya's narcissism as "primary," typical of any child's normal development (Freud 1991, 18–19). When Vanya matures, his feeling of self-contentment gives way to the growing need for another male person – Stroop. Stroop, as we are told, "values [Vanya's] heart's noblest aspirations, [and] will never deny [him] his understanding and affection" (p. 74).

With Nabokov's protagonist, the situation is totally different. Being a penniless and friendless Russian emigrant in Berlin, he lives under constant stress. He lacks confidence and is lonely. He looks in the mirror once, but the sight of "[a] wretched, shivering, vulgar little man in a bowler hat" is repulsive to him (p. 26). The little man commits suicide, giving birth to the mysterious Smurov and his shadowy admirer. Not being adequately loved, Smurov goes through yet further fragmentation. The fact that the name of Kuzmin's character – Vanya Smurov – is broken down by Nabokov into an attractive girl, Vanya, and Smurov-the-narrator, can be seen as a typical instance of Nabokov's playing games with his readers. On the other hand, it can be viewed as the ultimate proof of Smurov's self-fragmentation. In the long run, it is not the reader who is deluded, but Smurov himself, who – because of the missing or misleading mirrors – remains unaware of his outlines, confusing Vanya with his missing half. At the end of the story, however, both men are happily reunited:

> As I pushed the door, I noticed the reflection in the side mirror: a young man in a bowler carrying a bouquet, hurried towards me. That reflection and I merged into one. I walked out into the street.
>
> (p. 97)

Only his falling in love with himself finally makes Smurov "invulnerable" to the threats of the outside world: "[w]hat does it matter that I am a bit cheap, a bit foul, and that no one appreciates all the remarkable things about me – my fantasy, my erudition, my literary gift . . . I am happy that I can gaze at myself. . ." Thus he conveniently readjusts Plato to his own needs (p. 103).[17]

It is no accident that Nabokov's *Bildungsroman* about Narcissus's quest for identity was fashioned after Kuzmin's *Wings* – the story about the moral development of a homosexual. What Nabokov's "emigrant" and Kuzmin's "homosexual" do have in common is their isolated position with regard to the rest of society.[18] In many ways, Nabokov's Smurov is the same Vanya Smurov from *Wings*, but placed in the context of an emigrant. While Kuzmin's Smurov gradually comes to grips with his "estrangement" from society by reaching out for similarly oriented people; in order to survive in extreme conditions (like being uprooted and living in a foreign country), Nabokov's Smurov directs his love totally toward himself. If for Kuzmin's Smurov narcissism is only an intermediate stage in his growing up, then for Nabokov's Smurov it is the only state which allows him to sustain his integrity and survive. Smurov's behavior is in accordance with Freud's observation that a person's "narcissistic attitude" increases his/her resilience and diminishes his/her "susceptibility to influence" (1991, 3).

Narcissism – love of oneself – is in many ways similar to homoerotic love, because in both situations the lover and the beloved are of the same gender. In his seminal study, "On Narcissism: An Introduction" (1914), Freud suggested that narcissism often accompanies what he terms "other disorders," like homosexuality (1991, 3, 18). Freud was not alone in this assumption. In the 1910s and 1920s a number of scholars (Löwenfeld, Rank, and Sadger among others) believed in a direct correlation between homosexuality and narcissism. Sadger, for example, described homosexuality as "the narcissistic perversion *par excellence*" (Ellis 1936 III/2, 363–364). It is most unlikely that Nabokov can have been totally unaware of these discussions. It is noteworthy that in their discussions of narcissistic traits, the scholars drew their conclusions both from their work with actual patients and from analyses of literary texts.[19] Science and literature were going hand in hand in their construction of the twentieth-century myth of Narcissus.[20] It will suffice to mention that in *The Eye* Nabokov explored the traumatic effects of emigration on the mental state of a young person – which he would know only too well himself[21] – long before the famous revelations of Heinz Kohut, who showed that any "external shifts, such as moves from one culture to another; from private life into the army; from the small town to the big city" are traumatic to one's ego and serve as a precondition for one's growing need of exaggerated love for oneself (1978, 623).[22]

Conclusions

As this chapter shows, *The Eye* is, in many ways, a product of Nabokov's transferal of Kuzmin's *Wings* into the cultural setting of the late 1920s and early 1930s. Both authors were exploring a similar theme – alienation – but in different contexts: the context of Russia at the turn of the century for Kuzmin, and the context of emigration for Nabokov. By creatively appropriating one of the important cultural texts of the preceding tradition, Nabokov was able not only to "write back" to its opponents but also to rid himself of imitative features, unavoidable at the stage of apprenticeship, and glide smoothly into a more gratifying craftsmanship. *The Eye* is a perfect example of what Thomas Greene has termed "heuristic imitation": "Heuristic imitations come to us advertising their derivation from the subtexts they carry with them, but having done that, they proceed *to distance themselves* from the subtexts and force us to recognize the poetic distance traversed" (Greene 1982, 40; original emphasis). Hence, Nabokov's discourse of alienation was informed not only by the mythology of the Silver Age (via Kuzmin), but by the contemporary discourse of narcissism as a scientific phenomenon, and by his own experience as an emigrant.[23] The result of such amalgamation was a literary character that later became the hallmark of Nabokov's fiction.

Smurov is the first lonely "sexual lefty" among Nabokov's numerous "perverted" characters. A happy homosexual couple from *Mashen'ka* [*Mary*] (1926) is an exception rather than the rule. Latent or evident perversion of any kind in Nabokov's characters – such as Sebastian Knight, Charles Kinbote, Humbert Humbert, to name but a few – appears to be a product of their social isolation, and not the other way around. For certain, in *The Eye*, Smurov's narcissism and alleged homosexuality are unequivocally presented as a direct consequence of his enforced emigration and alienation. Suffering from finding himself in the unrewarding position of a rootless Russian emigrant in a hostile Berlin, Smurov does not feel himself at home in the company of his compatriots. His pupils openly dislike and despise him. The owner of the book shop, Weinstock, seriously believes that Smurov is a Soviet spy, while Vanya's family strive to expose him as a liar or a petty thief. It is only after having been irrevocably rejected by Vanya that Smurov throws himself under Kashmarin's protection. Latent homosexuality, therefore, becomes, for Nabokov, an additional marker of the emigrant-outsider, signaling his exceptional position vis-à-vis an unfriendly environment.

Notes

1 I wish to thank V. Ambros and C. J. Barnes and the anonymous reviewers for their helpful comments on this chapter. I had finished writing this chapter by summer 1996 and was unaware that Olga Skonechnaia was exploring Kuzminian subtexts in Nabokov at the same time: see her "Liudi lunnogo sveta v russkoi proze Nabokova." *Zvezda* 11 (1996): 207–214.

> "To take a deep breath and up to the shoulders // place my stretched arms in the wings,// [then] from the windowsill to slide into the air // and fly despite [the laws of] science [. // . . .] I am afraid I'll not survive the flight. . . // No, I've survived. I sit on the floor in darkness, // I am dazzled, and there is a buzzing in my ears, // and a blissful ache in my shoulders." (Unless otherwise indicated, translations from Russian are my own.)

2 Ivanov's opinions were shared by Georgiy Adamovich and the Merezhkovsky-Gippius circle (Berberova 1996, 286).
3 All quotations from *Wings* are from Kuzmin (1980); page references are given in parenthetical notes in the text.
4 There was also a family connection through Nabokov's latent identification

with the author of the first Russian novel about homosexuals. In the early 1900s Nabokov's father, Vladimir Dmitriyevich (a recognized authority on criminal law), argued on many occasions for the decriminalization of homosexuals, maintaining (not unlike Kuzmin) that "homosexuality was neither inherently abnormal nor morally reprehensible" (Engelstein 1994, 67–71). V. D. Nabokov's interest in homosexuality was not purely theoretical, for many members of his family, including his son Sergey, were homosexual.

5 See Timofeev's explanation as to why Kuzmin used the name of Dostoevsky's character in his book (1993).

6 All quotations from *The Eye* are from Nabokov (1966); page references are given in parenthetical notes in the text.

7 "Petropolis" reprinted the following of Kuzmin's works at the time when Nabokov moved to Berlin: *Seti* (3rd edn, 1923): *Plavayushchie-puteshestvuyushchie* (3rd and 4th edn, 1923): *Kryl'ya* (4th edn, 1923) and *Glinyanye golubki* (2nd and 3rd edn, 1923); see Malmstad 1989, 178 n7.

8 Matilda's parting with her husband and her immediate starting of an affair with Smurov evokes the reckless tone of Kuzmin's poem "Ariadna" (*Parabolas*) [1923], "У платана тень прохладна, \\ Тесны терема князей, — \\ Ариадна, Ариадна, \\ Уплывает твой Тезей! \\ ... Чередою плод за цветом, \\ Синий пурпур кружит вниз, — \\ И, увенчан вечным светом, \\ Ждет невесты Дионис."

9 This passage probably alludes also to Kuzmin's novella, *Kartonnyy domik* [*The House of Cards*] (1907), where the name Matilda Petrovna appears for the first time: "If you find it amusing when Matilda sits on your stomach and says she's a chimera, when in one evening you have ten of the silliest tête-à-têtes of the most compromising kind, when you listen to as many as twenty poets – then we've had a very good time. But, between ourselves, all that has palled to a considerable degree" (Kuzmin 1980, 143).

10 On references to *Travelers by Land and Sea* in Nabokov's "Lips to Lips" see Barnstead 1986.

11 See Irina Paperno's discussion of a similar love-triangle in Kuzmin's "The Trout Breaks the Ice" (1989).

12 See, for example, Blok (1931, 189); Ivanov (1994, 104–105); Markov (1977, 402–405); Shakhovskaya (1991, 40–41) among many others.

13 See Markov (1984).

14 Half way through the narrative, Vanya is told that Stroop "can be reached at the Four Seasons Hotel" in Munich (p. 75).

15 Plato stipulates that "[e]ach person selects his love from the ranks of the beautiful according to his own style" (*Phaedrus* 252D).

16 For a more detailed discussion of this theme, see Gillis (1978).

17 It is usually assumed that it was Nabokov's intention to portray Smurov as a failure – both as an artist and as a human being (Johnson 1985; Field 1987, among others). I disagree with this. By carefully piecing himself together, Smurov–Narcissus attains a degree of integrity and peace within himself that is favorable to creativity. Smurov, as a character at any rate, did not fall into oblivion. He came back to life in the satisfyingly self-centered Fedor Konstantinovich Godunov-Cherdyntsev of *The Gift* (unlike the "nameless" Smurov this character is not only given a name, but a patronymic and a double-barrelled surname), who, by the end of the book, is a picture of real happiness and confidence:

> It is easier for me, of course, to live outside Russia, because I know for certain that I shall return – first because I took away the keys to her, and secondly because, no matter when, in a hundred, two

hundred years – I shall live there in my books – or at least in some researcher's footnote.

Apart from the fact that both narratives are recounted by the interchanging Ich/Er-narrators, the protagonists in both novels are young Russian émigré writers; both novels also take place in the Berlin of the mid-1920s. The mysterious Marianna Nikolayevna of *The Eye* reappears in *The Gift* as Marianna Nikolayevna, Zina's mother. Fedor's latent homoerotic attachment to Koncheev – the scene of the naked Fedor meeting with the dressed up "Koncheev" with a stick [sic!] in the "Grunewald" (Part V) is particularly suggestive – is usually overlooked by the critics. Fedor's lonely sunbathing in Grunewald might have been informed by similar scenes of Michel's suntanning from André Gide's novel, *The Immoralist* (1902). In this novel, Michel resorts to naked sunbathing in a secluded spot (leaving his devoted wife at home) as a means of recovery from TB, the disease that was an outward manifestation of his inner suppression of homosexual desires (Sontag 1977, 21). It is not fortuitous that Nabokov's Sebastian Knight (*The Real Life of Sebastian Knight* 1941) also suffered from a mysterious disease that eventually drove him away from his girlfriend, Clare Bishop. Gide's groundbreaking work was known to Kuzmin and apparently also to Nabokov.

18 On Kuzmin's Smurov as an "outsider" see Schindler (1992).
19 See Ellis (1936, 3: 347–375), Rank (1971, 69–86), Kohut (1978, 615–617); the studies of Ellis and Rank were published prior to Nabokov's writing of *The Eye*.
20 Hermann Hesse's *Narziss und Goldmund* [*Narcissus and Goldmund*] about the spiritual and sensual progression of the young Goldmund was published in the same year as Nabokov's *The Eye*.
21 Nabokov's 1965 foreword to *The Eye* betrays his intimate links with his protagonist. In it, Nabokov describes Mukhin – Smurov's lucky rival for Vanya's attention – as "a nasty prig, fought in 1919 under Denikin, and under Wrangel, speaks four languages, affects a cool, worldly air, and will probably do very well in the soft job into which his future father-in-law is steering him" (pp. 8–9). The actual text of *The Eye* does not offer any support for such an "unfair" characterization, unless we assume that this foreword was written by an aging Smurov himself. The foreword finishes almost with a "threat": "The plot will not be reducible in the reader's mind – if I read that mind correctly – to a dreadfully painful love story in which a writhing heart is not only spurned, but humiliated and punished" (p. 10).
22 See Andrew Field's discussion of Nabokov as Narcissus (1987, 12, 27–30, 58, 80–82, 139); Field, however, does not consider *The Eye* in the light of the myth of Narcissus.
23 The question of whether *The Eye* was intended as a parody of Kuzmin is a tricky one. Even if it were meant as such, Nabokov's contemporaries certainly failed to recognize its "target text" and Nabokov did not assist them in this endeavor. It would seem that Nabokov (who was notoriously secretive about the works that truly influenced him in the course of his career) took a long time to rid himself of the influence of this particular predecessor. Kuzmin's presence can be detected not only in *The Gift*, but in the strangely homoerotic poem "How I love you" [Kak ya lyublyu tebya] (1934) which bears a striking resemblance to corresponding portions of Kuzmin's long poem "The Trout Breaks the Ice" (1928). Nabokov's rather fond recollections of his homosexual uncle, Vasiliy Rukavishnikov, in *Drugie berega* (1954) are reminiscent of the

canonical descriptions of Kuzmin. Kuzmin can also be recognized in Konstantin Ivanovich Chateau (*Pnin* 1953), "a subtle and charming scholar ... [with] mild melancholy caribou eyes, the auburn goatee ... [and] long frail fingers," whose article Pnin forwards to his Akhmatova-like future wife in the 1920s. In his article, Chateau (not unlike Kuzmin in *Wings* and Nabokov in *The Eye*) "brilliantly refutes ... [the] theory of birth being an act of suicide on the part of the infant" (Nabokov 1989, 125, 183). Maybe it was only in *Pale Fire* (1962), whose main theme is, apparently, what Harold Bloom terms the "anxiety of literary influence," that Nabokov managed to shed Kuzmin's influence, and any other influence for that matter. In this later parodic re-writing of *The Eye*, Charles Kinbote fails spectacularly in his endeavor to influence and enliven the imagination of his illustrious neighbor, John Shade, in spite of his frenzied activity (involving incessant discussions, eyeing, spying, and eavesdropping). Not only does he fail to see any traces of his personal story in Shade's last poem (the only word that resonates through the whole piece is "shade"!), but even his perceived physical resemblance to Shade is completely bogus. Shade does not look like Kinbote but like Judge Goldsmith, a resemblance which costs him his life in the end. Shortly before the tragic accident, Kinbote – not unlike Kuzmin's *lyrical hero* in "The Trout Breaks the Ice" – rescues his "dearest friend" Shade from the influence of his "mediocre" wife by inviting him to his house to recite his completed poem. Like Kuzmin's protagonist, he literally leads Shade (whose feet are numb) to his house. Not surprisingly, he brings him death instead of life. After Shade's death Kinbote, agonizing over his literary "non-influence," flies away and possibly commits suicide.

4

GETTING ONE PAST THE GOALKEEPER

Sports and games in *Glory*

David H. J. Larmour

Introductions

Glory [*Podvig*], the story of the travels and maturation of a young émigré, takes Martin Edelweiss from a childhood in pre-revolutionary Russia, through a meandering flight to Switzerland after the revolution, to his university days at Cambridge. It also recounts Martin's first sexual experience with the middle-aged Alla, his unsuccessful love affair with a girl called Sonia, his friendship with an English student called Darwin and his falling in with anti-Bolshevik émigrés. The novel ends with Martin's seeking "glory" by crossing over the border into the Soviet Union, for some grand, but unnamed, purpose. This is a journey from which Martin never returns.

As a glance at the bibliographical entries in *The Nabokovian* shows, *Glory* has received less attention from scholars than most of Nabokov's other works. There are reasons for this. For one thing, it was the last of the Russian novels to be translated into English, as late as 1971. It also has a significant autobiographical element – childhood experiences, time in Cambridge and visits to Switzerland – and this caused it to be viewed, perhaps primarily, as a quarry from which personal details about the author could be mined. The search for biographical information in such a text turns out to be more like entering a minefield than a quarry: Andrew Field, an expert in this area, remarks that the variation between accounts of the same incident in *Speak, Memory*, *A University Poem*, and *Glory* "forcefully reminds us how futile it is to seek to fix Nabokov in his own novels" (1967, 118).

And then, it has often been said that *Glory* lacks some of the features of the mature Nabokovian text, like complexity for instance. Hyde, for example, divines "a certain thinness" about *Glory* (Hyde 1977, 51), and says that its appeal "resides in its fairly simple statement of themes which later become more complex" (p. 53). What is interesting is how frequently the novel's autobiographical content is linked with its perceived failings, or, at least, its lack of appeal to a general and a scholarly audience alike. Hyde views it as "written for an émigré audience" to an extent greater than any of the other novels (1977, 53), while Field suggests that the autobiographical material "may be one factor which serves to inhibit the author's imagination" because *Glory* "is the longest Sirin work which does not challenge the reader with subtle multiplicity of meaning" (Field 1967, 118). The assumption here is that the presence of personal details or the acting upon the author of the autobiographical urge has had a deleterious effect on the textual production of this novel.

But, for all its supposed thinness and simplicity, when Leona Toker investigates the novel's metaphysical ideas, she discovers that *Glory* is "as complex as any of the later works" and argues that it is "the first novel to adumbrate Nabokov's cautious metaphysics, a novel that masks eschatological anxiety with apparent simplicity and a lyrical tone" (Toker 1989, 88). If, as Nabokov himself says in his Introduction (p. xiv),[1] this novel was "diabolically difficult to construct," it is perhaps deserving of closer scrutiny. And indeed, when it comes to the underpinnings of Nabokovian ideology and their connections with the world of actual experience, it is precisely the presence of the autobiographical parallels which makes this text especially worth investigating. Brian Boyd, discussing the plot, notes that "*Glory* is the first Nabokov novel shaped to match the lack of structure in an individual life" (Boyd 1990, 357–358). And presumably not just any old life; while there is, of course, no simple correspondence between Martin's life and that of the author, reading Chapter 9 of Boyd's biography ("Becoming Sirin: Cambridge, 1919–1922" [1990, 164–195]) makes it difficult for the reader to disassociate the two. Although Martin Edelweiss is not, in any simplistic sense, to be equated with Vladimir Nabokov, the ideological assumptions and aporias, the polarities and hierarchies, which the text discloses to us cannot be disassociated either from the world of lived experience in general, or from this author's real-life concretization of experience in particular.

The authorial Introduction functions as a bridge between the text and these realms of actual experience, but, at the same time, through the mechanisms of the game, it works to prevent critical scrutiny of the novel's ideological manipulations. The Introduction carefully sets up interpretative parameters for the reader, using several superlatives, which seem intended to ensure that we pay attention (pp. xi–xii), especially to certain features of the main characters: Martin is "the kindest, uprightest, and most touching of all my young men" and is "nicer" and "more naive" than the author "ever was." "Little Sonia" has "lustreless black eyes and coarse-looking black hair" and is "the most oddly attractive of all my young girls, although obviously a moody and ruthless flirt." This appears to promote a sympathy for Martin, the young male, while Sonia, the young female, is delineated with an ambiguous mixture of desire and dislike, straight out of the Catullan *odi et amo* school. While Martin gets at least four positive epithets, Sonia receives a similar number of negatively-charged ones. We notice immediately that only Martin's character is described, whereas Sonia is also evaluated for her looks and attractiveness. We are also given nudges towards a "politically correct" interpretation of events in Russia and their aftermath: the émigrés are described as "three staunch patriots, dedicated to counter-Bolshevist work," with the words "staunch" and "dedicated" carrying positive connotations which alternatives like "die-hard" and "fanatical" for instance would not. The émigrés are situated, politically speaking, in the realm of "liberal thought" which, the author takes pains to tell us, had a "vigorous existence among Russian expatriates" – American intellectuals, he adds in a rather sweeping generalization, were "conditioned by Bolshevist propaganda" into believing that all Russian émigrés were either Soviets or Tsarists. The novel *Glory*, we learn, was serialized in a magazine run by people just like these "three staunch patriots." These details appear to privilege the "liberal" political position (i.e. the "enlightened liberalism" of the comfortably off with a vested interest in promoting gradual or cosmetic social change) over the two extremes of Soviets and Tsarists, suggesting that the émigrés and the author occupy the enlightened middle ground of moderation and common sense, a sort of parliamentary "golden mean." They also raise the possibility that, like the "staunch patriots," this novel is also "dedicated to counter-Bolshevist work."

The Introduction has several more pointers for the reader: Darwin, Martin's Cambridge friend, and Professor Moon are totally invented, but the characters Vadim and Teddy are based on actual acquaintances the author knew at Cambridge (p. xi). This introduces the dichotomy of fiction and fact, emphasized later by the author's description of himself as "the wizard who made Martin" (p. xii). The artifice of the author is responsible for Martin's lack of interest in politics and his lack of talent. Nabokov tells us that it would have been very easy for the author to have made Martin an artist, a writer (p. xiii): "how hard not to let him be one, while bestowing on him the keen sensitivity that one generally associates with the creative creature; how cruel to prevent him from finding in art – not an escape ... but relief from the itch of being!" Nabokov compares the result to a chess problem he once composed, one which was "diabolically difficult to construct." This all emphasizes the role of the author as game-maker. Peter Hutchinson, in his study of the games authors play, notes that Nabokov frequently gives advance notice of gaming in his titles (such as *King, Queen, Knave*) or in his prefatory remarks (as in the case of the short story, "The Vane Sisters"), as well as in the text itself (Hutchinson 1983, 36).

We are given advice as to how to read the "fulfillment" or "glory" which Martin seeks: "it is the glory of high adventure and disinterested achievement; the glory of this earth and its patchy paradise; the glory of personal pluck; the glory of a radiant martyr" (p. xiii). Freudian readings are firmly discouraged: it would be reckless to connect "Martin's plunge into his fatherland with his having been deprived of his father" or "to point out, with womby wonder, that the girl Martin loves and his mother bear the same name" (p. xiii). This presents the reader with an apparent dilemma: are Nabokov's remarks to be taken as a parodic anticipation of typical Freudian readings, or as a hint as to where meanings may be found? If we disregard authorial intention, of course, the question becomes moot: a Freudian-based interpretation would probably follow similar lines and, more importantly, what the text raises only to dismiss must be scrutinized.

Nabokov ends his prefatory remarks with a lengthy sentence telling us where the "fun" of *Glory* is to be sought (p. xiv):

> the echoing and linking of minor events, in back-and-forth switches, which produce an illusion of impetus: in an old daydream directly becoming the blessing of the ball hugged to one's chest, or in the casual vision of Martin's mother grieving beyond the time-frame of the novel in an abstraction of the future that the reader can only guess at, even after he has raced through the last seven chapters where a regular madness of structural twists and a masquerade of all characters culminate in a furious finale, although nothing much happens at the very end – just a bird perching on a wicket in the grayness of a wet day.

The Introduction thus offers an encapsulation of the main devices of the narrative which follows. It demonstrates how matters of ideological content are subordinated to – or, more accurately – obfuscated by the playing of the game. The pointed remarks about the characters, and the very definite assumptions about women and politics which color them, give way to a focus on the artificiality of the text and the manipulations of the master artificer who made it. Once this is established, and the novel's characters and events are divorced from such elements of the phenomenal world as political struggle, parent–child relationships, and sexuality, the reader is invited to join the game. Geoffrey Green, drawing on Freud's "Splitting of the Ego in the Process of Defence" and "Analysis Terminable and Interminable," astutely speculates on the nature of such Nabokovian distancing: "Might it be said of Nabokov's writing that it creates alternative 'situations in reality' that may serve as 'approximate substitute[s]' for the 'original danger[s]' that were encountered in life?" (Green 1989, 371). The linguistic brilliance of the final sentence describing the "fun" of *Glory* indicates that the safe, artful game is, in fact, already underway: the artificiality of the narrative is foreshadowed in such phrases as "*illusion* of impetus," "the old *daydream*," "an *abstraction* of the future that the reader can only *guess at*," the "*masquerade* of all characters" and the "furious *finale*." All these terms create the impression of artifice and illusion. The reader, it seems, can only "guess at" the connections between the world of the narrative and the world of phenomenal reality. The sentence, which continues for several lines before reaching a full stop, overwhelms the reader with information in the same artful way as the narrative does, with its allusions, its chronological and geographical shifts, and its rhetorical devices.

This emphasis on playing the game, however, sets off an alarm bell at the same time as it threatens to ensnare the reader in its interpretative net. The alarm is raised by the disjunction between the final sentence and the more openly ideological comments which preceded it. The final sentence contains references to sporting games which anticipate the numerous descriptions of Martin's athletic activities ahead: "the *ball* hugged to one's chest," the reader who has "*raced* through the last seven chapters," and the "bird perching on a *wicket*" all evoke the playing of games. Even the "back-and-forth switches" suggest the give-and-take which characterizes many such activities. Moreover, this drawn-out sentence, with its overtones of sexual climax ("hugged to one's chest ... twists ... furious finale ... nothing much happens at the end ... a wet day"), links sports and sex in a nexus of semiological significance. Thus the reader is alerted that, in the upcoming narrative, the scenes of sporting games may well be a key to some aspects of what the narrative attempts to marginalize: the real-life implications of its ideological assumptions. In a text which relies for its operations on the structures of games, those characters and scenes closely associated with sports may reveal to us the central conflicts of the narrative.

Sports and games

Martin Edelweiss is marked by his sporting activities: tennis, football, boxing, and mountain-climbing. For some guide to interpretation of these elements in *Glory*, we can look to other works. Sports and games are, in fact, a standard part of Nabokov's textual repertoire; Rowe devotes a chapter to exploring their presence, and their sexual symbolism, in numerous novels. In *Lolita*, there is, for instance, a long description of Lolita playing tennis (Rowe 1971, 211–215). Nabokov himself indicated that "Lolita playing tennis" was one of the "nerves of the novel" (Nabokov 1955, 318, cf. 232–236) and Rowe traces the theme, noting that "the sustained *double entendre* is very subtle," but also the presence of "some rather gross potential puns" (1971, 145). He raises the possibility of construing the rally "as a single sex act" and winning "as attaining a climax."

The beauty of the symbolism, Rowe suggests, lies "in the fact that none of it – however suggestive – can ever be irrefutably demonstrated" (Rowe 1971, 146). Similar use is made of tennis in *King, Queen, Knave* (Rowe 1971, 146; Nabokov 1989a, 188), amid a bevy of sporting terms for sexual activity. Football, or some such team game, makes an appearance in *Bend Sinister* (Nabokov 1990, 66–67; cf. Rowe 1971, 153–154), with the goal as a sexual metaphor. In *Laughter in the Dark*, when Rex is trying to persuade Margot to have sex with him, their conversation is interrupted by an account of how the ice-hockey goal-keeper "slid slowly toward his tiny goal," how he "pressed his legs together" and how "the noise had reached its climax: a goal had been scored" (Nabokov 1989b, 151–152). Clearly, sports and sex are intricately bound up in Nabokovian discourse.

In *Glory*, there are three extended scenes in which Martin participates in a sporting activity: the tennis match in Chapter 10 (pp. 46–47), the football match in Chapter 26 (pp. 108–111) and the impromptu boxing bout with Darwin in Chapter 28 (pp. 122–125). Each of these scenes is of pivotal importance for the development of the plot and of Martin's character, especially in the realm of sexual experience. The tennis match in Chapter 10 is preceded by Martin's budding attraction to Marie, the maid, which is temporarily dampened when Martin's mother suggests that Marie smells. Martin watches a courting couple and then sees some women playing on the tennis court, noting how "clumsy and helpless" they are when they play (p. 46). The game of tennis is thus metonymically linked with sexual activity.[2] We learn that Martin thinks he is an excellent player, one who "had assimilated the concord essential for the enjoyment of all the properties of the sphere" (p. 47). When he is matched against the experienced professional player from Nice, however, Martin is soundly beaten. Afterwards, he mentally replays every shot, transforming defeat into victory, and realizes how hard it is "to capture happiness" (pp. 47–48). This phrase is an indication that the tennis match has potentially more significance than a simple game or even a sexual experience: it somehow stands for life itself and the quest for happiness. That sporting victory or defeat should be connected with personal happiness is an intriguing notion. The very next scene of the story has Martin travel to London, where he is immediately "victorious" in sexual terms: he spends his first night with a prostitute – who has the almost unbelievably trite name of Bess – and awakens in high spirits the next morning, even though she has stolen ten pounds from his wallet (p. 51). A defeat on the tennis court at the hands of a male opponent, then, is followed by, and closely linked with, a victory in the "game of sex" with a woman; but at the same time the fact that she has preyed upon his wallet imports an element of ambiguity into Martin's "conquest." The happiness captured by victory is followed by a loss brought about by trickery.

In the second sporting scene, the soccer match follows upon two significant events: first, Martin has learned, not without a certain sense of betrayal, that his mother has got remarried, to his uncle (pp. 101–102); second, Martin has had a sexual encounter with Rose, another tritely English name. The "goddess of the tearoom" has told him she is pregnant and Martin has dutifully proposed to her. Darwin, however, goes to talk to the waitress, finds out she is not actually having a baby (thus Martin is again victimized by a combination of sex and trickery), and tells Martin to stay away from her (pp. 102–105). Darwin connects the liaison with Rose to Martin's role as goalkeeper in the upcoming college soccer match: he is worried that he may not be able to concentrate on his performance in the nets (p. 104). The description of the soccer match itself is full of sexual innuendo: first, in a chronological shift, we hear how Martin would recollect his childhood reveries before sleep, in which he used to see himself as a "crack footballer" (p. 108). The word "crack" is not necessarily innocent in a Nabokovian novel, as Rowe points out in the case of Humbert's words "– crack players will understand what I mean" (Nabokov 1955, 235) – in his discussion of Lolita's rhythmic coordination on the tennis court (Rowe 1971, 146). The *Glory* passage continues as follows:

> It was enough for him to close his eyes and picture a soccer field or, say, the long, brown, diaphragm-joined cars of an express that he was driving himself, and his mind would gradually catch the rhythm, grow blissfully serene, be cleansed, as it were, and, sleek and oiled, slip into oblivion.
>
> (p. 108)

and a few lines later:

> ... the new series of reveries he had recently evolved ... would also grow solid and be filled with life, as his dreams about soccer matches had grown solid and incarnate, those dreams in which he used to luxuriate so lengthily, so artfully, when, afraid to reach the delicious essence too quickly, he would dwell in detail on the pregame preparations...
>
> (p. 109)

This is suggestive of masturbatory fantasy, in which the pleasure of orgasm is enhanced by delaying ejaculation. Games and masturbation are linked elsewhere by Nabokov: in *Pale Fire* (Nabokov 1962, 124), Kinbote uses the term "games" to refer to masturbation (Rowe 1971, 151). The phrasing "grow solid and be filled with life" and "grow solid and incarnate" suggests an erection.

Martin is disappointed that Sonia does not even look at him, although this is the first time he has appeared before her in his "soccer array," and when the match starts he looks round to see if Darwin and Sonia are watching (p. 110). As the account of the game gets underway, the text again alludes to Martin's childhood fantasizing and the language takes on a homoerotic resonance, as he imagines a footballer on the opposing team charging up the pitch towards the goal he is defending:

> Thus he would protract the delight ... and now he could hear the panting of the attack as the redhead broke loose – and there he came, his shock of hair bobbing ... and now the ball was already in his hands...
>
> (p. 111)

The account culminates in the statement that Martin "kept his goal virgin to the end of the game," thereby ensuring that his team wins with a goal at the other end, just before the final whistle (p. 111). Martin's net, of course, maintains its virginity by not being penetrated by the ball(s) of the other team. After the game, Martin finds Sonia in Darwin's room, and is elated to find that Sonia has just rejected Darwin's proposal. Again, sporting prowess, sexual desire, and happiness are associated with each other, as Martin feels a

> rush of radiant torrent that had burst through the locks, he remembered the tricky cross he had collected so nicely, remembered that the Rose business was settled, that there was a banquet at the club that evening, that he was healthy and strong, that tomorrow, the day after tomorrow, and for many, many days more life would go on, replete with all kinds of happiness.
>
> (p. 113)

Martin seizes Sonia and kisses her, just as Darwin enters the room. In this case, paralleling the first sporting incident, Martin's victory in the football match is followed by a victory over Darwin in the sexual game for Sonia. It soon becomes clear, however, that in this triangle of desire we have more than a simple rivalry between two males for a female prize.

The third sporting scene occurs when Martin and Darwin are out in a punt on the river: Martin sees Rose on the bank and ignores Darwin's injunction not to greet her. Darwin promptly moors the boat and arranges a fight. Martin at first thinks it is all a joke, but changes his mind when he gets hit hard. The ringing in his head "sang of Sonia, over whom, in a sense, they were fighting this duel" (pp. 123–124); the phrase "in a sense" is right, for we never get a clear explanation of Darwin's behavior. There is a detailed description of the fight, which ends with Martin collapsing on the grass. Darwin grins, puts his arm around his shoulders and together they trudge to the river. They keep asking "each other in low solicitous tones where it hurt and if the water did not sting" (p. 125). Afterwards, the two friends lie together on the cushions as the boat floats down the river in a romantic scene which strikes Martin as reminiscent of the wounded Tristram floating "alone with his harp."[3] This episode is followed in the narrative by Martin's return to Switzerland, where he is the object of his mother's admiration: "She was satisfied with the happiness at hand – of his being with her now, healthy, broad-shouldered, tanned; of his slamming away at tennis, speaking in a bass voice, shaving daily, and making young, bright-eyed Madame Guichart, a local merchant's wife, blush as red as a poppy" (p. 129). Shortly thereafter, Martin decides, on his twenty-first birthday, to go to Berlin, where Sonia now resides.

These sporting incidents function as models for the operations of the novel as a whole. For Martin, his relationships with women and with his male friend Darwin are a kind of game, with sexual and social fulfillment as the prize: in the first scene, Martin plays against an anonymous opponent and then has sex with the equally anonymous Bess; in the second scene, Martin's team is victorious in the football match and he scores a victory in his game with Darwin for the hand of Sonia; in the third scene, Martin's defeat by Darwin sends him back to his mother and then on in pursuit of Sonia again. The football game has an important social resonance, perhaps explaining Martin's departure from England: he is the goalkeeper on the team, an essentially passive role, suitable for a marginal figure like him – if he keeps the balls out, he is praised, while if he lets them in, he is condemned. The game can only be won, though, by other members of the team, when they put the ball into the net of the opposing side. If Martin stays in England, he will always be a goalkeeper, never a striker. On the soccer field, he is part of the winning team, but not a winning individual, not even the individual who scores the goal. Defeat in tennis by the professional from Nice or in boxing by Darwin is also a kind of social defeat. The outsider is forced to compete on the locals' turf and according to their rules – he rejects Vadim's patriotic exhortation to simply kick Darwin in the balls (p. 122) – and is duly defeated by a kind of skill and sophistication which he does not have. Through the sporting episodes, then, the text reveals profound anxiety about the sexual and social identity of Martin Edelweiss.

Martin and women

In spite of the smokescreen of such insistent playfulness and gaming, the sexual games of the novel and the discursive portrayal of women (and men) are open to varying (re)interpretation, not necessarily following the guidelines offered in the author's Introduction. What are the implications of viewing the women in the novel as ideological constructions? Just about every female character – Sofia, Alla, Bess, Sonia, Rose – fits a stereotype.

Women, moreover, are basically spectators or pawns in Martin's games. He is incapable of establishing a meaningful relationship with any of them. As Andrew Field comments (1967, 118), the novel is "most centrally about the inability of Martin Edelweiss to form any sort of lasting relationship" and this is what leads to his great exploit (p. 119). Toker suggests (1989, 97) that Martin's glory is achieved at the expense of human commitments. The urge to interpret Martin's sexual identity in the light of Freudian paradigms is almost irresistible; the text itself seems actively to solicit such approaches, even if the remarks in the Introduction seek to discourage them:

> ...only a desperate saphead in the throes of a nightmare examination may be excused for connecting Martin's plunge into his fatherland with his having been deprived of his father. No less reckless would it be to point out, with womby wonder, that the girl Martin loves and his mother bear the same name
>
> (p. xiii)

But, after all, the reader has the right to interpret the text using the methods she sees fit, and why not use the one which the authorial introduction brings to our attention, even if only – apparently – to dismiss it? Nabokov's antipathy to Freud and psychoanalytic interpretations is well-known and well-documented, and, one might say, a little too well celebrated among the critics. Indeed, the author's magisterial response to Rowe's work typifies the state of the official dialogue between the Nabokovian text and Freudian analysis (Nabokov 1971). This is a dialogue the author aims to frustrate by claims, such as the one he makes in the Introduction to *Despair*, that he has planted red herrings for the "eager Freudian": "the attractively shaped object or Wiener-schnitzel dream that the eager Freudian may think he distinguishes in the remoteness of my wastes will turn out to be on closer inspection a derisive mirage organized by my agents" (Nabokov 1966a, 8). These expressions of hostility have not scared off everybody, however, and there have been several illuminating studies of novels and short stories (Shute 1984; Green 1988, 1989; Elms 1989; Welsen 1989). Nor has it gone unnoticed that Nabokov's open hostility to Freud has only served to cement the links between the two: as Green puts it, "to ban Freud so vociferously is to give him substance, thing-ness, within Nabokov's world of textual things" (Green 1989, 374). If, moreover, in the search for clues to textual ideology, one is to refuse to play the author's game or at least to play it exclusively by his rules, then such interpretative strategies are indeed "fair game." In fact, if we view the attacks on Freud as symptomatic, then the interpreter's attention is drawn to those aspects of the text which the dominant discourse most strenuously negates, denies, and displaces.

In his analysis of "Cloud, Castle, Lake" (a short story Nabokov wrote in 1937, just five years after *Podvig*), Elms discerns "apparently unconscious depictions of a maternal figure, a symbolic return to the womb, and a forcible expulsion from it" (1989, 355). This story concerns a Russian émigré, Vasili, who is greatly affected by the sight of a lake in a forest and who finds a "kind of inn" on its shore. He decides to stay there for the rest of his life. The piece ends with him giving up his job in Berlin, presumably with the intention of returning to the lake. Nabokov commented elsewhere that "he will never find it again" (Field 1967, 197; cf. Elms 1989, 360). Elms convincingly posits a network of "claustral imagery" in the story, suggesting "Vasili has found his own consoling womb with a view" (1989, 359), and connecting the story with the author's real-life forced exile from Russia and his "loss of an intensely close relationship with his mother when he was a small child" (1989, 362). The description which Elms gives of the short story could easily be applied to *Glory*: "discovery of a nurturant, womblike paradise which he associates with memories of his childhood, memories of a longed-for but inaccessible woman, and memories of his lost homeland" (1989, 362).

The similarities between short story and novel are indeed striking. First in the matter of presentation: Elms notes that in "Cloud, Castle, Lake" there is a mixture of subtle symbolism and more explicit sexual imagery, which may be the author's idea of a Freudian – or anti-Freudian – joke (1989, 357). This is very much the technique in *Glory*, where the suggestive mingles with the obvious. Second, the emphasis on the landscape: throughout the novel, Martin is acutely sensitive to his natural surroundings and is drawn inexorably to the "dense forest with a winding path disappearing into its depths," mentioned first on the second page. Recalling Freud's theory about the dream landscape as the maternal genitals, as Elms does in his reading of the short story (1989, 357), it is intriguing to speculate on the significance of all the landscape descriptions in *Glory*. Connolly comments on the obsession with the "absent other" in Nabokov's early fiction and notes how a distant land can serve as the object of such an obsession (1992, 248n). In *Glory* at least we appear to be dealing with an "absent (M)other," to quote Elms, for the landscape descriptions exhibit the characteristic features of the "simple claustral complex." Toward the end of the novel, Martin returns to the land, working on the "happy, fairytale farm" in rural France (p. 165). His skin becomes the color of terracotta (p. 163), and this is a premonition of his return to his homeland: earlier, on p. 64, Russia was styled a "splendid amphora" and the Soviet Union as a "clay kitchen pot" by Archibald Moon. The dark forest which Martin enters at the close of the novel is, of course, the claustral enclosure par excellence. Third, there is the emphatic presence of the mother: the novel begins with an account of the close bond between mother and child, which appears to have its origin in Nabokov's own relationship with his mother. Nabokov's mother encouraged him to feel that he and she were psychologically very similar, according to *Speak, Memory* (Nabokov 1966b, 36–39; cf. Elms 1989, 363) and Martin's mother "always had the feeling that everything else they talked about created for Martin, through her voice and her love, the same sense of divinity as lived within her" (p. 11; cf. p. 7). Fourth, the theme of the return to the lost homeland: in the short story, this is impossible; in the novel, however, Martin makes the journey, but at the cost of his life (Green 1988, 51).

Nabokovian ideology, as visible in this particular text, appears to propose that the development of masculine subjectivity depends to a significant degree upon repudiation of the mother and femininity. This is the real quest in which Martin Edelweiss is engaged. Inevitably, this involves a repudiation, or at least a devaluing, of women in general, as embodiments of the despised femininity within the subject himself. The organizing consciousness of the text helps considerably here, by presenting female characters who are highly stereotypical. Alla is the predatory older woman, and, at the same time, a substitute for the beloved mother. Bess, the prostitute, and Rose, the waitress, are little more than cut-outs from the pop-up book of stereotypes (their names are generic working-class): the former is a thieving prostitute, the latter the deceitful girl who dupes a man into marrying her by claiming she is pregnant. Sonia is the capricious and contradictory coquette: the Introduction, after all, tells us that she is (in spite of being "oddly attractive") a "moody and ruthless flirt" (p. xi). Sonia is unattainable but desirable; she is also threatening, however, because she has the capacity to undercut Martin's acquisition of masculine gender identity: she calls him "flower" (making fun of his last name, Edelweiss, 131) and "doggy" (p. 118), and to his dismay takes no interest in his sporting activities (pp. 99, 110).

Martin and men

In a culture of hegemonic and patriarchal masculinity, manhood is performed for the approval, not of women, but of other men, who evaluate the performance of the masculine gender role. In *Glory*, Martin is very early on (p. 13) afraid of seeming "unmanly," and daggers and pistols are mentioned no fewer than five times within the first twenty-seven pages. In such a system, women function primarily as the currency through which this homosocial activity is enacted. On p. 27, young Martin, fascinated by Silvio and the other seamen, with their daggers and pistols, competitively marks out Alla as the woman he would save in the event of disaster.

Eve Kosofsky Sedgwick (1988) has adapted René Girard's paradigm of triangular desire to an erotic triangle in which two males bond "homosocially" through competition for a shared female object of desire. The relationship between Martin and Darwin is of pivotal importance in Martin's performance of manhood. They are rivals for the same woman, and are communicating by being rivals. The violence of the boxing is what brings them finally together. Nancy Morrow suggests that certain characters "may become the player of a 'dreadful game' because he or she can never become the imitated other. As a result, a game arising from mediated desire can never lead to harmony and reconciliation. The rivalry that erupts between the subject of mediated desire and the imitated other often leads to irreconcilable conflict, even violence" (Morrow 1988, 11). Martin appears to be just such a character. At the end of *Glory*, however, there is an implied reconciliation: with Sonia and all the others having faded into the background, Darwin is left standing as a shadowing figure almost analogous to Martin, and seems to coalesce with him, as he walks off into the fir forest along the same winding path that Martin has been heading towards all along (p. 205).

Are Martin's problems with women connected with Darwin? In a sense they are; it is not a simplistic case of Martin preferring Darwin to Sonia in baldly sexual terms. Rather, the text is unable to suppress the homoerotic desire encoded in the narrative, just as it cannot completely hide those desires and fears connected with the mother which were outlined above (p. x). The text attempts manfully to marginalize the homoerotic element, but cannot quite control it. The novel has one explicitly homosexual character, the academic Archibald Moon, who is introduced as the "unsayable," only to be ridiculed and rejected: Martin homophobically recoils from his mild physical gesture on p. 97 ("Moon without any excuse stroked Martin's hair with trembling fingers"), along with his "dead" vision of Russia. The words "without any excuse" indicate the disposition of the narrative consciousness towards Moon's actions, but offer no detailed explanation of what may have motivated them. Martin defines himself in opposition to Moon the homosexual and to his fossilized and sterile Russia which is just a decorative bauble (pp. 64, 97). The performance of masculinity has frequently been associated with homophobia, succinctly defined by Michael Kimmel as "the repudiation of the homosexual within – never completely successful and hence constantly reenacted in every homosocial relationship" (Kimmel 1994, 130).[4] Nonetheless, the figure of Moon, although ridiculed like his scholarly counterpart Kinbote in *Pale Fire*, imports the theme of homoerotic desire, much as the explicit rejection of Freudian readings in the Introduction actually encourages such speculations. It is worth recalling that the Introduction informed us that Moon and Darwin are "totally invented" characters: as such they are entirely the product of the authorial organizing consciousness and therefore particularly revelatory of the text's ideological structures.

Given the all-male environment of Martin's athletic activities, it is hard not to see some unconscious homoeroticism in the sexualized language in which these activities are described. Interestingly, elsewhere in the

Nabokovian corpus sporting activities do, from time to time, connote homosexual desire: Rowe (1971, 148–149) notes connections with swimming in *King, Queen, Knave* (Nabokov 1989a, 78, 80, 203) and in *Pale Fire* (Nabokov 1962, 291), whose homosexual character Kinbote practices table tennis (p. 22), calisthenics (p. 26), wrestling (p. 98; cf. p. 118) with boys. Kinbote also claims to be an "enthusiastic rock-climber" (p. 118); Martin likes to climb mountains too (pp. 85–87). One might reasonably speculate then on whether the friendship with Darwin is in fact central to Martin's sexual and social identity and to his crisis of fulfillment. Darwin is, after all, and somewhat surprisingly, the person we see last in the narrative.

Conclusions

The identity which Martin Edelweiss is conditioned to desire is inevitably contradictory. Rooted in notions of patriarchal masculinity, it is inexorably drawn to the feminine, but with a mixture of desire and repulsion, much like that noted earlier in the remarks about Sonia in the Introduction. The text also represses homoerotic and oedipal desire and connects the two. As an émigré, Martin has equally ambiguous attachments to the Russia where he was born and the England where he is a student. In neither case can he reach a happy accommodation. Russia has changed into the Soviet Union and he cannot blend into England, as he is an outsider. Martin needs both the émigrés and Darwin to maintain his fragile sense of masculine identity and his place in the world, but can only resolve the contradictions by abandoning them both (along with Sonia and his mother) and following the forest path to the place where his identity is whole and unfractured. Unfortunately, this place no longer exists. The text does not seek to resolve the web of contradictions in which Martin Edelweiss finds himself enmeshed. It simply trails off, removing Martin from the reader's gaze. The three main characters, in spite of the very definite things the author has to say about them in the Introduction, are never fully rounded and remain somewhat nebulous entities. It is this very indeterminacy, however, which allows the scope for various interpretations of them, their doings and their desires, as different framing discourses engender different readings.

Notes

I would like to thank my colleague Susan Isabel Stein for her helpful comments on earlier drafts of this chapter and for discussing aspects of psychoanalytic criticism with me.

1 Page references to *Glory* will be given in parentheses in the text without repeating author and date.

2 Tennis appears throughout the text: at p. 54, Martin defeats some of Sonia's young male friends; at pp. 129–130, Martin's tennis-playing excites his mother's approval; at p. 99, it fails to arouse any interest in Sonia; at pp. 136–137, Martin teaches tennis in Berlin and on p. 135 there is a reference to a tennis court where he used to play with his mother, now buried under a new building; on p. 151, Martin has a mistress whom he met at the tennis club; on p. 170, Martin meets Gruzinov by the tennis court; and at p. 175, Martin finds Gruzinov watching a lively game of tennis between two young men.

3 There are obvious allusions to the story of Tristan and Isolde; Galya Rylkova has suggested to me that this tale, particularly its Wagnerian version, was particularly popular among homosexuals because it portrayed the notion of suppressed and unfulfilled desire.

4 Galya Diment (1995, 736) notes Nabokov's "strong disapproval of homosexuality (even though a number of his close relatives were homosexuals)."

5

THE CREWCUT AS HOMOEROTIC DISCOURSE IN NABOKOV'S *PALE FIRE*

Paul Allen Miller

Although far from being a professional scholar of Nabokov, I have read *Pale Fire* many times over the last sixteen years, and one image that has always stayed brightly illuminated in my mind is that of Bob, Kinbote's unfaithful young lover, standing mournfully before Judge Goldsmith's house after being thrown out for bringing a red-haired floozy into Kinbote's masculine den of ping-pong and carrot crunching. The description of Bob[1] standing there with skis slung over his shoulder has always struck me as an outrageously funny and yet hauntingly melancholy moment that sets the tone for the whole novel. The passage begins as a description of a photograph Kinbote has of himself and Shade, but as is so often the case in this text, the narrative voice quickly becomes sidetracked by its own, more obsessional concerns[2]:

> I am wearing a white windbreaker acquired in a local sports shop and a pair of lilac slacks hailing from Cannes. My left hand is half raised ... and the library book under my right arm is a treatise on certain Zemblan calisthenics in which I proposed to interest that young roomer of mine who snapped the picture. A week later he was to betray my trust by taking advantage of my absence on a trip to Washington whence I returned to find he had been entertaining a fiery-haired whore from Exton who had left her combings and reek in all three bathrooms. Naturally we separated at once, and through a chink in the window curtains I saw bad Bob standing rather pathetically, with his crewcut, and shabby valise, and skis I had given him, all forlorn on the roadside, waiting for a fellow student to drive him away forever.
>
> (p. 17)

What I want to propose here is that one of the reasons for this scene's continuing resonance is that it exemplifies a kind of unique semiological nexus of at least five sets of thematically central binary oppositions which structure the novel's ideological backdrop or, in Jameson's terms, its "semantic conditions of possibility" (1981, 57): homosexuality versus heterosexuality; the effeminate versus the virile; the European versus the American; refined intricacy versus naive simplicity; and aristocratic culture versus lower class barbarism. The master binarism around which all the other terms turn, and the only one which regularly shifts valences, is that of homosexuality versus heterosexuality. It, as Eve Sedgwick has pointed out, serves as an ideological switching point which both coordinates and disrupts the movement of the other ostensibly subordinate, though relatively autonomous, ideological oppositions not only in the novel but also in the North American and European culture of the last century (Sedgwick 1990, 11, 34, 72–73).[3] What follows, however, is less an exercise in queer theory, a field to which it owes countless debts, than an attempt at ideological mapping and thus deconstruction in a novel both phobic and desiring.

Nabokov, as is commonly admitted, was an aesthetic formalist, and in an ideally ordered classical universe we would expect these five sets of oppositions to be homologous with one another. And certainly, in terms of popular American stereotypes, the European, the effeminate, the homosexual, the refined, and the aristocratic would all be thought of as essentially opposed to the image of an unrefined, red-blooded heterosexual boy spawned from the raw-boned earth of the prairie. This should come as no surprise. Such simple sets of homologous oppositions are, of course, part and parcel of the Americanocentric vision of Newt Gingrich, Pat Buchanan, and other religious and political fundamentalists, as they are of most exclusionary ideologies. Right-wing populists are hardly the first to see the world in this way. The Romans regarded the "culturally superior" Greeks in much the same fashion.

It is unsurprising, then, that one of the main sources of ideological tension, and hence narrative movement, in the novel comes from the fact that the vertical relations maintained between these various sets of superimposed oppositions are highly unstable. Indeed, Bob's crewcut and the scene in which it is evoked gains its poignancy precisely from the fact that it represents that impossible point in ideological space at which these sets of parallel lines converge, undoing not only the individual oppositions themselves but also the privileges accruing to each position within them. The crewcut, then, is the point of suture which both brings these opposed sets of values together and yet holds them apart, by articulating their inherently contradictory nature. It is the marker of an alienating doublebind that more than all the thematics of lost kingdoms, and more than the biography of Nabokov himself, marks this text as a novel of exile (Hyde 1977, 174–175, 184).

How can such claims be made about a mere haircut? It's fairly simple. For, as revealed in the now famous photos of accused Oklahoma terrorist, Timothy McVeigh, this particular coiffure wears its ideological markers on its sleeve. The crewcut in American life has certain clear ideological resonances. It is in origin a military hairstyle. It became fashionable in post-World War II America as a symbol of masculine simplicity, a recollection of the straightforward GIs who had fought to rid the world of European and Asiatic fascism, and who were now fighting the Cold War to stave off Russian Communism. It was the degree-zero of haircuts. It stood for unadorned "Americanicity,"[4] and thus, according to the binary oppositions outlined above, it should also have been a marker of heterosexuality. The crewcut represented the polar opposite of Kinbote's aesthetic, which abhorred simplicity and "sincerity" (p.112), just as Nabokov did himself (Hyde 1977, 183).[5] Nonetheless, what Bob's peculiar situation shows is that what *should* be the case and what *is* the case are often two different things. Bob is Kinbote's lover.

The idea that hairstyles and other systems of bodily adornment are capable of transmitting complex ideological messages is not new. From Lévi-Strauss's detailed examinations of the patterns of aboriginal tattoos (1971, 176; Jameson 1981, 77–79), to Barthes's *Mythologies* (1957), to the popular song "Hairstyles and Attitudes" by Timbuk 3, it is commonly accepted that, within the ideological and semiological constraints imposed by our cultural communities, the way we choose to look says something about who we want to be. A crewcut is an ideological statement. In addition, there is a long tradition in the west that links short hair with masculinity and virtue, and long hair with effeminacy and decadence. It stretches from the iconography of the cavaliers and the roundheads in the English Civil War, which Priscilla Meyer has shown is an important subtheme in the novel – with Charles Xavier of Zembla standing for Charles II of England (Meyer 1988, 102)[6] – to Saint Paul's admonition for men to keep their hair short while their wives should wear it long (*Corinthians* 1.11–14), and to Athenian Old Comedy's depiction of long-haired aristocrats as those who like to be sexually penetrated, as Chuck Platter has recently demonstrated (1996).[7] In Rome, long hair was a sign of both adolescence and pederastic availability.[8]

Yet in the Classical Latin literature which David Larmour has shown Nabokov knew so well (1990a; 1990b), there is also evidence of an alternative construction of the set of oppositions signified by short hair versus long hair, masculine versus feminine, and, to use a set of terms which Foucault and Halperin (1990) have demonstrated are anachronistic for the ancient world but not for *Pale Fire* or Nabokov, homosexual versus heterosexual (the ancients categorized sexual preferences in terms of active versus passive). This alternative construction can be most readily seen in Juvenal's second satire. Here we are treated to a hilarious send-up of the arch masculinist pretensions of certain stern Stoic philosophers to Roman *virtus* ("virtue" but also "virility"). These philosophers kept their hair cropped short, prided themselves on their rejection of feminine adornment, and lusted heartily after young boys and passive anal penetration:

> Your shaggy limbs and the bristling hair on your forearms
> Suggest a fierce male virtue; but the surgeon called in
> To lance your swollen piles dissolves in laughter
> At the sight of that well-smoothed passage. Such creatures talk
> In a clipped, laconic style, and crop their hair crew-cut fashion,
> As short as their eyebrows.
>
> (2.11–15)

In the case of Juvenal's philosophers, then, the virile simplicity of their puritanical demeanor ultimately reflects not the patriarchal heterosexuality of Rome before its infection with the effeminizing vices of the Greek east (a common Roman ideological fantasy).[9] Rather, it points to that kind of extreme valorization of masculinity and male homosociality which finds its ultimate expression in what Irigaray has punningly termed "hommosexuality" (1985, 140–141).[10] Consistent with this semiotics of virility, Kinbote labels his own sexual practices "manly" or "masculine" (pp. 79, 92), while denigrating the sexuality of women (pp. 13, 16, 148, 172, 210). The tendency for such an excess of masculinity to be turned into its presumed opposite, effeminized homosexuality (hence the now obsolete term inversion), is in turn illustrated throughout the novel by such descriptions as that of Joseph Lavender's collection of erotic French photos featuring "oversized ardors" and "a dapple of female charms" (p. 141), or of the way Oleg's "bold virilia contrasted harshly with his girlish grace" (p. 89). Hypermasculinity always verges on androgyny. The most spectacular example of this tendency of an intense focus on virility to convert itself into a kind of femininity is the case of Garh, who when we first meet her is a lusty Zemblan mountain girl whose advances the fleeing king firmly rebuffs (pp. 102–103), but who reappears in the index as "Also a rosy-cheeked goose-boy found in a country lane, north of Troth, in 1936, only now distinctly recalled by the writer" (p. 217; Johnson 1979, 36).

Bob, Kinbote's crewcut-coiffed erstwhile American lover, exemplifies a similar mixing of ideological and sexual codes within the symbolic economy of Nabokov's novel. Indeed, if we return to the passage in question we will find much the same pairing of seeming ideological opposites throughout the scene as was noted in the satire of Juvenal's Stoics. We begin with the opposition implied in the first sentence between Kinbote's "white windbreaker acquired in a local sport shop and a pair of lilac slacks hailing from Cannes." The windbreaker bears three ideological markers: its color; its local provenance; and its association with sports. White is a color which generally connotes purity. Its status as the absolute lack of color (even if that status is spectrographically incorrect) connotes simplicity, and its plainness clearly opposes it to the lilac of the pants. The windbreaker's local provenance marks it as American, and the fact that it was purchased in a "sports shop" links it with the world of vigorous athletic activity, which, in the late 1950s and early 1960s when the novel was being written, was an exclusively masculine domain. The sporting life is thus a site of normative virility and hence ostensible heterosexuality, but it can also be a marker of the same latent "hommosexuality" of which Irigaray speaks. It is ambivalent. Indeed one feels sure that Kinbote would have thrilled at the thought of a gymnasium full of crewcut-wearing young football players about to hit the showers (Fussel 1991).

The lilac pants, on the other hand, bear the exact opposite set of ideological markers. In color, they are bold rather than simple, and they are hardly masculine in association. The image of John Wayne riding off into the sunset wearing lilac pants is one that can only provoke hilarity. Their provenance is European rather than American, and the fact that they were bought in the resort city of Cannes associates them with the overrefined, aristocratic world and, from the perspective of American puritanical provincialism, the questionable morals of the French Riviera.

We see, then, all ten of the terms of our initial five binary oppositions lining up in about the fashion we would expect: virility, simplicity, a certain cultural barbarism, and "Americanicity" found on one side and the effeminized, the refined, the aristocratic, and the European on the other. The one loose cannon is the homosexual versus heterosexual opposition. It swings both ways and so threatens to undermine the ideological edifice of the novel as a whole. Moreover, this pattern of oppositions is pervasive throughout the text. If we look just a few lines later in the same passage we find mention of "a treatise on certain Zemblan calisthenics" in which Kinbote hoped to interest young Bob before he betrayed him with his "fiery-haired whore." The term *calisthenics*, of course, puts us firmly back in the realm of the sports shop where the white windbreaker was purchased, but the term Zemblan, however imaginary its derivation, locates us at not too great an ideological distance from the Riviera.[11] The ambiguity is fertile, as it were, because the exercises Kinbote has in mind are more stimulating than your garden variety jumping jack, though perhaps not all that different in spirit. Indeed, this treatise would appear to be a kind of Zemblan *Kama Sutra*.

Such a reading is confirmed by a number of later passages in the novel that associate vigorous masculine activity, often of a sporting nature, with homoeroticism. Thus in Kinbote's commentary on line sixty-two, in the midst of recounting his vision of a black cat "sporting a neck bow of white silk," we find the following disquisition:

It is so easy for a cruel person to make the victim of his ingenuity believe that he has persecution mania, or is really being stalked by a killer, or is suffering from hallucinations. Hallucinations! Well did I know that among certain youthful instructors whose advances I had rejected there was at least one practical joker; I knew it ever since the time I came home from a very enjoyable and successful meeting of students and teachers (at which I had exuberantly thrown off my coat and shown several willing pupils a few of the more amusing holds employed by Zemblan wrestlers) and found in my coat pocket a brutal anonymous note saying: "You have hal.....s real bad, chum," meaning evidently hallucinations...

(p. 71)

This is a very rich passage, weaving together as it does manifest paranoia, nostalgic remembrance, and a denial of hallucinations in the form of hallucinating the word *hallucination* in a text where *halitosis* is manifestly intended. Indeed, it bears all the marks of that complete obfuscation of the referent in the moment of free play which is the hallmark of postmodernity, and of the complex ideological threads out of which the postmodern is woven (Jameson 1985, 255–256). Nonetheless, those ideological threads are still there to be unraveled, and what I want to pay close attention to in this passage are the Zemblan wrestling holds.

The homoerotic context in which those holds are mentioned is first made clear by the fact that reference to them comes immediately after Kinbote's avowal that he has found it necessary to rebuff the advances of several young instructors. It is made all the clearer both when those holds are qualified as "amusing" and when we realize that Kinbote's face was apparently so close to that of his "willing pupils" that his breath caused some severe discomfort. The word *amusing* is used elsewhere in the novel to denote the presence or possibility of a homosexual liaison. Thus in a later note in which Kinbote is monomaniacally recounting the escape of King Charles from Zembla, we find out that Charles stumbles upon a "restaurant where many years earlier he had lunched with two *amusing*, very *amusing* sailors" (p. 104; emphasis added). Hence, it would seem that the Zemblan wrestling holds referred to with the same adjective above are analogues to those very Zemblan calisthenics in which Kinbote had hoped to interest young Bob.

The world of virile sport, of rough and ready masculine activity, then, is a world of possible homosexual encounters in *Pale Fire*, as it was in the Greek *gymnasium*.[12] This fact is made all the clearer in another passage where Kinbote explicitly contrasts sport with heterosexuality: "Charles Xavier had gone to an all-night ball in the so-called Ducal Dome in Grindelwood: for the nonce, a formal heterosexual affair, rather refreshing after some previous sport" (p. 76). Likewise the most common metonym used for Kinbote's homoeroticism is the recurring motif of the ping-pong table. Early on, we learn that Kinbote keeps two ping-pong tables in his basement and that this fact is drawing comments from his fellow professors (p. 13). On the next page, those same ping-pong tables are unmistakably linked with Kinbote's sexual adventures: "I explained I could not stay long as I was about to have a kind of little seminar at home followed by some table tennis with two charming identical twins and another boy, another boy" (p. 14).[13]

That Kinbote had in fact taken liberties with his students is evident from the fear he expresses when called into the office of the head of the department and told that a boy had complained to his advisor. The complaint, it turns out, was *not* about Kinbote's advances, but the latter's sense of relief clearly shows that he knew that a sexual harassment charge was possible:

> There was also the morning when Dr. Nattochdag, head of the department to which I was attached, begged me in a formal voice to be seated, then closed the door, and having regained, with a downcast frown, his swivel chair, he urged me "to be more careful." In what sense, careful? A boy had complained to his adviser. Complained of what, good Lord? That I had criticized a literature course he attended.... Laughing in sheer relief, I embraced my good Netochka, telling him I would never be naughty again.
>
> (pp. 15–16)

The teasing rhetoric which only slowly reveals the true nature of the student's complaint is clearly designed to make plain to the reader the nature of Kinbote's anxiety (Walton 1994, 100–101). His fear of being outed, however, in no way alters his behavior, for we later learn that he is now auditioning partners for his third ping-pong table (pp. 113–114).

It takes little imagination to see how the sport of table tennis with its bouncing balls and paddles can be easily transformed into a metonymic evocation of Kinbote's pederastic desires. That spanking was one such activity becomes clear later when he writes of Bretwit's inadvertently revealing to Gradus that the king had left Zembla, "I could have spanked the dear man" (p. 128).[14] In any case, ping-pong, like wrestling and calisthenics, is a well-defined part of the novel's erotic vocabulary.

In a still later passage where Kinbote describes how he first met his "versatile gardener" who was to provide him with rubdowns and other services (pp. 53, 114), the gardener's attractive display of his own virile body serves as a salve to Kinbote's wounded feelings after he had apparently been caught committing an indiscretion at the college pool – a site for athletic activity where numerous nearly naked masculine bodies would normally be found:

> This gifted gardener I discovered by chance one idle spring day when I was slowly wending my way home after a maddening and embarrassing experience at the college indoor pool. He stood at the top of a green ladder.... His red flannel shirt lay on the grass.... He started work at my place the very next day. He was awfully nice and pathetic, and all that, but a little too talkative and completely impotent which I found discouraging. Otherwise he was a strong strapping fellow, and I hugely enjoyed the aesthetic pleasure of watching him buoyantly struggle with earth and turf or delicately manipulate bulbs.
>
> (pp. 205–206)

This passage combines all the major elements we have been discussing: manly sport; the gardener's simplicity (he is after all a manual laborer); homoeroticism; and "Americanicity," inasmuch as the gardener is black and therefore presumably not of European extraction (p. 155). Yet the mix is unstable; like Bob and his crewcut, the gardener, with his virility and his simplicity, would seem to be worlds away from Kinbote's lilac pants purchased in Cannes. The fact that he is not foreign to Kinbote's desires reveals the essential instability of our five initial oppositions.

Indeed, the association of homoerotic feelings with attractions to either the socially marginal or those who eschew cultural refinement is pervasive throughout the novel, making our seemingly stable notions of virility, simplicity, sexuality, and cultural identity ever more difficult to define. Thus in addition to the gardener, we find Charles at one point admiring the "good-natured faces, glossy with sweat, of copper-chested railway workers," who we can presume were similarly shirtless (p. 106), at another speaking of drunken young revolutionary soldiers "taking liberties with a young page" (p. 86), not to mention the amusing sailors cited earlier and a "black giant" who had "brutally enjoyed" a "fickle young" stableboy (pp. 209–210). By the same token, when Kinbote recounts the king's failed attempt at marriage and the production of an heir we find Charles succumbing to the pleasures of a raft of circus performers, whose very names signify both low social status and aristocratic decadence, and one of whom is directly termed a brute:

> [Queen Disa] found out all about our manly Zemblan customs, and concealed her naïve distress under a great show of sarcastic sophistication. He congratulated her on her attitude, solemnly swearing that he had given up, or at least would give up, the practices of his youth; but everywhere along the road powerful temptations stood at attention. He succumbed to them from time to

time, then every other day, then several times daily – especially during the robust regime of Harfar Baron of Shalksbore, a phenomenally endowed young brute (whose family name, "knave's farm," is the most probable derivation of "Shakespeare"). Curdy Buff – as Harfar was nicknamed by his admirers had a huge escort of acrobats and bareback riders, and the whole affair rather got out of hand so that Disa ... found the palace transformed into a circus.

(pp. 148–149)

The circus smells Disa found in the palace were no doubt not much different from those Charles himself complains of when recalling the drunken revolutionaries "taking liberties with a young page" – "And what a smell of leather and goat in the spacious chambers once redolent of carnations and lilacs!" (p. 86). Just as the difference between virile and effeminized, and in conventional terms that between homosexual and heterosexual, becomes more and more confused, so does the difference between simple and refined, aristocratic and barbarian. In short, the very difference between the elite and the herd, the civilized and the philistine, on which, as William Gass approvingly notes, so much of Nabokov's art depends, begins to collapse.[15] When lilacs and circus smells become all but indistinguishable, so presumably do crewcuts and pants bought in Cannes.

One of the most striking examples of this collapse of social and cultural distinctions in the novel's crucible of pederasty can be illustrated by comparing two scenes of fondling in the novel. The first involves an old groom named Grimm, a moniker evoking both a haggard scowl and the cruel peasants and forest people that populated the world of fairytale before being sanitized for modern consumption. Grimm we find out had "had a way of fondling" a young boy named Christopher when no one was around, a way that Christopher apparently quite enjoyed (p. 157).[16] This fondling by the old groom, reminiscent of Foucault's peasant of Lapcourt and the game of curdled milk (1978, 31–32), can in turn be compared to another scene of "fondling," where the social and ideological markers are reversed. It occurs in the midst of one of Kinbote's harangues against Gradus's supposed terrorist organization, the Shadows:

Spiteful thugs! They may be compared to hoodlums who itch to torture the invulnerable gentleman whose testimony clapped them into prison for life. Such convicts are known to go berserk at the thought that their elusive victim whose very testicles they crave to twist and tear with their talons, is at a pergola feast on a sunny island or *fondling* some pretty young creature between his knees in serene security laughing at them!

(pp. 107–108; emphasis added)

This passage clearly aims at establishing an opposition between pederasts and thugs which would underwrite the earlier discussed homology between the oppositions, hetero- versus homosexual, and aristocratic culture versus barbarism. Yet as the description of Grimm, as well as of the thugs' focus on their accuser's testicles, reveals the opposition cannot be maintained. Once again, it seems, homoeroticism swings both ways.

This rhetoric of the simultaneous assertion and undermining of social, cultural, and sexual homologies can be found most strikingly in the case of Gradus. At first, he would appear to occupy in every sense the opposite end of the ideological spectrum from Kinbote. Thus at one point we are told that the would-be regicide is disgusted by the sexual advances of young Gordon Krummholz at the villa of Joseph Lavender (a shade darker than lilac), advances to which the fugitive king had willingly succumbed. "The young woodwose had now closed his eyes and was stretched out supine on the pool's marble margin; his Tarzan brief had been cast aside on the turf. Gradus spat in disgust and walked back toward the house" (p. 144). The whole atmosphere of this scene is bathed in the pale light of what, from a middle-American or normative bourgeois perspective, can only be described as a bizarre aristocratic effeminacy and decadence:

> He had nothing on save a leopard-spotted loincloth. His closely cropped hair was a tint lighter than his skin.... "That's the Grotto," said Gordon. "I once spent the night here with a friend." Gradus let his indifferent glance enter the mossy recess where one could glimpse a collapsible mattress with a dark stain on its orange nylon. The boy applied avid lips to a pipe of spring water and wiped his wet hands on his black bathing trunks.
>
> (pp. 142–143)

Gradus, however, is insensitive to young Gordon's charms. The lips seductively wrapped around the pipe of spring water had but the slightest effect. "Our preoccupied plotter did not register any of these details and merely experienced a general impression of indecency" (p. 142). The combination of insensitivity and moral revulsion clearly marks Gradus as a member of the world of thugs, rather than of gentlemen (pp. 142–143). He is portrayed as one with the philistine world of "frenzied heterosexualism" with its cynicism and glossy magazines that Kinbote decries (p. 126). Indeed Gradus is, in Kinbote's own words, a "Puritan," a term whose profound resonance with American culture and self-identity Nabokov certainly recognized (p. 109), and one to which we shall return.

There is another side of Gradus, however, one which points to a homoerotic potential precisely because of his low social standing and his consequent association with that kind of rough and ready hypervirility which we saw earlier in the "homosexualism" of the gardener, the copper-chested railway workers, those amusing sailors, Bob, and his crewcut. Gradus, of course, before becoming an assassin, had been a laborer in the Onhava glassworks, a hotbed of Zemblan revolutionary fervor. Kinbote's description of his craft, however, is laced with erotic double-entendres and sexual insinuations:

> He also worked as teazer and later flasher, at governmental fac-tories – and was, I believe, more or less responsible for the remarkably ugly red-and-amber windows in the great public lava-tory at rowdy but colorful Kalixhaven where the sailors are.
>
> (p. 109)

The words *teazer* and *flasher* are technical terms from the world of glass-making, referring respectively to the "stoker or fireman in a glasswork" and to the person who causes the "globe of glass to expand into a sheet" (*OED*). But they are also sexual slang, and at least one flasher in the collo-quial sense of the term appears in the novel, "the college porter who one day ... showed a squeamish coed something of which she had no doubt seen better samples" (p. 168). In addition, it is unlikely to be accidental that these "technical" terms appear in the context of Kinbote's nostalgic recollection of the public restroom in "rowdy but colorful Kalixhaven," where Charles had apparently cruised in happier times. That such is the correct reading of this evocation of the exiled king's sexual slumming can be confirmed by the presence of the sailors. These are the same sailors that were termed "amusing, very amusing" earlier in the novel, as can be seen by turning to the entry under *Kalixhaven* in the index, which reads "a col-orful seaport on the western coast a few miles north of Blawick (q.v.), 171; many pleasant memories" (p. 218). If one then turns to the entry under *Blawick* (p. 215), it describes a seaside resort and directs the reader to Kinbote's commentary on line 149 of Shade's poem, which is where the passage on the "amusing" sailors first appeared (p. 104).[17] Gradus, thus, by association becomes linked with a particularly low-rent side of Kinbote's sexuality. This motif culminates in what can only be described as a fantasy of anal rape, when at the end of the same note in which Kinbote describes Gradus's work as a teazer and a flasher in the public lavatory he launches into the following diatribe, "Gradus should not kill kings. Vinogradus should never, never provoke God. Leningradus should not aim his pea-shooter at people even in dreams, because if he does, a pair of colossally thick, abnormally hairy arms will hug him from behind and squeeze, squeeze, squeeze" (p. 111).[18]

Thus Gradus, like Bob's crewcut, becomes a nexus of competing and contradictory discourses. Ostensibly heterosexual and certainly barbarously lower class, Gradus seems to be everything Kinbote is not, and yet on the level of fantasy if not on the level of narrative fact (if such a distinction has any meaning in a text like *Pale Fire*), he nonetheless becomes associated with precisely that homoeroticism for which Kinbote explicitly states Gradus feels disgust. Gradus is discursively seduced in a way that makes the seeming distinction between him and Kinbote, as well as that between the baroque and the simple, the cultured and the barbarous, the homosexual and the heterosexual, and the roughly masculine and the decadently effeminized, appear to be nothing more than the product of an obsessive and pedantic imagination which insists on impressing its own absurdly reductive schema on a disorderly world that consistently eludes it. The classically ordered universe of strict homologism between levels of signification in short appears every bit as mad as Kinbote's reading of Shade.

One last opposition remains to be discussed: the American versus the European. Gradus, it will be recalled, was referred to by Kinbote as a Puritan with a capital P. This specific allusion to the religious sect most firmly tied in the popular imagination with the founding of the American nation links Gradus's ostensible simplicity, barbarity, and heterosexuality with the same traits of red-blooded American masculinity signified by Bob's crewcut.[19] This superficial homologism is confirmed on a number of levels throughout the novel. Thus at one point Kinbote speaks of the "popular nomenclature of American animals" as reflecting the "simple utilitarian minds of ignorant pioneers" (p. 132), while Shade, the image of Robert Frost and an essentially American simplicity in poetry itself (Meyer 1988, 133), terms the King of Zembla, as Kinbote has described him to the poet, "rather appalling," presumably referring to his pederastic proclivities (p. 153). At the same time, Goethe, the emblem of European sophistication, is specifically described as an author of pederastic poetry: "This line, and indeed the whole passage allude to the well-known poem by Goethe about the erlking hoary enchanter of the elf-haunted alderwood, who falls in love with the delicate little boy of a belated traveler" (p. 169). Likewise, Igor II, an early nineteenth-century king of Zembla is described in the index as having had a collection of statues of his "four hundred favorite catamites in pink marble, with inset glass eyes and various touched up details" (pp. 217–218). Thus Kinbote, as what Hyde has termed the bearer of the "myths of a decayed and deposed aristocracy, the ghost of the mind of Europe" (1977, 177),[20] as opposed to the "utilitarian minds of ignorant pioneers," consistently portrays his own set of cultural values as the natural and necessary corollary of his own homoeroticism. From this perspective a classically ordered universe can be reimagined in which the European, the effeminized, the homosexual, the refined, and the aristocratic are systematically opposed to the American, the virile, the simplistic, and the barbarous.

Yet just as systematically every time this typology is erected in the novel, its lack of foundation is exposed. Bob the crewcut-coiffed all-American boy is seduced. Demonstrations of manly sport become quasisexual encounters in which wrestling holds and calisthenics serve as metonyms for sexual positions. Kings are found having erotic frolics with sailors in public restrooms, and aristocrats fondling young boys on the beach are indistinguishable from grim old stable hands fondling young aristocrats. By the end of it, John Wayne in lilac pants sounds not nearly so absurd as when we began. The ordering, taxonomic ideology which made the world make sense, which underwrites the distinctions not only of feverish systematizers but also of sophisticated aesthetes are revealed as pathetic attempts to keep disorder at bay. Nor is one side of the oppositional column any more innocent than the other. Bob's seductive virility was always already ready to be supplemented by the Irigarayan "hommosexuality" which is its necessary product.

In some ways this whole systematic inversion of norms is perhaps best symbolized by what I like to think of as Kinbote's seduction of Tom Sawyer. The description is found in the index entry under *Kinbote*:

> his logcabin in Cedarn and the little angler, a honeyskinned lad, naked except for a pair of torn dungarees, one trouser leg rolled up, frequently fed with nougat and nuts, but then school started or the weather changed...
>
> (p. 219)

The image of the shirtless boy (like the gardener) standing in or near a mountain stream, with his fishing pole over his shoulder and one leg of his jeans rolled up over his knee is something out of a Norman Rockwell painting. It's an American idyll of childhood innocence and simplicity, a pastoral Eden. But Vergil's shepherds got lonely and Nabokov's do as well. This Tom Sawyer, we find, was fed with nougat, nuts, and probably more. He was seduced. Seduced but not raped. The American ideal of unsophisticated innocence and purity is sodomized, but as Bob and his haircut show, and the token bribes of a little candy reveal, it wanted it all along. Its purity and simplicity was a pose every bit as much as that of Juvenal's philosophers. But so was the sophistication of its seducer. The European and the American, just like the Greek and the Roman, or the hetero- and the homosexual, each require the other for their identity and hence always necessarily undermine their own specific claims to priority and position (Walton 1994, 100). The dominant term in each case is dependent on the submissive and vice versa, and the pressure exerted on them in *Pale Fire* is so intense they can only implode. In the end, the collapse of these artificial distinctions leaves us all in exile from the world of comforting but dangerous certitudes, all frantically trying to make sense of a nonsensical world, and all too often trying to find a hated and despised other that will allow us to prop up our own ever more fragile senses of cultural, sexual, and personal identity.

Notes

1 For more on Bob, see pp.69–70. Page references to Nabokov's text will be given in parentheses in the text without repeating author and date.

2 For the interweaving of the rational and the frankly bizarre, see *inter alia* pp.7 and 18. On Nabokov's use of homosexuality to denote solipsism, see Meyer (1988, 203). On the failure of previous attempts to deal with the topic of homosexuality in *Pale Fire* and the tendency to see it as a metaphor for something else, see Walton (1994, 89–96).

3 I had not yet read Sedgwick's excellent book when I first wrote this chapter. Consequently, what follows is less an application than an expansion and confirmation of her hypothesis.

4 For a defense of a similarly ridiculous neologism, see Barthes's *Mythologies* (1957, 206)

5 On Kinbote as a "voice" of Nabokov himself, see in addition to the passages already cited: p.94, for the declaration that " 'reality' is neither the subject nor the object of true art which creates its own special reality having nothing to do with the average 'reality' perceived by the communal eye"; p.153, for the notion that "true art is above false honor"; and p.162, the disparaging of "Freudian fancies." These are all quite Nabokovian sentiments, uttered by a madman. Meyer qualifies Kinbote as a "parody" of Nabokov himself (1988, 63, 108). The author's deployment of this rhetorical strategy of the *mise-en-abîme* in regard to his own subject position is one of the aspects that definitively marks this as a postmodern text.

6 See also her interesting observation, "Nabokov's use of the buried treasure of the history of the Restoration is a recompense in art for the assassination of his father. He wreaks his revenge by likening the Cromwellians to Gradus, by showing revolutions to be conducted by simpleminded thugs" (1988, 108).

7 See also his unpublished paper on female depilation and the iconography of the well-trimmed pubis as an image of disruptive sexuality brought under control.

8 Tibullus 1.4.37–38; Murgatroyd (1990, 144–145); see also the character Giton in Petronius's *Satyricon*.

9 See Catharine Edwards's extensive discussion (1993, 94–97).

10 Lacan first uses the term "hommosexuel" in his *Séminaire XX* to designate the phallic conception of love as opposed to that *jouissance féminine* which is "au-delà du phallus," that is to say "beyond or in excess of the phallic" (1975, 69, 78–79).

11 In addition, the term *calisthenics* is Greek in origin, combining the roots *kalos* (beautiful) and *sthenos* (strength). It easily calls to mind the well-oiled bodies of the Greek gymnasium, the site of both manly prowess and pederastic desire.

12 On contemporary gay male gym culture and its complex patterns of signification and efforts to distinguish itself from straight gym culture, see Halperin whose discussion, while enlightening, is overly schematic in its desire to separate the two phenomena from one another in an absolute fashion (1995, 32, 116–118, 221n, 225).

13 Note the use of repetition in this passage as well as in the earlier one on the "two amusing, very amusing sailors" (p.104). This trope seems to be a method for marking erotic discourse in the novel.

14 For those who doubt the erotic potential of such spanking in a literary context, I can only suggest that they read Robert Coover's *Spanking the Maid*.

15 See Meyer's argument that the smugness or cruelty detected by some readers in Nabokov's work is merely a device to help the reader develop "the necessary critical distance" (1988, 23). It is unclear, however, that, even if such were a

complete accounting of the author's intentions, this fact would negate the actual content of those formal devices.

16 A related but not quite identical image can be found in the comparison of the "fingers of fate" to those of "a *grim* old shepherd checking a daughter's virginity" (pp. 165–166; emphasis added).

17 For a good general discussion of the riches the index contains, see Johnson (1979).

18 On the repetition, see note 10.

19 Puritanism in the novel is linked with revolutionary thugs, be they Gradus's Shadows or Cromwell's roundheads (Meyer 1988, 102–103)

20 For *Lolita* presenting "America ... through foreign eyes" and for parallels between Humbert and Kinbote, see Meyer (1988, 12, 219).

Part III

LOLITA

6

SEEING THROUGH HUMBERT

Focussing on the feminist sympathy in *Lolita*[1]

Tony Moore

> It is a question of focal adjustment, of a certain distance that
> the inner eye thrills to surmount, and a certain contrast that
> the mind perceives with a gasp of perverse delight.
>
> (*Lolita* 17)[2]

Brief argument

I read Vladimir Nabokov's *Lolita* when it was first published expecting a
riot of excitement not readily available in my life then. I was an English
public schoolboy harboring primitive private urges, a member, along with
children and illiterate juvenile delinquents, of one of three groups
Nabokov scornfully cites to characterize some boorish readers drawn to
his novel in the mid-fifties.[3] Quite a few of us in Britain viewed it as a dirty
work before seeing a page. Yet even my untutored, insensitive response
must have absorbed some ambiguous sense of criticism of "the special
experience 'H. H.' describes" (Nabokov 1989, 5), to borrow Dr. John
Ray's oleaginous evasion, for, as far as I can remember, I got no cheap
thrills; the book dampened my commitment to prurience and left me floundering in search of other outlets for my rampant, morally deplorable
teenage lusts. Forty years on, I took up *Lolita* again with a graduate class
of thirty-five American women, whose enthusiastic reception of the book
convinces me that Humbert Humbert, notorious pedophile and blatantly
manipulative narrator, has had a hard time from critics since he first
appeared; he is overdue rehabilitation. I realize that coupling him and
feminist sympathy will be dismissed as an outrageous oxymoron by many
who have vilified him. Yet *Lolita* subverts the conventions of male ownership and control in Humbert's memoir and sabotages that character's
attempts to shift blame for his obsessive criminal perversion onto women's

innate being. The narrative exposes the Humbert who tells much of the tale as a prisoner of his own male rhetoric. His alibis are betrayed by weaknesses revealed in his presumption of power, over both Dolores Haze and his writing.

Like many fine postmodern texts, *Lolita* is not what it pretends to be. Nabokov uses Humbert as the focus of much dissembling during the eight weeks the character devotes to his memoir. It is not a revolting tale told by an obsessive pervert of his vile perversion. It is not the total of its criminal narrative raw material: pedophilia, rape, incest, sexual slavery, repeated child abuse, kidnapping, wife battering, and murder. It is not defiantly callous in promoting a flippant, joking response to these serious and intractable matters. It is not an attempt to justify the unjustifiable by an increasingly desperate narrator whose reductively narrow sexual self-absorption obliterates the interests and feelings of a young American girl. It does not denigrate Dolores nor abandon her to side with a sex monster. It is not a pornographic fiction. It is neither a love story nor an anti-feminist fiction.[4]

Lolita is none of the above in spite of brave attempts, mounted regularly since publication, to make the novel carry these and similar offensive readings, through attacks that are usually blind to the book's complexities. Although parts of the book can bear expert witness to one or more of such views, hostile reactions are based mainly on the misconception that the whole narrative is a justification of Humbert's behavior. Much critical opinion is led astray into accepting the surface meaning of his first person account entirely at its declared value, taking him and his endlessly knowing posture at his words' worth and confusing his version of events with the events that others would recognize. His phrases may seem to be those of the same man, whose rich verbal stock would have little value without his ubiquitous first person pronouns. But they turn out to be configurations, much more complex than are found in many memoir-novels, of different consciousnesses, some of which Humbert controls fully or partially and some he does not control at all.

Humbert determines his own presence in three forms: (1) the character who has the solipsistic experiences with Lolita; (2) the teller who has distanced himself from, and changed his attitude to, these experiences before he starts his tale, but withholds an overt statement on this development until the fifty-sixth day of his creative enterprise; and (3) the artist who moves even further outside his solipsism as he writes and reads his memoir. So while Humbert's narration ostensibly maintains a broadly straight chronological line, it splits time and runs at different speeds as it holds three sets of perceptions endorsed by him at some stage or another. The tale's *now* is simultaneously: (1) the accurately reported state when he was "moved to distraction by girl children" (p.19), which he wished then would never end, "Let them play around me forever" (p.21); (2) the life which is past and from which he has become separated "by the time of my arrest" (p. 16), and wishes had been different, "Oh, Lolita, had you loved me thus!" (p. 14); and (3) the parenthetically noted present of his narration, which he treats sometimes as an oral and at others as a written act, "Ladies and gentlemen of the jury,..." (p. 9), "I leaf again and again through these miserable memories,..." (p. 13). Clues to these time shifts occur in the first six chapters, where all these citations are found along with the hint on how to view them contained in my epigraph. These are unlikely to be given sufficient weight, though, by most first-time readers, who probably become preoccupied with Humbert's preoccupation with nympholepsy, as well as distracted by his mesmerizing performance as a character. His changes of mind are the origin of some inconsistencies of attitude and emotion in his story, often noted and attributed variously by commentators to Humbert's slick verbal deviousness, hypocrisy, or miraculous deathbed moral enlightenment. But we need not rely only on semantics; there is much evidence to go on within Humbert's various styles. Humbert deserves a better press than he often gets for the integrity with which these changes in his position are corroborated within the verbal texture of his writing. The substance of his language dynamically reflects his varying interior states for, as a consummate romantic artist, his styles become the signature of his mobile consciousness. Changes embedded in the linguistic properties of his memoir participate centrally in adjusting its meaning at different points, whether or not this is his wish. In addition, Humbert's unstable perspectives are compounded by two further voices that he does not manipulate, those of *his* – as he claims – Lolita, and the judgmental Nabokov. They make contributions to his writing that provide interpretive keys not sanctioned by him, since he is kept ignorant of their presence in his pages.

Consequently, readers are required to discriminate at least five sets of attitudes which merge and diverge and become mutually challenging and mutually modifying. *Lolita*, often mistaken for a singular, unified and univocal text, comprises plexiform narrative materials existing in a state of disturbance and fluidity requiring constant "focal adjustment" (Nabokov 1989, 17) by readers to understand the teller's relationships and their own, all of which move as reading progresses, to the illusions and allusions in the tale's rich interweaving of styles.[5] Only when the tale is completed are we provided with the hindsight needed for full retrospective reorienation. In an elegant self-contradiction, the novel masquerading as the defense of an author allegedly set on averting a death sentence comes to full maturity by giving birth to readers quick enough to master the disorientation the condemned man engenders.[6] The narrative's complicated vacillations of perspective eventually submerge the distinctiveness and autonomy of the flamboyantly obtrusive voice of Humbert the sexual pervert and child abuser, which dominates the bulk of his pages, and become the means by which the text revises and repudiates its reprehensible, exclusionary attitudes. Humbert rebuts his own twisted nature and falsehoods in a reconsidered view of his story that articulates sympathy and endorsement, instead of condescension and disparagement, for Dolores.

This essay does not claim to expose all the secrets kept hidden from commentators until now. *Lolita* remains a delightfully baffling book that seems bent on subverting critical faculties as it revels ostentatiously in laying false trails and in shifting, rather than fixed and absolute, answers to its narrative riddles. Nor does the argument go quite as far as suggesting that *Lolita* could be co-opted in clear support of many of today's liberal feminisms. But it does explain some focal adjustments that can be made to sustain a strong reading that rests on the book's moral foundation and is, consequently, completely out of sympathy with the narrator's chauvinist presumptions in much of the book.

Narrator and narrated

The Humbert who tells much of the tale is imprisoned within his own masculine rhetoric. He cannot avoid the obvious and crucial disadvantage he shares with all first person narrators who aim to mislead others from the imagined security of their own delusions: he is both the narrator and the narrated. He is constantly displaced by, and deceived within, his writing. As he struggles to control us by insisting his memoir contains the authentic life led by him and his characters, his narrating both empowers and imprisons him. The freedom he takes with his pen to shape events leaves him a marked man. His efforts to take full possession of the tale are frustrated; he is trapped not only within his obsession, but also within the fluid and mobile memoir he writes as it generates readers equipped to make the focal adjustments demanded by the tale's complexities.

Humbert expects to show a sophisticated, cultured hero worthy of our compassionate understanding and endorsement, but words fail him time and again. His self-portrait puts on display a character constricted in the straitjacket of conventional masculinity, insistent that the urges of his malevolent male will are an imaginative response to the inhuman mysteries of woman and her female sexuality. I reread *Lolita* while I was also reading Camille Paglia's *Sexual Personae;* there are some striking, although fortuitous, parallels between the two books.[7] The unwitting mimicry of Paglia's central concerns in Humbert's prose is so close and extensive that I almost found it necessary to check who speaks in which book. The "true nature" of his "chosen creatures ... is not human but nymphic (that is demoniac)" (p. 13). The nymphet is discerned by the "ineffable signs," clear only to the artist or madman – "the little deadly demon among the wholesome children; *she* stands unrecognized by them and unconscious herself of her fantastic power" (p. 17). Paglia glories in the claim that "sex is daemonic" (Paglia 1991, 3), not evil, or rather both good and evil, like nature itself (Paglia 1991, 4). Both writers recognize a realm of power that invades the human world yet seems unconnected to human origins or human ends and remains outside the control of conventional developed social reality in the West. Humbert thinks he harnesses this power; but he is at its mercy, as he is transported to another realm which he feels is supreme, incapable of definition: "For there is no other bliss on earth comparable to that of fondling a nymphet. It is *hors concours*, that bliss, it belongs to another class, another plane of sensitivity" (Nabokov 1989, 166). Yet, at the same time, it is hellish, like the worst torment imagined by humankind: "Despite ... the vulgarity, and the danger, and the horrible hopelessness of it all, I still dwelled deep in my elected paradise – a paradise whose skies were the color of hell-flames – but still a paradise" (p. 166). Conflicting impulses animate Humbert's created world. Exultation and dread give birth here to encomia interrupted by a panic response to the darker mysteries involved in woman outside and beyond man's control, acknowledged in *hors concours*. Perhaps "[s]ex is the point of contact between man and nature, where morality and good intentions fall to primitive urges" (Paglia 1991, 3). Humbert has been taken out of his own individuality on the morning of his Enchanted Hunters orgy when he gloats "that every nerve in me was still anointed and ringed with the feel of her body – the body of some immortal daemon disguised as a female child" (Nabokov 1989, 139). He experiences Lolita as a Paglian daemonic archetype:

> Daemonic archetypes of woman, filling world mythology, represent the uncontrollable nearness of nature. Their tradition passes nearly unbroken from prehistoric idols through literature and art to modern movies. The primary image is the femme fatale, the woman fatal to man. The more nature is beaten back in the west, the more the femme fatale reappears, as a return of the repressed. She is the spectre of the west's bad conscience about nature. She is the moral ambiguity of nature, a malevolent moon that keeps breaking through our fog of hopeful sentiment.
>
> (Paglia 1991, 13)

"The beastly and the beautiful merged at one point" (Nabokov 1989, 135). There is much contradiction and ambivalence in Humbert's account of "nymphet love" (p. 135); yet, despite his paean to nymphets, he sticks mostly to his conception of female flesh as the devil's work, equated with original sin. The Old Testament history's traditional pessimistic view of humankind born unclean with a propensity for evil is very much alive in him. Dolores walks into the Haze living room – to be turned into the instrument of his extended orgasm – "holding in her hollowed hands a beautiful, banal, Eden red apple" (pp. 57–58). They play about with this forbidden fruit and he measures success with his furtive self-manipulation when "the least pressure would suffice to set all paradise loose" (p. 60). Then, in daydreams about the unlimited access to Lolita opened by the prospect of marriage to her mother, he celebrates an ideal sexual freedom when all restrictions on him are subsumed by his lover: "before such a vastness and variety of vistas, I was as helpless as Adam at the preview of early oriental history, ravaged in his apple orchard" (p. 71). Humbert strengthens this Adam-Lileth-apple excuse in exoneration when he draws attention to Dolores's choice of the gingham dress "with a pattern of little red apples" (p. 111) the day he takes her away from Camp Q and again after their first motel sex.

"Lo and Behold" (p. 162). His alibi further corroborates its universal origins in his preoccupation with physiological sex differences. His references to, but inevitable failure to explain, the different biological realities that separate him from his nymphet are responses to the hidden in woman. He reveals symptoms of an advanced state of what Paglia diagnoses as an endemic male condition: "men's delusional certitude that objectivity is possible is based on the visibility of their genitals ... [which] is a defensive swerve from the anxiety-inducing invisibility of the womb" (Paglia 1991, 22). She elaborates on the ineradicable consequences of these natural facts:

> The female body's unbearable hiddenness applies to all aspects of men's dealing with women. What does it look like in there? ... Mystery shrouds woman's sexuality. The mystery is the main reason for the imprisonment man has imposed on women. ... Sex crimes are always male, never female, because such crimes are conceptualizing assaults on the unreachable omnipotence of women and nature.
>
> (Paglia 1991, 22)

So Humbert's attempt to dominate and incarcerate Dolores is an un-learned behavioral characteristic, originating in a compulsion to conceptualize the threatening difference in reproductive organs. He gropes his way in dense psychological undergrowth with no visible means of support. He not only keeps her in captivity for two years because of the anxiety induced by her mysterious femaleness, but also twice imagines finding out what it looks like in there! He conjures up her insides as a kind of pre-coital light show in the car journey to their first motel night as he observes that her "lovely prismatic entrails had already digested the sweetmeat" (Nabokov 1989, 116). And in the second chapter of Part Two, by now accustomed to devouring all that he wants, he drools regret that he cannot get at the juicy, succulent, and sweet mixed grill promised by her offal. "My only grudge against nature was that I could not turn my Lolita inside out and apply voracious lips to her young matrix, her unknown heart, her nacreous liver, the sea-grapes of her lungs, her comely twin kidneys" (p. 165).

Humbert is a skillful advocate for nature, besides this complaint that it does not provide for all his appetites. "The daemonism of chthonian nature is the west's dirty secret" quips Paglia in a Humbertian apothegm (Paglia 1991, 6).[8] Humbert speaks out against taboos that normally frighten or overwhelm us. He applies much of his wicked humor and richly witty rhetorical resources to washing his filthy secret on the public page and reminding us that his sexual desires are deep, dark, dirty, and destructive. That is the trouble with Humbert: he is tauntingly immoral, deeply unpleasant and exploitative; but his memoir engages our better selves in its unfathomable complexity and devious subterfuge. We can hardly avoid reacting against his prose as it enacts the abuser's process of deliberate and sustained coercion of the victim to do the will of the victimizer. His erotic fantasy brings a wonderful whiff of cleansing stale air into the Norman Rockwellian images of the American clean-cut family circle. "I am just your *old man*, a dream dad protecting his dream daughter" (Nabokov 1989, 149). Judgments are refined, not blunted, by the brazen deceit of his linguistic pressure and extra vigilance is brought into play against abuses which are usually ignored or condoned with polite silence.[9]

Narrative function of Dolores

"Lolita had been safely solipsized" (p. 60), claims Humbert in a solecism embodying the essence of his sense of entitlement. He invents an incongruous, spuriously authentic intransitive verb with which to fix her status as object. He passes counterfeit coinage in characteristic lexical sleight of hand smoothed by alliteration. This deceptively simple sentence, with its etymological pun carrying multiple significances, incorporates, as it acknowledges and turns to creative advantage, the main rhetorical convictions of Humbert the child abuser. He either cannot or will not grant pre-adolescents and readers, events and language, any predominant values in and for themselves; they are manipulated only to keep them oppressed within his subjectivity. The pervert has to use perverted narration to realize his perverted world.

But Dolores cannot be "solipsized." No language he can devise is fixed enough to subordinate her entirely; in fact she emerges most strongly when Humbert least expects it and completely undermines the credibility of his understanding of his experiences in Part One. For instance, he expresses in eager hyperbole his detumescent relief on the couch: "Blessed be the Lord, she had noticed nothing!" (p. 61), deaf to his own words that have just given clear outward confirmation of her agitated libido, "she cried with a sudden shrill note ... and blinked, cheeks aflame, hair awry!" (p. 61). His lust keeps him ignorant that the object of his desire is aroused herself. Then again, Dolores's voice is present and articulate throughout the climactic episode at the Enchanted Hunters. Expectations of titillation may throw readers' concentration off balance during the diversion through twenty-six pages of cunning manipulation between the plan of rape, "My scheme was a marvel of primitive art" (p. 106), and some unspecified consummation, "by six fifteen we were technically lovers" (p. 132). Consequently, the heroine's polyphonous cries for help probably pass by most readers first time, just as they do Humbert, twice – at the time his story occurs and as he writes his memoir. She is troubled by ambivalent and conflicting feelings resulting from her first penetrative sexual experiences with Charlie Holmes at the camp and, unable to make much sense of the turbulent mixture of furtive excitement, pride, enjoyment, curiosity, and guilt stimulated by her initiation into this part of the adult's forbidden world, she looks repeatedly for adult guidance. She tries pseudo adult talk, " 'Fact I've been revoltingly unfaithful to you, but it does not matter one bit, because you've stopped caring for me anyway' " (p. 112); baby talk, " 'Bad, bad girl' said Lo comfortably. 'Juvenile delickwent[']]" (p. 113); Humbertian jocular pastiche, " 'I am a friend to male animals ... I am absolutely filthy in thought, word and deed' " (p. 114); Charlotte's coy and pretentious syntax, " 'C'est. Except for one little thing, something I simply can't tell you without blushing all over' " (p. 115); and direct appeal, " 'Oh I've been such a disgusting girl. . . . Lemme tell you–' " (p. 123). Her persistence flagrantly contradicts Humbert's notion of a nymphet on an island of entranced time, yet his erotic fantasy so enslaves him it blots out all else at the time of the experience and also when he writes recollecting in captivity.

Of course, his tunnel vision is a joke that runs throughout the novel, providing artistic plausibility for most of the outlandish developments in the storyline. But Nabokov creates some exquisite moments by foregrounding this trait and subverting his narrator at the twin peaks of his triumph. Humbert's physical and narratorial climaxes are diminished within his own words. Dolores asks to be kissed and offers "hot, opening lips," forward behavior so out of keeping with his conception of nymphets that he has to reclassify the experience as "but an innocent game on her part, a bit of backfisch foolery" (p. 113). Locked into his "hermetic vision" of the virginal – "my nymphet, my beauty and bride" (p. 123) – he is oblivious to the preposterous position he puts himself in. The dramatic irony is thickly spread at his expense when he palms off a sleeping pill as a virility aid to the unvirginal homo- and heterosexually aware sub-teenager who has already enjoyed servicing Charlie that morning: "I had hoped the drug would work fast. It certainly did. She had had a long long day, she had gone rowing in the morning with Barbara ... – and had been active in other ways too" (p. 122). He is so bound up in himself that Dolores's bold initiative in masturbating him in the early morning after an uneventful night brings her no credit. Her boisterous, uninhibited enjoyment of a newfound freedom earns a supercilious sneer, "My life was handled by little Lo in an energetic matter of fact manner as if it were an insensate gadget unconnected with me" (pp. 133–134). This emerging but still immature sexuality shows on the simplest level that the female character is neither subjugated nor humiliated at this point. Yet her part in the sex is so unsettling to Linda Kauffman in her 1992 essay that she wants to censor it from the book: "it is doubtful his claim that Lolita seduced him is true; more important it is unverifiable" (Kauffman 1992, 60).[10]

This is an example of the critical perversity that *Lolita* still attracts. Nabokov chooses to stress the difference between literature and life and does so with imagination and clarity. The conspicuously bogus verisimilitude of Ray's "Foreword" primes readers for entry into a fictional maze with no easy way out. The narrating character as a boy of thirteen who "wanted to be a famous spy" (Nabokov 1989, 12) is father to the man who enjoys "trifling with psychiatrists; cunningly leading them on; never letting them see that you know all the tricks of the trade" (p. 34). Humbert points out repeatedly in his early chapters that he is not to be trusted. He is not an ordinary liar but a Cretan liar, so habituated to dissembling that even he is unsure at times if he is telling the truth about telling lies or telling lies about telling the truth. Such explicit reminders that this novel cannot be verified should delight us. The fictionality of Humbert's story is advertised with more blatant honesty than most characters receive from their creators. "Imagine me; I shall not exist if you do not imagine me" (p. 129) brings home the tenuous connection between this fictional author's memoir and outward "reality."[11] Not much fiction, and none of Humbert's narration, can be subjected to empirical verification.

However, there is an internal consistency in the part Dolores plays in this scene which makes her role of seducer tenable and substantiates her narrative function in providing a view of events that undercuts Humbert. She is venturing into the mysteries of adult sex, uncertain but intrigued and so signaling, in another irony crushing the putative author, the end of her nymphancy. She lives in the mundane "world of tough kids" (p. 134), a reality unconnected to his "intangible island of entranced time" (p. 17). Humbert's values are personal, solipsist in the extreme, only concerned with the nympholept's self, so he is unconscious that his erotic symbol is in full flight from him well before the moment he is sure he possesses her. She willingly participates in what she prosaically calls "doing it" three times in the Enchanted Hunters bed between 6:15 and 10 am. These are the first and last occasions she *fucks with*, or in conjunction with, Humbert, with the male as an object to her, just as she is to him.[12] Her good-hearted natural response from this position of equality is affirmed by the relaxed account she gives of her sexual adventures to date (pp. 135–137) and is still apparent just after they check out as she jokes, "I ought to call the police and tell them you raped me. Oh, you dirty, dirty old man" (p. 141). Humbert, even in his mindless insensitivity to Dolores as a separate complex individual, acknowledges that his obsession will become self-consuming. He is aware that he has slaughtered at birth the prospect of endless stimulated desire and requited pleasure, "It was something quite special, that feeling: an oppressive, hideous constraint as if I were sitting with the small ghost of somebody I had just killed" (p. 140). After his extended orgasm he had been enraptured by his "own creation, another, fanciful Lolita – perhaps more real than Lolita" (p. 62). Now he knows his fleeting erotic fantasy will not nourish and sustain him for long.

Narrative judgment

Dolores is even less "safely solipsized" in Part Two, as we see once we make the focal adjustments that refute Humbert's bilious discourtesies trying to turn her into "a most exasperating brat" and "a disgustingly conventional little girl" (p. 148). She *is* conventional, in wanting what other adolescents have and to stop "doing filthy things together and never behaving like ordinary people" (p. 158). She learns she can put no faith in those she ought to trust, as she is denied all the normal prerogatives of a middle-class white girl growing up within a recognized social system. It is remarkable after what Humbert puts her through that she sustains her crush on Quilty and encourages him as a lover, seems to enjoy sex with him, and can outwit Humbert in resource and deceit to get it regularly. In preparing for the school production of *The Hunted Enchanters* and afterwards at Kasbeam, Champion, and Wace, she is mistress of the adult art of adultery, nicely giving the lie to her own understated claim to be "a fast little article" (p. 222). "By permitting Lolita to study acting, I had, fond fool, suffered her to cultivate deceit" (p. 229). There are many more delicious ironies deflating Humbert as she plans and executes the new journey west to Elphinstone in conspiracy with Quilty. This enterprise charges her with renewed vitality. "And there she sat, hands clasped in her lap, and dreamily brimmed with a diabolical glow that had no relation to me whatever" (p. 214). The daemonic archetype is again *hors concours*, but for another's benefit. This second quest transposes the places of hunter and hunted in Part One; Humbert the enchanted hunter becomes the hunted enchanter. Dolores and Quilty write the rules for the games in the central section of Part Two, where she emerges as the successful strategist and playmaker, with skills that leave Humbert floundering as the crazed victim. The girl is robustly cheerful during the charade up to her hospitalization, while Humbert describes the perpetual torments he suffers as he wills into existence his worst fantastic fear of becoming a deceived lover. She wins the upper hand in their weird relationship; victim turns taunter, shrewdly exposing the limits to the hero's much claimed adult intelligence.

Does Nabokov make Humbert's perversion so attractive it could create depraved, inordinate, and lustful desires and corrupt male readers more susceptible than I was as a schoolboy? Is his narrative complicit in and even contributive to collective injuries on girls like Dolores? And does he help make victims of them all? Paglia points to an opposite, beneficial, and renewing effect of all art that shocks.[13] She provides one understanding of how Humbert's untrustworthy writing can have self-thwarting effects. His inspired defense of the legally and morally indefensible remains a fiction, but it exposes by extension the dark chthonian drives in the oppressive male when on "that plane of being where nothing mattered, save the infusion of joy brewed within [his] body" (p. 60). His characterization supports the validity and urgency of Paglia's assertion, which she propounds to justify raw sex in art. "Nature is waiting at society's gates to dissolve us in her chthonian bosom" (Paglia 1991, 39). She throws a direct challenge to those who advocate any kind of cultural policing with a variation on Aristotle's analysis of the benefits of catharsis in classical tragedy:

> Out with stereotypes, feminism proclaims. But stereotypes are the west's stunning sexual personae, the vehicles of art's assault against nature. The moment there is imagination, there is myth. We may have to accept an ethical cleavage between imagination and reality, tolerating horrors, rapes, and mutilations in art that we would not tolerate in society. For art is our message from the beyond, telling us what nature is up to.
>
> (Paglia 1991, 39)

"*Lolita* has no moral in tow" (p. 314) asserts Nabokov dogmatically, but I remain unconvinced, except in the limited literal sense too self-evident to need stating, that the book does not trail a message; were one visible we would have been denied the furious and continuing critical debate I outlined at the start. But there is an obvious difference between having no overt moral and having an amoral position.[14] I discern the judgmental Nabokov often disowning Humbert's foolish vanity and distancing his narrative from his character's obfuscatory disregard for right and wrong. For example, there is a pre-emptive strike, an Old Testament type emblematic pointer to the irreparable wrong Dolores suffers, placed within Ray's obituary announcement, through which readers are given a consummate sense of a neat ethical fictional ending even before Humbert begins his tale: "Mrs Schiller's death in childbed, giving birth to a stillborn girl, on Christmas Day 1952" (p. 4). The vainglorious deception in the narrator's fancies that allows him to believe he has created "another, fanciful Lolita – perhaps more real than Lolita" (p. 62) spins out of his control and reaches an insane terminal condition when his reach for fluent language is snatched from his previously sure grasp. Broken syntax and lame prose rhythms enact the mania in babble about his natural child's child receiving the benefit of his perpetual potency: "bizarre, tender, salivating Dr. Humbert, practicing on supremely lovely Lolita the Third the art of being a grandad" (p. 174).

"Can we really be surprised that readers have overlooked Nabokov's ironies in *Lolita*, when Humbert Humbert is given full and unlimited control of the rhetorical resources?" (Booth 1983, 390). Wayne C. Booth takes it for granted that he cannot be denied. But I react to the critic's wrong-headed assertion with "excuse me, yes, because he is not, not by a long stretch." The book is remarkable for the complex ways, some of which I have mentioned, in which the narrative tempers or mitigates its focalizing character's control. Nabokov's text lacks the imaginative sympathy with which postmodern authors often present seriously flawed, sexually absorbed or deviant leading characters.[15] *Lolita*, in contrast, fosters criticism of Humbert that becomes increasingly substantial as the narrative glosses, controls, and finally rebalances the character's licentious thought patterns. This narrative's jaundiced view of its storyteller's limitations emerges through Part Two in subtle and unsubtle, small and large devices. Humbert, the master of allusion, has his favored method of displaying literary superiority turned against him by those who surpass his skill, confident he will not recognize their references. He is up against bright, inventive and literate adversaries, both inside and outside his story, with the sense of decency to give him a sporting chance in their word games. Yet his lust obstructs his concentration when the clues lie thickest on the ground. Take the visit to the Wace summer theatre. "I remember thinking that this idea of children – colors had been lifted by authors Clare Quilty and Vivian Darkbloom from a passage in James Joyce, and that two of the colors were quite exasperatingly lovely" (p. 221). Humbert can be excused blindness to the anagrammatic appearance of Vladimir Nabokov pointing at him ironically. But his boasted familiarity with the European literary canon might have encouraged him to make more of Quilty's theft from Chapter 9 of *Finnegans Wake*. Nabokov leaves Joyce's fingerprints all over this scene to invite a parallel between two painfully obtuse characters, Shem the Penman and Humbert the autobiographer. Joyce's rainbow girls play a tug-of-love and marrying game – "Angels, Devils and Colours" – adding sexual spice by making the Angel's drawers heliotrope, the color the Devil (Shem) must guess.[16] The author allows his narrator to reach the right end of the spectrum with the soubriquet "my own ultraviolet darling" (p. 221), but denies him the further enlightenment that would have come with more assiduous pursuit of the correspondences with Joyce's victim. Joyce makes the inadequate intelligence of Shem obvious with his repeated failure to find the answer to the girl's riddle; "what she meaned he could not can" (Joyce 1939, 225) and Nabokov gives Humbert a close family resemblance to his precursor. "It's driving her dafft like he so dumnb" (Joyce 1939, 225) is echoed by " 'Sometimes,' said Lo, 'you are quite revoltingly dumb...' " (Nabokov 1989, 221) as she enjoys her barefaced lies and Humbert's discomfort. He creates a fanciful tormenting fiend now who, like Lolita earlier, is more real than the real thing: " 'I thought,' I said kidding her, 'Quilty was an ancient flame of yours,...' " (p. 221). He only had to connect Quilty to his own parody of "Her boy-fiend or theirs, if they are so plurielled, cometh up as a trapadour" (Joyce 1939, 224), to uncover an intertextual clue pointing to Dolores's duplicity.[17]

A scathing Nabokovian wit keeps Humbert oblivious that Lolita is liberated from his clutches on the Fourth of July, Independence Day; although he notes "there was some great national celebration in town, judging by the firecrackers" (Nabokov 1989, 245), he remains too myopic to make the connection even when the landlady dates Quilty's check out (p. 249). Some flaws in the defense he might have pleaded had he come before the jury become apparent. Assuming he might have some "unbiased readers" (p. 285), even they may suspect, yet be unable to prove, economy with the truth in the inspired verbality of his self-representation as an homme fatal, "a great big handsome hunk of movieland manhood" (p. 39). But no one can mistake the negative authorial judgment on his narcissism, and on all the self-aggrandizing priapic fantasies of the narrator and others who share his attitudes, when Nabokov grants Humbert a ludicrous excess of masculinity in allowing him to exaggerate the likely size of his penis by close to 100 percent: "I was to her not a boyfriend, not a glamour man, not a pal, not even a person at all, but just two eyes and a foot of engorged brawn–" (p. 283). The average length in its erect state of the white European male member is six and a half inches (Porter 1985, 34). This verbal enlargement of his small piece of flesh reduces to absurdity the legend of the phallus, depending as it does on a willing suspension of disbelief, a collusion to deny the reality that no penis can live up to its fabulous mythical importance. So Nabokov diminishes the singularity and power for which the phallus is generally a metaphor in male-centered literature in the same graceful and complex irony that cuts Humbert down to size.[18]

Narrative revision

Kauffman, a self-styled "materialist-*feminist*" (Kauffman 1992, 68), attacks *Lolita* for endorsing Humbert's "rhetorical ruses" to suppress Lolita's presence:

> the novel [Lionel] Trilling heralded as the greatest love story of the twentieth century in fact indicts the ideology of love and exposes literature's complicity in perpetuating it. The answer to the question, "Is there a woman in this text?" is no. But there was a

female, one whose body was the source of crimes and puns, framed unsettlingly between the horror of incest and aesthetic *jouissance*, between material reality and antimimesis, between pathos and parody. That body was not a woman's; like Lolita's stillborn baby, it was a girl's.

(Kauffman 1992, 76)

This conclusion to her combative essay rests on some false and questionable premises and occasional abuse of the text. Her fierce opinions need to be subjected to keen scrutiny and some rejected outright, for it is she who erases Dolores. Kauffman disqualifies herself as a reliable witness by castigating a book Nabokov did not write; she either misrepresents or ignores many of the last forty pages of Humbert's memoir. Consider the letter Dolores sends from Coalmount, printed in full as it was written (Nabokov 1989, 266). This is the only occasion in the novel when she is heard unmediated; Humbert does not interfere and allows her "small matter-of-fact voice" (p. 266) to speak without the patronizing prejudice that he throws in the way of "Farlow's hysterical letter" (p. 265), delivered at the same time. The dignity in the brisk account of her position is impressive; she is devoid of self-pity and recrimination: "I have gone through much sadness and hardship./ Yours expecting,/ Dolly (Mrs. Richard F. Schiller)" (p. 266). Her simple tact in broaching her need for money seems to strike Humbert immediately. He spares her words the splenetic commentary he has customarily poured on anything other than his own thoughts and feelings. The real Dolores is before him ready to take the place of the fallacy.

Kauffman's desire to kick Humbert is difficult to follow, since he spends much of the novel putting himself down. The character's active reconsideration of his sexual and narratorial perversions reaches a crucial point in that short chapter (Nabokov 1989, Part Two, 31), occupying a single paragraph in less than a page, which recounts near the start "I reviewed my case. With the utmost simplicity and clarity I now saw myself and my love. Previous attempts seemed out of focus in comparison" (p. 282). Humbert then names "his" love properly as he claims how much it matters that "*Dolores Haze* had been deprived of her childhood by a maniac" (p. 283; emphasis added). Immediately he reclassifies his love as lust and goes on to a chapter of "other smothered memories" (p. 284) in which Lolita's words are reported directly in quoted monolog and dialogue and with third person attribution of her realization that "even the most miserable of family lives was better than the parody of incest" (p. 287) Humbert had offered. I am not as convinced as some that this point marks a stage in Humbert's moral evolution; but his decision to scrutinize his nympholepsy here is unarguable.[19] Memory is about therapy as well as remembrance, and mends itself with its own focal adjustments. In Part Two, Chapter 32, he voluntarily employs what today is called recovered memory. This professionally endorsed contemporary tool is anachronistically apposite here in Humbert's tale; it allows both the abuser's memories and his victim's voice to be heard as they reflect back on experiences mediated previously only through Humbert's eulogies.

Kauffman's polemical argument seems to be pressed in service of a wider cause. Her contempt for the pathology in Humbert's characterization may lead her to employ hostility to Nabokov's entire fiction as part of a campaign against institutionalized male oppression in the world outside the narrative. But since *Lolita* is not another case of men silencing women, her offensive dissipates rather than stimulates concern in the important debate on how women have been unnaturally weakened by a history of sexual exploitation. There is no "complicity" between this novel and its narrator's manipulation; there is no obliteration of Dolores; nor, finally, is there passive endorsement by this character of his criminal history. He comes to see that his mind has been obsessed only with its own figments and disavows his elaborate artifice through a significant move in his last two-and-a-half pages. Humbert recalls a scene, "a last mirage of wonder and hopelessness ... soon after her [Lolita's] disappearance" (p. 307), when he had listened to the noises of ordinary humanity rising from a small mining town as he looked down on its "friendly abyss" (p. 307):

> I stood listening to that musical vibration from my lofty slope, to those flashes of separate cries with a kind of demure murmur for background, and then I knew that the hopelessly poignant thing was not Lolita's absence from my side, but the absence of her voice from that concord.
>
> This then is my story. I have reread it. It has bits of marrow sticking to it, and blood and beautiful bright-green flies. At this or that twist of it I feel my slippery self eluding me, gliding into deeper and darker waters than I care to probe.
>
> (p. 308)

This is one of the most illuminating moments in the book, calling for a decisive focal adjustment through retrospective reorientation.[20] The narrator looks into his memoir from the high vantage point of the penultimate page and acknowledges his theft of the girl's childhood. He no longer writes in the indecorous, thrusting "fancy prose style" (p. 9) he vaunted from the first page. He puts aside alliteration and word games, although that first sentence has enough assonance and elegant balance to testify this is Humbert's stylish natural voice, rather than one of many impersonations his earlier writing shows him able to turn on. His language is tasteful and reticent, devoid of the Humbertian trademarks of parody, self-parody, cynicism, satire, disdain, double entendre, and scornful desire to display how many more books he has read than his readers. This relatively restrained prose comes after, and as a reaction to, a reconsideration of his own floridly told case-history, which has exposed the true nature of his pretenses and delusions. His reading has given him a fresh focus, empowering him to separate fact from fantasy, his own banal reality from the uncertainties created in his fiction, narrative development from maudlin self-justification. He has uncovered the deceptions and suppressions, "his slippery self" in motion in his own writing and silently encourages readers to do the same so they can understand their relation to the story as well as his. If *we* reread, Humbert implies, we shall get behind his deviant words to where the writer has been and see the origins of his writing. He becomes part of the dead past "like the bits of marrow [...] and blood" sticking to his story, yet the text he has created needs to be completed by us as he passes away. Humbert was right to perceive that there was "nothing for the treatment of my misery but the melancholy and very local palliative of articulate art" (p. 283). Art undoes the self by the simultaneous doubling of identity and annihilation, for the process of writing becomes a process of self-obliteration. Joyce anticipates this discovery when he mocks autobiographers, disputing the notion that the best way to justify the self is to embark on confessions. In a chapter in *Finnegans Wake* before that which Humbert remembered in Wace, Shem writes with the ink of his own excrement, "through the bowels of his misery," on "the only foolscap available," his own flesh, only to find that he disappears:

> flashly, faithly, nastily, appropriately, this Esuan Menschavik and the first till last alshemist wrote over every square inch of the only foolscap available, his own body, till by its corrosive sublimation one continuous present tense integument slowly unfolded all marryvoising moodmoulded cyclewheeling history (thereby, he said, reflecting from his own individual person life unlivable, transaccidentated through the slow fires of consciousness into a dividual chaos, perilous, potent, common to allflesh, human only, mortal) but with each word that would not pass away the squidself which he had squirtscreened from the crystalline world waned chagreenold and doriangrayer in its dudhud.
>
> (Joyce 1939, 185–186)

He literally writes himself, scrawling his flesh upon his flesh. His real identity unfolds from, yet is obscured by, the obscene matter that hides the self behind itself only to expose itself more flagrantly in incontinent self-disseminations.

Similarly, Humbert, a polypseudonymous heir to Shem's penmanship, becomes guilty of involuntary and indecent exposure. His autobiography enacts the disfiguration of his life: the "squidself" is "squirtscreened" by its own ink that will not pass away since his writing must use it in repro-

106

ductive activity. The "dudhud" is the inevitability of failure of his attempt to obscure; the deed is a dud in the making, a weakness inherent in its patriarchal dadhood.[21] This became apparent once he assumed the reader's role. Thus distanced, he realizes his story exposes him, and that readers warrant better than his earlier strategies of manipulation; decoding of the "hideous hieroglyphics ... of [his] fatal lust" (p. 48) is part of the entire experience of his work. Clear recognition of the inevitable fictionality of his writing destabilizes his own narrational performance, which now doubles back on itself and encourages revised critical assessments. He gives these a further nudge with his unambiguous self-sentence: "Had I come before myself, I would have given Humbert at least thirty-five years for rape, and dismissed the rest of the charges" (p. 308). Maudlin insincerity? A facile appeal for sympathy? Unlikely remorse? This prose contains no hard evidence that Humbert has discovered an absolute moral sense, but neither does it strike hollow notes of sham Humbertian attempts to exorcize guilt or a stagemanaged deathbed conversion. Trilling's question of whether an inveterate liar is capable of a genuine confession of full responsibility invalidates itself. It is not necessary to give up scepticism about the narrator's full repentance to recognize the revised view of the narrative encouraged here by the more straightforward style of the memoir.[22]

Humbert's admission that he has reread his writing makes this sequence the inspiration for the decisive focal adjustment, a small paradigm of the larger reflective scrutiny the entire text requires before readers can fill in for themselves its gaps and fully locate its moral foundation. The book has to be read again before it can be read properly the first time. With the benefit of hindsight, we see that the narrator provides Dolores with psychological space of her own, repositions her centrally in the book, and fulfills his parting rhetorical promise as he faces his own extinction to "make [her] live in the minds of later generations" (p. 309). She lives in the mind, not as his exotic creation "another fanciful Lolita" (p. 62), but, with negligible verbal trickery, as she is in the discourse of her letter and in the memoir's last direct encounter: familiar, conventional, and warmly human. In the Hunter Road scene (pp. 269–280) she has already experienced enough to make her very old, "hopelessly worn at seventeen," dazed and resigned, "with her ruined looks and her adult, rope-veined narrow hands" (p. 277). The mind remembers her as the literal foregone conclusion of Humbert's maniacal perversion. Although he cannot undo what he has done and write himself straight, she breaks free from those solipsized, warped sections of the memoir which aimed to suppress her as the nymphet waif. No longer a mere dummy to Humbert's male ventriloquism, she emerges into the foreground of the narrative as a young woman with independent fictional life.

Postscript

My heart goes out to the abused colleague and distressed women readers movingly described in Elizabeth Patnoe's fine and challenging essay. But I shudder at the consequences of literary judgments shaped by attention to anecdote, however compelling, and by public discussion of private anguish, however terrible the personal loss suffered. *Lolita* is paper and ink, not flesh and blood, and commentators may find good reason to avoid being drawn into Oprahatic exposure of the trauma of some readers, and away from the text.

Many critics, whether enthusiastic or hostile, read the novel as a memoir about dangerous coercive social forces with which the central male character is irrevocably aligned. Support is then found in such reading for a spectrum of ideological causes, and Patnoe describes these fairly as misreadings. Yet it is not this text that promotes many of these misreadings, but predetermined polemics. Even if it is unrealistic to look for apolitical criticism, is it unreasonable to ask for social concerns to be balanced by sustained attention to what the author writes? I have argued that throughout the novel the narrator's false assumptions of total control are undermined and that the end of *Lolita* is especially revealing. By then Humbert has actively given up his belief in a superior imagination that entitles him to manipulate his narration, other characters, and all readers. His sense of control is consciously acknowledged *by him* for what it always has been – criminally deluded. This may not satisfy those who would prefer the tragic matter that he narrates, notably incest, sexual slavery, and spousal abuse, to be glossed with unequivocal moral judgment. This fiction has no clear answer to these pressing social problems, but that does not prove it is unaware of them. Its reticence may show how well it understands their complexities.

Notes

1 I am delighted to acknowledge the generous help given by colleagues in the Department of English at Boston University. Suzan Mizruchi fired me with enthusiasm for the project and guided it through the early stages. Julia Prewitt Brown, William C. Carroll and John T. Matthews disagreed penetratingly with a late draft and provoked me to reshape parts of the argument. All my readings of complex prose narratives are pervaded by John Paul Riquelme's teaching.
2 The edition of *Lolita* in use throughout is the Vintage paperback (New York: Vintage International, 1989). All subsequent citations are given parenthetically with page numbers alone.
3 See Nabokov's Afterword "On A Book Entitled *Lolita*" (*Lolita* 316). I was a day scholarship boy, so I am exempt from the rest of Nabokov's peevish slur.
4 See, among others: Trilling (1958); Barnes (1959); McNeely (1989); Kauffman (1992). More comprehensive surveys of criticism can be found in Schuman (1979); Page (1982); Rampton (1984, bibliography 213–230); Tammi (1985, bibliography 365–382).

5 Humbert's "focal adjustment" is used in context in the epigraph to this essay, the title of which nods towards the coinage "focalizations" in Genette (1972, 189–194).

6 See Roland Barthes's "The Death of the Author" with its famous battle cry striking at the heart of traditional literary values: "the birth of the reader must be at the cost of the death of the Author" (Barthes 1977, 148).

7 Paglia's Chapter 1 "Sex and Violence, or Nature and Art" (1991, 1–39) helped me to identify Humbert's mythic male postures and to define the path of my argument.

8 "Chthonian" is one of Paglia's key terms for that which dwells in the underworld of the earth's bowels: "the blind grinding of subterranean force" (Paglia 1991, 5).

9 Christopher Ricks argues for the importance and potency of lying as a special paradoxical force creating pressure that recoils to emphasize the truth: "[lying] strikes at the roots of language and may strike, self-incriminatingly, at itself" (Ricks 1987, 373).

10 I use the later version of Kauffman's essay. An earlier version was published in 1989. See Kauffman (1989).

11 "Reality," Nabokov reminds in his Afterword "On A Book Entitled Lolita," is "one of the few words which mean nothing without quotes" (p. 312).

12 By implication I take issue with Catharine MacKinnon. "Sexual objectification is the primary process of the subjection of women. It unites act with word, construction with expression, perception with enforcement, myth with reality. Man fucks woman; subject verb object" (MacKinnon 1983, 25). In order for her proposition to hold she suppresses the lively American English construction to fuck with: subject verb conjunction object, used equally by men and women subjects.

13 Only Words (MacKinnon 1993) makes an eloquent, vitriolic statement of the case against this view. MacKinnon maintains that speech acts can be implicitly part of violence; in context they can commit violence.

14 There is evidence outside this narrative that Nabokov believed he had created "a highly moral affair." See his correspondence with Edmund Wilson (Nabokov and Wilson 1980, 296, 298).

15 Some examples chosen at random are: Cholly in Toni Morrison's The Bluest Eye (Morrison 1970); Alexander Portnoy in Philip Roth's Portnoy's Complaint (Roth 1967); Sebastian Dangerfield in J. P. Donleavy's The Ginger Man (Donleavy 1958); Harry Angstrom in John Updike's Rabbit, Run (Updike 1960) and the three subsequent Rabbit novels.

16 Carl Proffer points out that Humbert lifts too; his "ecstatic description of his first night alone with Dolores is a paraphrase of a passage from the Nickspub scene of Finnegans Wake" (Proffer 1968, 135). See Eckley (1985) for a fuller account of Joyce's use of the game.

17 I benefit from the impressive scholarship in Alfred Appel's indispensable edition The Annotated Lolita. But his predeliction for the peremptory in critical statements, sealed with the author's approval, aims to bury enquiry which needs to be kept alive. The infallible judgments in his notes should be read skeptically. Here is just one example where this formidable couple is not to be trusted: "...said Nabokov, for, 'Generally speaking, FW is a very small and blurry smudge on the mirror of my memory' ... The 'children-colours', however, constitute the only intentional allusion to Finnegans Wake in Lolita" (Appel 1991, 414).

18 Much of this paragraph is lifted from the present writer's "How Unreliable Is

Humbert in *Lolita*" in *Journal of Modern Literature* XXV:1 (Fall 2001) © Indiana University Press, 2001, and is used with permission.

19 See, for instance, Alexandrov (1991, 168 and 184). He claims this chapter "shows that [Humbert] has come to understand his error" in confusing fact with fancy.

20 Alexandrov's chapter cites this scene as "Humbert ... abandoning the entire category of 'nymphet'" (Alexandrov 1991, 164). But he sees a double point of view, rather than the three sets of Humbert's perceptions for which I argue, in the memoir; so I attribute different significances to this revelation.

21 I owe this to John Paul Riquelme. See Chapter One, "Twists of the Teller's Tale: *Finnegans Wake*" (Riquelme 1983, 1–47).

22 See Trilling (1958).

7

DISCOURSE, IDEOLOGY, AND HEGEMONY

The double dramas in and around *Lolita*[1]

Elizabeth Patnoe

There is general agreement, among those professionals who work with adult survivors, that the effects of abuse might show themselves in the form of low self-esteem, lack of assertiveness, depression, and problems in sexual and maternal relationships. However, when we look at the research done on the socialization of women, and the norms set for female behavior (in Western culture) we find that many of the behaviors and "traits" that would be seen to characterize "neurotic" women, such as those listed above, would also be used to prescribe sex-role-appropriate behavior in women.

(Jones 1991, 76)

Where [the women's movement] is strong, incidence figures rival the shocking U.S. statistic that one in three women before the age of eighteen has been sexually abused; where the women's movement is weak, incidence figures drop, and social concern about it is minimal.

(Virginia Goldner, in Jones 1991, viii)

Culture

She walked up to me, and she asked me to dance. I ask her her name. In a dark-brown voice she said Lola, *L-O-L-A*, Lola, Lo, Lo, Lo, Lo, Lo–la.

As a ten-year-old, I was intrigued by the Kinks' song about a boy liking a girl and then finding out something unexpected. What exactly was it? I didn't know for sure, but I liked its sound, its ability to urge movement at the slightest memory of its lyrics. I continued to love the name "Lola," a word that evoked memories of carefree childhood days – of sneaking squirt bottles on the school bus and dancing in the backyard. But during my first reading of *Lolita*, the name lost its playful allure, stopped making me want to sing along. Now it urges pause as I try to understand the speaker's use of "Lola" or "Lolita." The Kinks' "Lola," while about the doubling of cross-dressing, broaches issues of gender, sexuality, and interpretation, issues that also inform any discussion of *Lolita*, but I am interested in it for its exemplification of the power of intertextuality, of how one text – *Lolita* – can be even retroactively intertextualized with another – "Lola" – such that my pleasure in "Lola" is diminished, my vision of childhood changed, and my understanding of the diffuse doublings fueled by Vladimir Nabokov's *Lolita* clarified.

Nabokov's Lola experiences great pain because of Humbert's treatment of her, which we see in her crying every night after she thinks Humbert is asleep, in the scratches she leaves on Humbert's neck while resisting sex with him, and in her escape from him and the territory of his treatment – much of the United States. It is fitting that Lolita retreats to one of the country's borders, to a remote place where, presumably in part because its isolation precludes sophisticated medical support, she dies in childbirth. But, as if it is not enough that Humbert repeatedly violates Lolita and that she dies in the novel, the world repeatedly reincarnates her – and, in the process, it doubles her by co-opting, fragmenting, and violating her: it kills her again and again.

In 1966, *The Random House Unabridged Dictionary of the English Language* defined "Lolita" as "a girl's given name, form of Charlotte or Delores. Also Loleta." By 1992, *The American Heritage Dictionary of the English Language* offers a very different definition for "Lolita": "A seductive adolescent girl. [After Lolita, the heroine of *Lolita*, a novel by Vladimir Nabokov]." In a recent and exceptionally distorted representation of Lolita, the mythicized Lolita is not based on the novel's character who is abducted and abused, who dies at the end of the book, but a "Lethal Lolita" who attempts to murder her lover's wife. Amy Fisher has been repeatedly referred to as "Lolita" – in commercials for the three television movies about the shooting,[2] in newspapers, in *People*'s cover story, "Lethal Lolita," and even on the national evening news (CBS 12-1-92). In Japan, the term "Lolita complex" is widely used to refer to men's fascination with the sexuality of female youth – and to perpetuate the portrayal of women as ridiculously childlike. Maureen Corrigan of Georgetown University also distorted the Lolita character when, in a National Public Radio editorial, she equated one of Madonna's characters in the book *Sex* with Lolita. There, in another kind of doubling, Madonna poses as a full-breasted little girl in drop-bottom pink baby pajamas, who supposedly wants sex. What Corrigan describes as a Lolita is not the novel's Lolita, the Lolita who tries to call her mother from the inn, who scratches Humbert, who cries every night, and who finally escapes – just as my *Lolita* is not the same *Lolita* that *Vanity Fair* calls "the only convincing love story of our century" (Vintage 1989 cover). In "Time Has Been Kind to the Nymphet: *Lolita* 30 Years Later," Erica Jong says, "She has, in fact, defeated time – her enemy" (Jong 1988, 47), but time was never Lolita's enemy; it was Humbert's, one he imposed on her. And time's occupants – not time – continue to reincarnate Lolita only to batter her into their own self-validating construction, to be anything but kind to her.

Why didn't the Lolita myth evolve in a way that more accurately reflects Nabokov's Lolita? Why isn't the definition of "Lolita" "a molested adolescent girl" instead of a "seductive" one? The answer seems relatively clear, but its consequences are complex. This misreading is so persistent and pervasive because it is enabled and perpetuated intertextually, extra-textually, and intratextually. The text itself promotes misreadings of Lolita because, as Wayne Booth is one of the first to note, Humbert's skillful rhetoric and Nabokov's narrative technique make it difficult to locate both Humbert's unreliability and Nabokov's moral position (Booth 1983, 389–391). While the text offers evidence to indict Humbert, it is subtle enough that many readers overlook its critique of the misogyny illustrated in and purveyed by the rest of the text. Perhaps Nabokov minimized such signals in order to merge the novel's form and characterization with what is his attempt to illustrate and thematize what happens when an allegedly charming, clearly powerful character wreaks his egocentricity on a weaker one. Whatever Nabokov's rationale for providing such subdued messages in support of Lolita, they are often lost in an atmosphere that interprets and presents her oppositionally, and these antagonistic messages are compounded by a host of cross-cultural, diachronic narratives that precede and succeed *Lolita*, texts that purvey the notion that femaleness, femininity, and female sexuality are desirable, but dangerous – even deadly.[3]

Thus, instead of embracing the muted, violated Lolita, our misogynistic culture created and reified a violating Lolita. It made her as contrary to birth-giving and nurturing as possible: it made her lethal. Linda Kauffman says, "Lolita is as much the object consumed by Humbert as she is the product of her culture. And if she is 'hooked,' he is the one who turns her into a hooker" (Kauffman 1993, 160). Similarly, throughout the years, Lolita has become the product of our culture beyond the book's pages, where she has been made a murderess by characters far more powerful than Humbert. And these mythical machineries of evil Lolita narratives perpetuate a misogyny that imposes developmentally abnormal sexuality on some females and simultaneously punishes all females for any sexuality. By imposing this sexual responsibility and fault on females, they deem us unnatural, evil for having any sexuality, and, if we are young, doubly deviant, however developmentally appropriate our sexuality is.[4]

Ultimately, all females are caught in a culture that forcefully bifurcates them into characters who are or who are supposed to be both compassionate and lethal, asexual and hypersexual.

With so many co-opted Lolita myths impregnated in our culture, readers come to *Lolita* inundated with a hegemonic reading of evil Lolita and bad female sexuality, a reading that then overdetermines the book, that imposes itself upon its own text. The Lolita Story and its discourse have become an ongoing and revealing cultural narrative, a myth appropriated in ways that validate male sexuality and punish female sexuality, in ways that let some people avoid the consequences of their desires as they impose those desires on others. In this way, another source of the misreadings of Lolita is the reader, who is extratextual because he or she is outside the text of *Lolita*, who is intertextual because he or she lives between the narratives and images that bolster the misreadings of Lolita, and who becomes intratextual as he or she, submerged in these larger influences of cultures and intertextuality, brings them to *Lolita* so thoroughly that they become, for that reader, a very real part of the *Lolita* text.

This dual existence of one textual Lolita and another, very different, co-opted, mythical Lolita is just one example of the doubling in and around *Lolita*, of the doubling that results in fragmentations, splits, and violations of what many people experience personally or vicariously, of what many people witness, believe, and know. And the cultural systems complicit in the cleaving and appropriation of Lolita also fuel a machinery of doubling that promotes the doubling of readers, students, molestation survivors, female sexuality, and the roles and perception of women in general. While critics have addressed the character doubling of Humbert and Quilty, and while some of their notions are related to the doublings that I explore, my concern is with a whole system of doubling and with the various pegs within it. It is with the expansive doubling that is associated with both the mythic and the textual Lolitas, with the division and doubling of the public and private selves, the spoken and the silenced, the imagined or perceived or represented and the real – with what is often a destructive, oppressive, institutionally-condoned system of doubling that occurs in *Lolita* and that informs and is informed by it.[5]

Given a cultural context that both distorts and feeds upon Lolita, teachers, if they assign *Lolita*, must contend with the neglected doubling that occurs in these other realms and with how the book reflects on larger cultural pressures and processes. Perhaps one strategy for resisting and correcting these entrenched misreadings of Lolita, women, and of sexual molestation is to confront several of their sources. Intertextual sources that bolster the Lolita myth are perhaps the least threatening places with which to begin this challenge. Perhaps explorations of how our readings are partially constructed before we come to "the" *Lolita* text itself would ease readers into understanding how inter- and extratextual sources become intratextual, how their very personal readings are influenced by sweeping, insidious ideologies. Booth says *Lolita* misreadings "do not come from any inherent condition of the novel or from any natural incompatibility between author and reader. They come from the reader's inability to dissociate himself from a vicious center of consciousness presented to him with all of the seductive self-justification of skilful rhetoric" (Booth 1983, 390). But *Lolita* readers must also understand what is at the center of a cultural consciousness that encourages misreadings of *Lolita*. Once readers have some sense about how their readings are, at least in part, predetermined, perhaps then they can confront more intimate sources of misreadings, their own interpretive systems and assumptions. And then, perhaps readers will be more receptive to *Lolita*'s covert, intratextual messages that are frequently overlooked but are essential to our understanding of the way it functions in our culture. It would seem that the most effective resistance – whether it is to the hegemonic readings or to challenging them – would be met and take place in the "self" realm of the extratextual, in the most personal, private, and sometimes painful realms of readings and of texts. But if we can understand the part of the extratextual realm that influences the personal part of the extratextual, then perhaps we will better access and understand the interplay of our culture, ourselves, and the texts that become our texts.

To this end, I would like to see those of us who have been excluded from the hegemonic readings of *Lolita* resuscitate the character, reclaim the book, and insist upon our experiences with and around it so we can at least begin to counter the Lolita myth distortions, to resist some of the cultural appropriations of female sexuality. For me, this means processing several of my experiences with *Lolita*: as a young listener of "Lola," a nurse for children and teenagers, a student reader of *Lolita*, and with the text itself – particularly, here, with an excerpt from the Enchanted Hunters chapter in which the double-voicing is so complete and so manipulative that it results in a double-drama rarely seen in literature, but very much like the double-dramas too often played out in girls' and women's lives: the narration of an event that is countlessly described as "love-making" and seduction, but that can only be interpreted as rape.[6]

People

The resounding Lolita myths have influenced many responses to *Lolita*. Critics focus on the book's aesthetics and artistry, discuss it as an American travelog, view Humbert with compassion, as truly contrite, a tragic hero. Though diverse, these readings remain hegemonic, and they do not contend with gender issues, do not attempt to understand why and how the same text can be so pleasurable for some and so traumatic for others. While many of us celebrate the personal nature of literature, criticism has historically denied the subjective. For a long time women's voices in general, but especially women's voices of anger and pain, have not been sounded or heard. We have the critical history of reader response and personal criticism, but, for the most part, our discipline still disallows even the slightest hints of personal perceptions and reactions in scholarly work: we are expected to intimately engage with some of the most emotive stories ever told, but we are also expected to squelch certain results of that engagement even as we try to articulate some of the implications of that very same engagement. But we have been limited to those discussions and reactions deemed appropriate by the reigning cultural powers. Particularly noticeable in this movement is the critical history of *Lolita*, in which readers and critics almost always embrace what they consider the book's pleasures, almost always skirt its pains – Lolita's pains, as well as the readerly traumas associated with this novel.

Perhaps these issues have not been adequately addressed because readers who do not have such disturbing desires cannot imagine, cannot bear or bare the thought of them in themselves or others, and so deny or minimize such imaginings, avoid contending with them. One man I know seemed staunchly located in Humbert's narrative audience, defending him, insisting he does not rape Lolita, and calling her an "experienced seductress." I said that, while she had had sex, it was with her peer, which suggests at least the chance for a more developmentally normal, mutually-empowered experience. He said, "If my daughter ever fooled around at that age" and stopped short. I replied, "If your daughter were Lolita, you'd call it rape." He shook his head, exhaled audibly through his nose, and said, "Touché. Now I see what you mean."

Many other men praise the book's artistry, Nabokov's brilliant language. One associate said he loved the book – his favorite – for its artistry.[7] I asked him how he could feel so much pleasure from a book with this content. He said, "It's just a book." But this book is not "just a book" for everyone. For many people it represents some aspect of their reality, what has happened to them or their loved ones – or what they fear might happen. But this man seemed so seduced by the book's form that in every visible way he trivialized Lolita's experience and dismissed the trauma many readers experience with this text.

I witnessed how this book is not "just a book" for some people when, nestled into a booth one afternoon, some women and I began discussing the implications of *Lolita*. Three of us were especially passionate as we discussed its narrative strategy, its characterization, our responses. Our fourth colleague occasionally nodded her head, but remained quiet. About fifteen minutes into our talk, she abruptly rose to go home. The closest of her friends among us walked her to her car and upon her return told us why our colleague had gone: when she was a child, her father woke her, carried her from her bed to the bathroom, made her bend forward over the tub, and raped her. When she cried out, her father stuffed a washcloth in her mouth. With blood dripping down her legs, he forced her to perform fellatio on him. When she refused to swallow his semen, he squeezed her nostrils shut until she did. When he was finished, he picked her up by the elbows, held her face to the mirror, and said, "Do you know why Daddy did this to you? Because you are such a pretty pussy."

Is this shocking to you? Do you feel that in my writing it and your reading it, this person's trauma has been re-enacted? It has – through her, through and for me, and for you. And I imposed this trauma on you, thrust it into your eyes without your consent. If you feel upset, then perhaps you can imagine how our fourth colleague felt and how others might respond to texts and discussions that catapult them into chasms of deep, secret pains – including discussions less vivid and texts far less shocking than this one.[8]

While conspicuously few critics have expressed charged sympathy for Lolita's trauma,[9] most neglect to confront the trauma Humbert inflicts on Lolita, and none contend with the trauma the book inflicts on readers. Indeed, if critics discuss trauma at all (excepting those noted in notes 14, 17, and 18), they focus on Humbert's trauma. Critics range from judging him harshly yet with much compassion,[10] to strongly sympathizing with and even identifying with him,[11] to "rooting" him on, sympathizing and identifying with him to the point of sharing his pleasures – artistic and sexual.[12] Concurrent with this is the critical move that seems to offer frightening pleasure to those who view Lolita with derision.[13] While examinations of the book that focus on more typical questions of theme and structure can enhance our understanding about some parts of this complicated text, as countless critics focus on the book's pleasure and neglect its trauma, they also neglect many of its readers and enable the violator's pleasure, reinforce it, invite it to continue without confrontation. Thus, in addition to particular critical comments that purvey the Lolita myth, the collectivity of *Lolita* criticism in some way becomes complicit in the aesthetization of child molestation perpetrated by individual people and by the culture at large.[14]

And by not contending with readers' or with Lolita's trauma in the classroom, the criticism, or the culture, the trauma is at once both trivialized and intensified for individual readers because they suffer it alone, without forum. People who have been molested have lived what Elsa Jones calls a "double reality": "In my view one of the major negative consequences of being abused as a child lies in the confusion generated for the child between what she knows to be true and what her world acknowledges to be true" (Jones 1991, 37). Similarly, some readers of this text also live a double reality in the classroom, a place where personal, often disturbing texts are routinely, matter-of-factly, and authoritatively explored, even enforced.

Pedagogy

On the way to class, one of my peers told me that as he read he kept saying to himself, "Yes, yes.... But, then I'm a male, so I understand Humbert."[15] The first hour or more of class consisted of discussions much like published ones, about the puns, the time of narration, the time of action, the narrative audience – about everything except what Humbert really does to Lolita. One man read the frotteurism couch scene aloud, without any apparent sense of how the reading may have affected the discussion dynamics. In the second hour, the discussion, quiet and controlled, moved to whether, in the course of his narration, Humbert had come to a true understanding of and repentance for what he had done. Some men said they did not condone Humbert – and then talked at length about how we should have compassion for him, how he really comes to love Lolita, how he rehabilitates and wishes he had left her alone early on. Eventually I asked – with some measure of incredulousness – whether anyone else had had an unmitigated reaction against Humbert.

I appeared to be in the minority. Many of the women in the class remained quiet, including a usually expressive one who later told me she had been molested by her father. One woman had a strong reaction against Humbert, voiced it once, then told me later that she felt silenced by the men – and so silenced herself. Another woman, a writer, focussed on Nabokov's use of language. Another argued that understanding Humbert would help us understand and deal with our own desires.[16] After class, some of us talked about feeling judged because others implied that we had insufficient compassion for Humbert, suggested that we violated the text when we could not subjugate our real reader experiences to the "desired" authorial or narrative reader experiences.[17]

Discussing this text seemed to exacerbate the typical classroom dynamic in which the teacher – however much he or she may try to share authority – remains the authority, such that almost independently of what this teacher did or did not do, in this class, what is often assumed to be or represented as the "male" perspective became the dominant perspective. As a result, those students with painful experiences – students who, in vital ways, might have been most able to understand the implications of this book – felt and were disempowered. Sitting there, in humane academia, reading this prolonged account of how a young girl is sexually enslaved for two years, there seemed no room for these responses, these lives. After class, when one of my male associates told me that I cheated the text, that my reaction was "too moral," that it silenced him, then I really wanted to yell.[18] But I stayed implosively silent, feeling embarrassed for saying anything against Humbert, even as I felt angry – with Humbert and with some of the men in class for being unable to permit, accept, even tolerate our responses, responses that I considered rational and reasonable in content and articulation. And yet, if, as Virginia Goldner reports, "one in three women before the age of eighteen has been sexually abused" (Jones 1991, viii), can texts like *Lolita* be taught without exacerbating the trauma of relatively large numbers of mostly female students? And without dealing with what often becomes another silencing, disempowering presence in a whole host of discourses?

This class resounded with student splitting, with students responding to the text one way outside the classroom and another way within it, one way within ourselves and another way without. I am certain that some students split as they felt and denied or hid their trauma. Other discussants might have doubled as they felt and denied their pleasure, as they made public declarations against Humbert's behavior while growing privately pleased by it. And, while I am working from a generally female perspective in my attempt to contend with larger issues of pedagogically- and textually-induced trauma, I want to know more about how *Lolita* and other texts produce and exacerbate male trauma. Might some male readers of *Lolita* feel bullied? Misrepresented? Wronged? Might some be distressed by other men's arousal? By their own arousal? Might some fear that all women will think that all men want to violate girls? Might they fear for the women and girls about whom they care? Fear that their reactions might betray their peers who argue relentlessly on Humbert's behalf? And how might men who have been sexually abused feel, men who often have no forum in which to process their experiences, whose trauma is silenced perhaps more than any other? Think of how they must have doubled.[19]

The classroom is perhaps one of the most public arenas for traumatic readings. Yet, amidst a flurry of attention to various sorts of harassment and violence, pedagogical theory and methods have not yet sufficiently addressed personal trauma transmitted through and perpetuated by perfectly academic discussions and canonized texts. It is not difficult to see why some might want to overlook or repress traumatic reactions. Perhaps silence is a site, source, and sign of strength for some people. And there is the risk of classroom chaos, of cascades of shocking personal revelations, of dangerous pseudo-therapy sessions. But if teachers assign traumatic texts, it seems they are obligated to acknowledge and at least reasonably try to accommodate students' responses to them – if not entirely, then in part; if not on an individual basis, then within a general and perhaps less threatening discussion of what responses such texts "might" evoke. In the process of trying to contend with trauma, there is always the possibility of exacerbating it, but the risk of exacerbation must be greater if teachers impose and then ignore the trauma, if they banish it to some secret solitude or silence. Silence should be an option in, not a function of, such discussions.

We may not love *Lolita*. Many of the women I have talked with about it have very negative feelings about it, and many cannot re-read, write about, or teach it. But the book remains required reading in some class-rooms, and were it never again assigned, we would still have to contend with its resonances and the culture that supports them. I understand why some people prefer to maintain their externally silent reactions to these issues, but I also hope that others see that voicing our responses is essen-tial, that it is time ▮▮▮▮▮▮▮ those who cannot see that, beneath Humbert's dominant ▮▮▮▮▮▮▮ e is a kid molded to fulfill a role in a dest▮▮▮▮▮ very day becomes, in one way or another, a very real nightmare for countless children. It is time for us to grapple with the couch scenes, to redress ourselves. While con-tending with *Lolita* and other Lolita texts, we can advance our under-standing of broader issues of classroom and readerly trauma – and of pedagogically-imposed trauma in general – and we can contend with the whole set of Lolita myths and discourses. We can discuss the politics of representation, ingestion, response, and influence, and we can expose the complex relations of power, sex, and gender that are represented in and sometimes perpetuated by these texts. While the general and critical communities have repressed the ideological contestation imbued in this book, have turned it into a site of gross cultural appropriation – and in ways that may not have surprised or been condoned by Nabokov – we need to renew the contestation. As we do this, we will take an important step in refusing a cultural milieu that violates and punishes women, that denies, trivializes, and fragments the female personal – especially trauma – while hegemonically advancing the male personal – especially pleasure.

Texts

One of the primary debates about *Lolita* is whether we can believe Humbert's claims about Lolita. Humbert acknowledges and reveals his unreliability throughout the book, and, having been frank and honest, he expects us to believe him when he claims reliability. But I cannot believe two important claims of which he tries to convince us: that Lolita seduces him the first time they have intercourse, and that he comes to truly love Lolita as a person.[20]

When Humbert recounts his first non-frotteuristic sex act with Lolita, he insists that Lolita seduces him, but a variety of textual signals suggest that Lolita and Humbert are not seeing eye-to-eye throughout the event. Because I will explicate this passage in detail, let me reproduce it for you here:

> Frigid gentlewomen of the jury! I had thought that months, perhaps years, would elapse before I dared to reveal myself to Dolores Haze; but by six she was wide awake, and by six fifteen we were technically lovers. I am going to tell you something very strange: it was she who seduced me.

Upon hearing her first morning yawn, I feigned handsome pro-
filed sleep. I just did not know what to do. Would she be shocked
at finding me by her side, and not in some spare bed? Would she
collect her clothes and lock herself up in the bathroom? Would
she demand to be taken at once to Ramsdale – to her mother's
bedside – back to camp? But my Lo was a sportive lassie. I felt her
eyes on me, and when she uttered at last that beloved chortling
note of hers, I knew her eyes had been laughing. She rolled over to
my side, and her warm brown hair came against my collarbone. I
gave a mediocre imitation of waking up. We lay quietly. I gently
caressed her hair, and we gently kissed. Her kiss, to my delirious
embarrassment, had some rather comical refinements of flutter
and probe which made me conclude that she had been coached at
an early age by a little Lesbian. No Charlie boy could have taught
her *that*. As if to see whether I had my fill and learned the lesson,
she drew away and surveyed me. Her cheekbones were flushed,
her full underlip glistened, my dissolution was near. All at once,
with a burst of rough glee (the sign of the nymphet!), she put her
mouth to my ear – but for quite a while my mind could not separate into words the hot thunder of her whisper, and she laughed,
and brushed the hair off her face, and tried again, and gradually
the odd sense of living in a brand new, mad new dream world,
where everything was permissible, came over me as I realized what
she was suggesting. I answered I did not know what game she and
Charlie had played. "You mean you have never–?" – her features
twisted into a stare of disgusted incredulity. "You have never–"
she started again. I took time out by nuzzling her a little. "Lay off,
will you," she said with a twangy whine, hastily removing her
brown shoulder from my lips. (It was very curious the way she
considered – and kept doing so for a long time – all caresses
except kisses on the mouth or the stark act of love either "romantic slosh" or "abnormal.")

"You mean," she persisted, now kneeling above me, "you
never did it when you were a kid?"

"Never," I answered quite truthfully.

"Okay," said Lolita, "here is where we start."

However, I shall not bore my learned readers with a detailed
account of Lolita's presumption. Suffice it to say that not a trace
of modesty did I perceive in this beautiful hardly formed young
girl whom modern co-education, juvenile mores, the campfire
racket and so forth had utterly and hopelessly depraved. She saw
the stark act merely as part of a youngster's furtive world,
unknown to adults. What adults did for purposes of procreation
was no business of hers. My life was handled by little Lo in an

energetic, matter-of-fact manner as if it were an insensate gadget
unconnected with me. While eager to impress me with the world
of tough kids, she was not quite prepared for certain discrepancies
between a kid's life and mine. Pride alone prevented her from
giving up; for, in my strange predicament, I feigned supreme stupidity and had her have her way – at least while I could still bear
it. But really these are irrelevant matters; I am not concerned with
so-called "sex" at all. Anybody can imagine those elements of
animality. A greater endeavor lures me on: to fix once for all the
perilous magic of nymphets.

> (Part I, end of Chapter 29)

We can read this passage in at least two very different ways, believing
Humbert's claim that Lolita seduces him and directs him to the act of
intercourse, or challenging him by imagining Lolita's perspective, and
especially by considering that Lolita does not direct him to penetrate her.
Throughout *his* report, Humbert wants us to believe that Lolita knows
exactly what she does, that she directs him to intercourse, that Lolita is in
control: he tells us that he acts stupid; that she is a knowledgeable and
experienced teacher who has participated in a furtive world, a perilous and
depraved nymphet; that she is the one who makes presumptions with him.

But Humbert also participates in the doubling of this text and of child
molestation by doubling himself, by being one thing and pretending to be
another. From the onset, with his address, "Frigid gentlewomen of the
jury!," he implies that he will employ evidentiary rhetoric directed at
women, but, throughout this passage, his language is riddled with indirec-
tion and ambiguity, and he never absolutely defines the "stark act" so
central to the scene.[21] Throughout the narration as well as the time of
action, Humbert doubles: he "feigns" sleep and "imitates" waking; he pretends to be a powerless student while he is the powerful teacher; he says
that his "dissolution" was near, that "for a while [his] mind could not
separate into words the hot thunder of her whisper"; he has the sense that
he is in a "mad new dream world, where everything was permissible"; he
tells *us* that he "realized what she was suggesting," but he tells *Lolita* that
he "did not know what game she and Charlie had played"; he feigns
"supreme stupidity" and ignores Lolita's difficulties during the act; he says
he is not concerned with "sex" at all, but we know that compels him.
Clearly, Humbert, while wanting us to believe he is disempowered, is
empowered, and he manipulates the voice and the dialogue of this passage
in his effort to convince us that he is seduced, while there is covert evidence that this is not the case, that Lolita does not have intercourse in mind,
but an adolescent petting game.

First, Humbert says Lolita seduces him, but he begins the caressing, and
he does not indicate who initiates the first kiss. Shortly thereafter he says,

"As if to see whether I had my fill and learned the lesson, she drew away and surveyed me." If we can rely on Humbert's interpretation of Lolita's look, and if she is indeed drawing away to see if he has learned his lesson, then it seems logical to infer that Lolita thinks she *has* finished giving the lesson, that she has given Humbert what she thinks *should* be his fill after the first kiss. Furthermore, if Lolita intends to teach Humbert a lesson about kissing, then presumably she would initiate the lesson. If she does initiate it – and if Humbert wants us to believe she seduces him – then why doesn't Humbert tell us she initiates it? By not identifying who kisses whom first, Humbert enables the possibility that he kisses her. We also cannot be sure of Humbert's interpretation of Lolita's look and of why she moves away from him. Could she draw – or pull – away from Humbert in surprise? Could her flush be of fear?

Throughout this passage, Humbert says he realizes what Lolita suggests when she "put her mouth to" his ear, saying that she seduces him and implying that she initiates foreplay that she wants to culminate in intercourse. Again, if Humbert's goal is to convince the jury that Lolita seduces him to intercourse and if her whisper resounds like thunder, why doesn't he conclusively tell the jury what Lolita *says* instead of what she *suggests?* When Humbert says he realizes what Lolita's *suggesting*, his sly wording whispers two possible interpretations. First, Humbert could mean that Lolita directly invites him to participate in something – that she says, for instance, "Let's make out" or "Should we make out?" But Humbert's wording could also indicate that he – and not Lolita – makes the presumptions, that he infers what Lolita might be implying, not what she is actually stating.

Even though it would be easier for Humbert if we believed his claim that Lolita initiates and orchestrates the activities that lead to intercourse, the collective effect of Lolita's perspective and Humbert's commentary suggests that her lesson, her goal, her game, her "stark act" is not to have intercourse, but only to kiss and perhaps fondle. Humbert, of course, admits to feigning ignorance throughout this scene, and even how he speaks this to her suggests kissing and petting games, not intercourse: "I answered I did not know what game she and Charlie had played." For me, *game* evokes various pre-teen kissing games – or, at the very most, some kind of fondling activity. Again, Humbert strategically does not specify what Lolita says. Instead, he reports her as saying "you never did *it* when you were a kid?" (emphasis added), which reinforces the implication that Lolita is referring to a common kids' game. Perhaps Humbert really never played the game as a kid, but surely Lolita does not think that sexual intercourse is common among youngsters – while it would be quite likely that she would believe kissing or petting games are.

One key to identifying the indeterminacy in this passage is the phrase "stark act," which Humbert uses twice. First, he says that Lolita thinks that "all caresses except kisses on the mouth or the stark act of love [are] either 'romantic slosh' or 'abnormal.'" Later he says, "she saw the stark act merely as part of a youngster's furtive world, unknown to adults. What adults did for purposes of procreation was no business of hers." While, after the first reference, *stark* act may possibly – though not necessarily – mean intercourse, the second reference undermines this possibility by suggesting even further that Lolita plans to participate in kids' petting games. This would further explain why, after suggesting them, she is surprised to learn that he had not participated in them when he was young. Humbert facilitates this alternative reading by emphasizing the kids' context of the game when he lists the influences upon this "young girl" of "modern co-education, juvenile mores, [and] the campfire racket." While Humbert wants us to believe the "depraved" Lolita wants to have intercourse with him, he also exaggerates typical "juvenile mores" and campfire experiences.

Finally, whether Lolita has had intercourse with Charlie or not, Lolita gives Humbert no clear indication that she wants to have it with him. Somewhere even Humbert recognizes this: once again, he says, "She saw the stark act merely as part of a youngster's furtive world, unknown to adults. What adults did for purposes of procreation was no business of hers."[22] One of my associates interprets these lines to mean that Lolita believes intercourse is something about which youngsters know and adults do not care. If so, then why would Lolita want to seduce Humbert, an adult, to intercourse? My colleague claims it is to impress Humbert with her knowledge and experience. But, if she believes "it" is a common children's experience, then why would she think her experience would impress someone who also had been a kid and who, she presumes, had had similar childhood experiences? Finally, the double-voicing of the line "What adults did for purposes of procreation was no business of hers" is remarkably telling of Humbert's manipulative voice. Whether or not one accepts my associate's reading that Lolita believes intercourse is common in childhood and that she does not care about how adults procreate, Humbert's own words subvert his primary interpretation, and their double-voicing resonates loudly: *this is what adults say about kids, not what kids say about adults.*

For me, these lines and the following ones strongly suggest that Humbert knows Lolita cannot yet conceive, cannot comfortably accommodate a man – and that she is not interested in intercourse with him. The following passage is charged with possibilities:

> My life was handled by little Lo in an energetic, matter-of-fact manner as if it were an insensate gadget unconnected with me. While eager to impress me with the world of tough kids, she was not quite prepared for certain discrepancies between a kid's life

and mine. Pride alone prevented her from giving up; for, in my strange predicament, I feigned supreme stupidity and had her have her way – at least while I could still bear it.

These lines describe Humbert's ultimate power twist – the twist of what he actually does and of how he narrates his actions in his attempt to convince himself and us that Lolita is in control, that he succumbs to her, and that what he does here is on some level acceptable. When Humbert says he feigns "supreme stupidity" and has "her have her way" while he can "still bear it," he might mean that he lets her fondle him until he ejaculates (and they never have intercourse) or, what I think he *wants* us to believe, that she wants to have intercourse, and that, even though Lolita is not prepared for intercourse with an adult, though this causes her pain, her pride compels her to continue having intercourse until Humbert ejaculates. I propose, however, that Lolita's "stark act" could well be the more sophisticated component of her two approved activities – a petting game that she thinks adults do not play. If we read these same lines within another possible context of Lolita as a pre-teen – one covertly corroborated by the text – it is quite possible that they indicate that Lolita wants to impress him with this unnamed activity from "the world of tough kids" – note that "kids" is used thrice – and that she is absolutely not prepared for a different kind of discrepancy between children and adults: Lolita's perspective of the "stark act" versus Humbert's, petting games versus child–adult intercourse.

These same lines also allow for another very different but related reading of Lolita's perspective and experience, and, considered together, the alternative readings enhance each other. Humbert uses *life* twice in the end of the excerpt. Within the dominant, more figurative reading, *life* is a metaphor for *penis*. As such, the line, "My life was handled by little Lo in an energetic, matter-of-fact manner as if it were an insensate gadget unconnected with me" suggests a description of Lolita's genital fondling of Humbert, and "she was not quite prepared for certain discrepancies between a kid's life and mine" may refer to size differences in children and adults.

However, what if, in a kind of reversal of Humbert's narrative trend to be strategically symbolic and indirect, we pull back his covers and consider *life* more literally. Within this reading, these lines suggest that, when they pet, Lolita obliviously alters the direction of Humbert's future life, that she makes out with him as if their behavior is in no way going to affect Humbert's future. Of course, while Humbert's syntax places the blame for these changes on Lolita, it is his molestation of her that changes both of their futures. Furthermore, the second use of *life*, considering its literal definition based in length of time (not anatomy), reiterates that a youngster may be satisfied with petting games while an adult may not be. Merging both meanings of *life* and both meanings of *stark act*, and considering that *harsh*, *blunt*, and *grim* are synonyms for *stark* (*Webster* and *American Heritage*), this passage underscores that Lolita is at once not prepared for Humbert's size or his ejaculatory stamina during fondling, that her pride compels her to continue petting, that Humbert goes along with her game, feigning stupidity about her limitations and her intentions, and, when *her* way – the way of a kid's life, either the kissing or the fondling – is no longer enough for him, in an abuse of both her body and her "pride," he, without her consent, directs the stark activity *his* way: he penetrates her, and, as he rapes her, feigns ignorance about her pain while he thrusts to ejaculation.

I focus my interpretation of this passage on the passage itself, but the novel also supports my reading by predicting and even inviting it several pages before Humbert narrates the first time he and Lolita have intercourse. When Humbert picks Lolita up from camp to bring her, she believes, to her hospitalized mother, he reports that Lolita kisses him in the car. He says:

> I knew, of course, it was but an innocent game on her part, a bit of backfisch foolery in imitation of some simulacrum of fake romance, and since (as the psychotherapist, as well as the rapist, will tell you) the limits and rules of such girlish games are fluid, or at least too childishly subtle for the senior partner to grasp – I was dreadfully afraid I might go too far and cause her to start back in revulsion and terror.
>
> (p. 105)

Then, as Humbert and Lolita check into their room, Humbert reports a self-indicting dialogue: "She said: 'Look, let's cut out the kissing game and get something to eat.' ... 'What's the matter with misses?' I muttered (word-control gone) into her hair. 'If you must know,' she said, 'you do it the wrong way.' 'Show, wight ray.' 'All in good time,' responded the spoonerette" (p. 111). These lines precede Humbert's narration of the sex scene, but, clearly, they are meant to inform our interpretation of it.

This novel, this experience, this social issue, is fraught with doubling, and this passage, with its internal doublings that are both contradictory and mutually enhancing, doubles into itself in a way that enables two different readings: the critically dominant, unchallenged one that assumes Lolita seduces Humbert to intercourse, and an overlooked reading that Lolita proposes kissing and petting games with Humbert – but not intercourse. This relative indeterminacy frustrates some readers of the novel (though most seem to unproblematically accept the hegemonic reading), and certainly my attempt to account for the latter reading will frustrate some of my readers. Of course, Humbert's passage is inherently and intentionally indeterminate; it is conveniently doubled. He claims to leave out the details because they are "irrelevant matters," but he erases them because they are, indeed, quite relevant. Since he wants to acquit himself of the accusation of rape, wants to convince us that in this scene Lolita seduces him to intercourse, he must narrate in gaps, must not tell us who initiates certain acts, must use elusive language, must be self-protectively discreet.

In an earlier version of this chapter, I noted that "this formalist reading may seem to redeem the text and Nabokov because it identifies textual challenges to the violent seduction fantasy," but that I was "not ready to exculpate Nabokov, the text, or the likes of Lionel Trilling." I wrote, "Perhaps Nabokov wanted me to see the 'real' kid in this excerpt – or perhaps not. Certainly, where I see the raped child, others imagine a seductive little girl." I still cannot know for certain how Nabokov intended this passage to be read, but now I feel more sure that he would support my reading. After all, his text does support it. Nevertheless, in this passage Nabokov, with more force than anywhere else in the novel, narratively plies two perspectives. Through this interweaving, this doubling, he problematizes Humbert's claims and Lolita's liability – and he does this by testing the limits of what we now familiarly know as M. M. Bakhtin's notion of heteroglossia. Bakhtin says heteroglossia is:

> *another's speech in another's language*, serving to express author-
> ial intentions but in a refracted way. Such speech constitutes a
> special type of *double-voiced discourse*. It serves two speakers at
> the same time and expresses simultaneously two different inten-
> tions: the direct intention of the character who is speaking, and
> the refracted intentions of the author. In such discourse there are
> two voices, two meanings and two expressions. And all the while
> these two voices are dialogically interrelated, they – as it were –
> know about each other.
>
> (1981, 324)

This passage, with Humbert so insistent upon his own view while revealing such contrary yet valid, viable variations of Lolita's perspective, exemplifies an extreme kind of personal double voicing. In the course of this narration, the doubled form both produces and enacts a doubled content – a doubled action – and the narrative consequences are that this interconnected yet gaping double voicing reflects and produces a colliding *double drama*: two people, with two related yet relatively oppositional intentions, interact – and for the empowered one the outcome is seduction, while for Lolita, the very same interaction, the very same words, result in rape.

Some readers insist that, from the onset of this scene, Lolita wants to teach Humbert how to have intercourse, that she initiates and maneuvers penetration. While I disagree with this interpretation, even it describes an essential double drama: if Lolita consents to or even appears to direct her painful penetration by Humbert, she does so with Humbert's powerful director's hand; as he leads her to believe she is in control, he controls her – he gets power by appearing to give up power, exerts his will by appearing to relinquish his will. Finally, even within this reading of Lolita as pseudo-director, he directs her to consent to activities which he maneuvers and for which he knows she is not prepared. And this "consent" is problematic, first, because it is not clear that Lolita does consent to intercourse, and because, within the power-differential of this situation, it becomes impossible for Lolita – or for any twelve-year-old – to truly consent to what is about to happen, to consent as an informed, independent, empowered person who has a variety of implementable options from which to choose. We know the implications of Humbert's gaming with Lolita, of the power-differential which is doubly dramatized, and we know that Humbert's manipulations result in an extended bondage and violation of Lolita during which his will – his *life* – continues to penetrate and prevail.

Thus, regardless of the indeterminacies of this passage, all readings describe Humbert's coercion of Lolita, the exertion of an adult's sexual desires upon a child – rape. This ambiguity of perception and interpretation – this double drama which concurrently reveals and conceals various truths – is both continued and undermined when Humbert reports that Lolita says *with a smile*, "You revolting creature. I was a daisy-fresh girl, and look what you've done to me. I ought to call the police and tell them you raped me. Oh you, dirty, dirty old man" (p. 130). Are we to entirely believe the man who believes that Lolita's second expression of pain is "reproduced" for his benefit? Does she really smile when she calls Humbert a brute? Humbert's manipulation of rape into consensual sex involves an honest portrayal of some of his liabilities, which makes it easier for him to misrepresent other liabilities, easier for him to double.

Yet Nabokov reveals Humbert's role as screenwriter, director, and interpreter – as perverter – of the drama when Humbert says a few chapters after narrating the rape scene, "*The rapist* was Charlie Holmes; I am the *therapist* – a matter of nice spacing in the way of distinction" (p. 137; emphasis added). Indeed, although Humbert makes a distinction here between himself as "the therapist" and not the rapist, earlier he blurs the distinction and – in another example of Nabokov's linguistic craft – he covertly associates himself with a rapist. When discussing Lolita's "innocent game" of kissing him, Humbert says, "as the psychotherapist, as well as the rapist, will tell you" (p. 105), and Humbert goes on to tell you. He also refers to "the child therapist" in himself (p. 115). And later, of course, Lolita speaks with Humbert about "the hotel where you raped me" (p. 184) and says "I ought to call the police and tell them you raped me" (p. 130).

Nabokov continues to reveal Humbert's doubling – and unreliability – through language that exposes his ongoing pedophilia and debunks his insistence that he comes to love Lolita for her own sake.[23] He says of his meeting the pregnant, married Dolly:

> I had no intention of torturing *my* darling.... there she was with her ruined looks and her adult ... hands ... (*my Lolita!*), hope-lessly worn ... and ... I knew ... that I loved her more than any-thing I had ever seen or imagined on earth.... She was only the ... dead leaf echo of the *nymphet* I had rolled myself upon with such cries in the past ... but thank God it was not that echo alone that I worshipped.... I will shout my poor truth. I insist the world know how much I loved *my* Lolita, this Lolita, pale and polluted ... *still mine*.... No matter, even if ... her lovely *young velvety delicate* delta be tainted and torn – even then I would go mad with tenderness at the mere sight of your dear wan face, at the mere sound of your raucous *young* voice, *my* Lolita.
>
> (p. 253; emphasis added)

Even as Humbert proclaims his love for this Lolita, as he describes a young woman ravished by the experiences he has imposed on her, key words throughout his narrative reveal his continued obsession with *possessing* a *young* Lolita, with possessing her for the sexual attraction he found in her youth – and that he still finds in other youth. He continues to think about other girls sexually both in the time of narration and the time of action at the end of the novel: in the time of action, he looks lewdly at young girls playing near Lolita's house; at the beginning of the time of narration, he thinks about the girls in the catalog in prison; and at the end of his narra-tion, he writes this passage, saturated with quiet clues about what still obsesses him, with clues that make clear that he does not love Lolita spiri-tually, nor as an individual, that his feelings for her are pathologic and self-serving, and that he remains fixated on what he cannot have – a fantasy world and object that he unsuccessfully tries to disguise beneath the discourse of age and wear.

Humbert's objectification of and disregard for Lolita is reflected even in how he addresses and refers to her: throughout most of the time of action and the time of narration, Humbert calls her *Lolita*, while everyone else calls her by the name she prefers, *Dolly*. When he sees the pregnant Dolly, he calls her by her preferred name until he recognizes in her the "echo of the nymphet," until he envisions the young, "velvety delta" of *his* Lolita. Finally, just before the book ends, he refers to Dolly as, "*my little one. Lolita girl*" (p. 259; emphasis added), and his last words are "my Lolita" (p. 281). And yet, even with these clues, in the same way that Dolly's will, character, and voice are supplanted by Humbert's throughout the novel, her life, fate, and image continue to be supplanted, distorted, and used by a world that embraces and punishes its own version of Humbert's imaginary Lolita.

"Well, you drink champagne and it tastes just like cherry cola, C-O-L-A, cola." Suddenly, this "Lola" line intertextually and ironically reflects the duality of *Lolita* – the doubled discrepancies between and the manipulated mergings of an adult's world with a child's. It reflects how, for some readers, *Lolita* is traumatic and depressing – like the alcohol in champagne – yet, for many others, it is pleasurable and stimulating – like the caffeine in cola.

Whether this book remains part of the canon or not, its repercussions will reverberate for a long time. While it might be simpler to slap the book shut, this will not silence its echoes. Instead of retreating from its trauma, I believe we – students and teachers, women and men – should confront its messages and challenges, should address its personal and cultural implications. While recognizing that there may be gender-specific reactions to the Lolita myths and the book, we must not assume them. We need to consider whether these passages and others in *Lolita* are heteroglossia at its best or its worst, to bring our own backgrounded voices to the fore, to reclaim ourselves – our voices, our interpretations, our stories. As we do this, we can confront the myths that aestheticize and romanticize molestation, that pre-sexualize kids, that make pedophilia pretty. And we can explore why, with the devastations of forced and coerced sexual behavior so evident, any person succumbs to or perpetrates it.

Virginia Goldner says adequate treatment of sexual abuse "must do justice to the *double injury*: the injury of a particular person by a particular person or people, and the social injustice of the victim's exploitation because of the impersonal fact of her age or sex" (Jones 1991, ix; emphasis added). As we understand the double injuries, as we disclose and undo the doublings in and around this book – the doubling of the Lolita myth, of female sexuality, of responses to the text, of students, of survivors, and of the text itself – and as we share our differences with this text and others, perhaps we will better understand the nature of reading, of sharing readings, of textual traumas, of others and of ourselves.

Postscript

Tony Moore and I share some minor opinions and two major ones about *Lolita*: that it provides clues that Lolita and Humbert are not everything that Humbert reports them to be, and that it asks for "sympathy and endorsement" rather than "condescension and disparagement" for Lolita. However, while I feel that these clues and others are often overlooked by individual readers and that they have been ignored or misappropriated by a larger culture that has, like Humbert, co-opted Lolita on behalf of some of its own powerful sex compulsions, Moore concludes that they are clear enough to provoke a sufficiently compassionate engagement with Lolita and a sufficiently critical one with Humbert. Then Moore neglects some of these clues. As a result, although he suggests that he will present a revolutionary reading of *Lolita* and an advocatory, feminist one of Lolita, he offers a somewhat traditional reading, especially in relation to the main characters and to "Humbert's" narrative technique.

Moore's argument and conclusions are informed by his engagement with Humbert, especially his seemingly interrelated belief in and compassion for him. Moore claims that Humbert "has had a hard time from critics since he first appeared" and is "overdue rehabilitation." He frequently defers to an assumption about Humbert's reliability regarding Lolita's dialogue, appearance, and beliefs. For example, he cites some of Humbert's disturbing images of Lolita – such as his description of her internal anatomy – without problematizing them. He also argues that Lolita "fucks with" Humbert and that she experiences a "good-hearted natural response from [her] position of equality" in the Enchanted Hunters Motel. Although Moore qualifies his support for Humbert, he also belies the degree to which he supports or is convinced by Humbert in other, less obvious, ways. For instance, Moore's perspective on Humbert seems both implied in and compelled by Moore's merging his own voice with Humbert's – which Moore does, for example, in his last sentence, when he cites one of Humbert's visions and reiterates it as his own: "This book is about Lolita."

Our differences are also evident in our characterizations of Lolita. For instance, Moore seems to accept Humbert's narration of Lolita's sex life without much question, whereas I argue that Humbert's characterization of Lolita is an example of his self-serving double voicing and dramas that are more extensive than I have convinced Tony they are. Thus, although Moore deviates from much of the critical history of *Lolita* by criticizing some of the violence that Humbert does to Lolita – even calling it "rape" – and although Moore explicitly advocates Lolita, he finally characterizes her as far more empowered and self-constructed than I am convinced she is. Although Moore's title, "Seeing Through Humbert" suggests that he will guide readers to see between – or to better understand – Humbert's rhetorical sheets of paper and cloth, Moore reads this text a little too much through – or under the influence of – Humbert's vision for some of his arguments to be convincing to me.

I also find it interesting to see how differently Moore and I use and respond to anecdote in our chapters. I included the trauma anecdote not because I wanted it to be dismissed as a sensationalizing ploy, but so that it might induce a long-overdue consideration of the real trauma this novel has the potential to exacerbate and inflict, so that it might bring to the fore just how difficult this text can be – and how unpredictably difficult. To assign this text is not the same thing as to assign a text about adultery to a class that may include adulterers or a text about drug abuse to a class that may include drug abusers. For me, there is something especially violent and haunting about child molestation – no matter how aestheticized it might be in a canonized novel. This seems so self-evident that it may preclude mention – even as it has also been avoided in critical discussions. My provocation of the issue of readerly trauma associated with *Lolita* has produced some unsurprising objections. But if it is inappropriate to explore the question of readerly trauma in this way and in these contexts, then how and where should we explore it? – a question I hope will prompt further explorations of the issue.

But this is only one of my chapter's efforts. Generally, my hope is to expand the readings of *Lolita* and to consider how the Lolita texts (as character, novel, and films) have been mythically appropriated by much of the critical commentary about the book and by the culture at large. More specifically, I try to explore the narrative's double-voiced discourse and its resulting double drama in the story's action. Indeed, although Tony's essay and mine betray essential differences, our goals are not entirely incongruous. I see *Lolita* as a double-voiced text that supports parts of Moore's argument – but that supports other arguments more comprehensively. Although Moore engagingly presents some convincing and progressive commentary, I still believe *Lolita* is not "about Lolita," but about Humbert's Lolita – and I still believe that the cultural and critical co-option of Lolita and *Lolita* warrants attention. Although Moore and I say some very different things, I think we would agree that the most comprehensive sense of any text requires a passionate engagement with the multivocality both in and around it – beginning with *Lolita*.

Notes

1 For our fourth colleague. And with gratitude to James Phelan, Nils Samuels, and Marlene Longenecker for our provocative discussions about *Lolita* and for their keen responses to this chapter. An earlier version appeared in *College Literature* 22.2 (June 1995), and I would like to express my thanks to the editors for permission to reprint it here, with some additional material and minor changes in format.

2 One, "Casualties of Love: The 'Long Island Lolita' Story," "earned a 22 percent audience share and $3.64 million in revenues" (*People* 8-8-94).

3 Appel (1991, 332) reports that Nabokov was unfamiliar with the movie *The Blue Angel* in which Lola-Lola, a cabaret dancer, ruins the life of a professor who falls in love with her, but it is easy to speculate about the possibility of intertextuality between this 1930 film, its 1959 remake, and the 1955 publication of *Lolita*. *Lolita* readers and the Lolita myth also may have been influenced by the movie version of *Lolita*, which impacted notions of what is phenotypically beautiful in North American women and models. However,

while Nabokov wrote the screenplay for the movie, it is significantly different from the novel.

4 This punishment of female sexuality is all the more ironic since the alleged sexuality of "nymphets" is what makes them, by patriarchy's own definition, desirable. And the doubling continues because Lolita's alleged nymphet quality is supposed to be essential – thus, natural (and so why not common?); but it is also supposed to be abnormal and rare – thus, unnatural.

5 For a discussion of the Humbert/Quilty and the good/evil double, see Appel (1967, 114, 131, 134) and Frosch (1982, 135–136). See also Maddox (1983, 80), Alexandrov (1991, 161), and Tamir-Ghez (1979, 80). Critics who discuss the doubling of the readers' desire or perspective with Quilty include Appel (1967, 123), Packman (1982, 47), and Rampton (1984, 107). Haegert notes critics who claim that Nabokov was in part attempting to exorcise an unwanted "double" (1985, 779), among them Fowler and Pifer. They are joined by Centerwall, who argues that Nabokov was a "closet pedophile" (1990, 468).

6 Kauffman (1993) states "it is doubtful" that Lolita seduces Humbert, and Levine rejects the "misguided" arguments which "confuse virginity with innocence" (1979, 475), but critics usually claim that Lolita is a seductress and often, in the process, confound the issue of virginity with the question of rape. Some explicitly but cursorily defend her and then sympathetically incorporate Humbert's language into their own. See also Trilling, who says, "Perhaps [Humbert's] depravity is the easier to accept when we learn that he deals with a Lolita who is not innocent, and who seems to have very few emotions to be violated" (1958, 14); Field, who says, "Humbert is himself 'seduced' by the unvirginal little nymphet" (1967, 330); Frosch, who says, "Then, too, Lolita is not 'the fragile child of a feminine novel' but a child vamp, who ... is not a virgin" (1982, 132); Appel, who refers to the sex acts between Lolita and Humbert as "conjugal visits" and "seduction" (1967, 121); and Packman, who says that by the end of Part 1 "the initial striptease of the nymphet has been completed" (1982, 59). Others believe Lolita seduces Humbert but emphasize Humbert's responsibility, including Phelan (1989, 164). Typically, those who claim that Humbert rapes Lolita go on to subvert the claim by confounding love and rape. Gullette says that "each act" of Humbert's intercourse with Lolita is "a form of rape" (1984, 223), but describes Humbert as "loving children" (p. 221). Maddox confounds love with hate and moral perfection with imperfection when she says, "*Lolita* is a novel about love and death in two of their most pathological forms: child rape and murder," which, when we "encounter them in a text," "can be disturbing but convincing metaphors for a desire for moral and aesthetic perfection" (1983, 67). Tamir-Ghez refers to Humbert's "design to rape" Lolita, but says he does not rape her because "she complies," and then refers to "the first time he makes love to Lolita" (1979, 72 n.7, 80).

7 Of course, Nabokov wants this admiration, and he uses his artistic skill to enact another kind of doubling: to represent a playful tragedy, to carefully construct and then deny the same mimetic reality, to make the story artificial and real, to foreground the synthetic aspects of the work so much that, even as he asks us to participate mimetically, he undermines our mimetic engagement – such that those who largely engage mimetically with *Lolita* are criticized for not appreciating its art. See Phelan 1989 for definitions and applications of the synthetic, mimetic, and thematic components of narrative.

8 While Nabokov avoids sustained, graphic descriptions of Lolita's violations,

his words throw some readers into ripping, detailed memories of their own molestations.

9 Most notably, see Kauffman (1993). Also see McNeely (1989), Levine (1979), and Giblett (1989). See also notes 6, 14, 17, and 18.

10 Some of the critics who discuss readers' sympathy for Humbert include: Brand, who says "our access to Humbert's extraordinary consciousness makes us more sympathetic to him than we would be to anyone else who does what he does. Still ... Nabokov provides us with the moral terms with which we can convict Humbert" (1987, 19); Rampton, who says, "it is precisely the Humbert 'talk,' the marvellously intelligent discourse that devastatingly indicts not just himself but a whole society, that makes him so attractive and keeps us sympathetic and involved" (1984, 110); Tamir-Ghez, who says "even such paragraphs that point quite strongly at his guilt still make the reader sympathize, in the first place, with *him*" (1979, 70; also 66, 76, 81); Toker, who says that "Humbert is a callous predator" who eludes readers during "stretches" of the novel (1989, 203); and Phelan, who calls Humbert "undeniably perverse" and says, "We react to Humbert's doom not with pleasure but with sympathetic pity" (1981, 162). Many critics seem confused about how to judge Humbert, often betraying extended sympathies for him, yet curtly noting that his behavior is not to be condoned – as we will see in other quotes from some of these same authors.

11 See Appel (1967), who emphasizes Humbert's victimization, entrapment, pain, despair, and horror; Bullock (1984), who says Lolita "abandons" "Hum for other men"; Gullette (1984), who says Humbert's crime is aging "and wanting nevertheless to have a sexual life" (p. 221); Jong (1988), who says the villain in *Lolita* is time and that "Humbert is ... every man who is driven by desire" (pp. 46–47); Tamir-Ghez (1979), who calls Humbert a "man with whom the average reader can easily identify" who "wins us over" (pp. 71, 82); and Green (1966), who claims that "The sexually perverse enterprises ... are made funny, beautiful, pathetic, romantic, tragic; in five or six different ways we are made to sympathize with [Humbert] in them. Above all, they are made impressive" (p. 365).

12 Most notorious is Trilling's comment that "we have come virtually to condone the violation it presents.... We have been seduced into conniving in the violation, because we have permitted our fantasies to accept what we know to be rather revolting" (1958, 14). Others include: Appel, who says, "we almost find ourselves wishing Humbert well during his agonizing first night with Lolita at The Enchanted Hunters" (1967, 126); Bader, who says Humbert's "agonizing love for a slangy twelve-year-old is a delectable taboo" (1972, 63); Butler, who claims that during the couch scene "we may even fear for him the possibility of detection. Then, at the moment of orgasm, we experience a corresponding relief that the scene has passed without incident. And, finally, we may even let ourselves be swayed by Humbert's retrospective view of the scene as an artistic triumph" (1986, 433); Tamir-Ghez, who notes that "What enraged or at least disquieted most readers and critics was the fact that they found themselves unwittingly accepting, even sharing, the feelings of Humbert Humbert.... [T]hey caught themselves identifying with him" (1979, 65); and Toker, who says we identify and sympathize with Humbert, who pursues "a pleasure that few readers wish to give up, despite all the scornful treatment that such a pleasure may receive in various aesthetic theories" (1989, 202–203).

13 See Trilling, who "was plainly not able to muster up the note of moral outrage" and says "it is likely that any reader of *Lolita* will discover that he comes to see the situation as less and less abstract and ... horrible, and more

and more as human and 'understandable' " (1958, 14); Parker: "She is a dreadful little creature, selfish, hard, vulgar, and foul-tempered.... Lolita leaves him ... for a creature even worse than she is" (1993, 9–10); Appel: Lolita "affords Nabokov an ideal opportunity to comment on the Teen and Sub-Teen Tyranny. It is poetic justice that Lolita should seduce Humbert.... Lolita is a Baby Snooks who looms threateningly high above us all" (1967, 121); Bader, who says Lolita "responds shrilly to Humbert's love-making" and faults Lolita for being conventional (1972, 69); Brand: Lolita is a "little girl as vulgar, energetic, flirtatious, seemingly innocent and yet manipulative as the American commercial environment itself" (1987, 19); Jong: Lolita is "an impossible object: a banal little girl" (1988, 46); Fowler: Lolita is "quite at home as a semiliterate Mrs. Richard Schiller living in a shack and the love of her life was the disgusting Quilty, not Humbert" (1974, 174); and Gullette: "Both the cult of childhood and the discourse that has been labelled 'Freudianism' have exacerbated, if they have not created, the guilt an adult feels in longing sexually for a child.... And feminism has heightened the sense of potential exploitation in this longing.... The outcome, at any rate, is that in the Western world sex is patently another game one cannot play with children" (1984, 218).

14 Kauffman is one of the only critics I have found to truly contest what I am calling this aestheticizing of molestation: "Aesthetic bliss is not a criterion that compensates for those crimes; instead it is a dead end, meager consolation for the murder of Lolita's childhood" (1993, 163).

15 While there seem to be some gender-specific reactions to *Lolita*, both in students and in published critics, there are also clear and important exceptions to them – as evidenced in my notes.

16 This response seems a dramatic manifestation of what Fetterley calls "immasculation," when "the female reader is co-opted into participation in an experience from which she is explicitly excluded; she is asked to identify with a selfhood that defines itself in opposition to her; she is required to identify against herself" (1978, xii). This reader's response surpasses immasculation because it not only requires the reader to identify against herself as she accepts a male position, but she, in taking this stance, also positions herself in stark contrast and *opposition to* another, particularly vulnerable, female. Kauffman, citing Fetterley, notes that *Lolita* gives "feminist" (though, it seems "female" is more appropriate here) readers "the choice of either participating in their own 'immasculation' by endorsing aesthetic bliss, or of demonstrating their humorlessness and frigidity" and that "physical as well as aesthetic *jouissance* for Humbert requires anaesthesia or annihilation for Lolita" (1993, 155). While immasculation has been the norm in *Lolita* criticism, Kauffman, McNeely, and Giblett have begun to challenge it.

17 For an articulation of these terms, see Rabinowitz (1987). One would think that, since Lolita's pain is so acutely, though rarely, clarified, that critics would have better attended to that very large group of readers who identify with the experience of pain and trauma, not of pleasure. Most critics – male and female – focus on the pleasurable experience of reading, especially (both overtly and covertly) from a particularly male perspective, including: Packman, Toker, Field, Appel (1967), Butler, Jong, O'Connor, and Fowler. For those who problematize the reading experience, see Rampton and Tamir-Ghez. And, for those who directly confront the "male" reading experience, see Kauffman, McNeely, Levine, and Giblett.

18 See Booth (1983) for one of the earliest and most notable discussions about the book's morality. For discussions focussed on Lolita's perspective, see McNeely

(1989), Levine (1979), and Kauffman (1993), who says, "*Lolita* is not about love but about incest, which is a betrayal of trust, a violation of love. How have critics managed so consistently to confuse love with incest in the novel? My aim here is to show how ... the inscription of the father's body in the text obliterates the daughter's" (p. 152). And one of my aims is to show how the "father's" text obliterates the "daughter's" in several contexts: in the larger culture, the classroom, the actual *Lolita* text, and in its criticism.

19 While Fetterley (1978) discusses the ways in which women identify against themselves as "immasculation" (see n.16), a related but very different move occurs when men are expected and assumed to identify with the male "standard" when that standard violates who they are as individuals. Individual men may be "immasculated," not such that they are co-opted into participating in experiences from which they are explicitly excluded, but by being co-opted into participating in experiences in which they are assumed to be included but, given their individual reactions, are not. Are some male readers of *Lolita* asked to identify with a perspective that is in opposition to themselves as individuals even though it is often assumed to represent their gender?

20 See n.6 on Lolita as seductress and n.23 on whether Humbert abandons his pedophilia and comes to truly love Lolita.

21 This passage is a pivotal factor in most critics' assumptions that Lolita is the unvirginal seductress, but few have noted – let alone explored and complicated – its specifics. Among those few are Levine, who says Lolita's pain after the "honeymoon night" is probably due to her menarche, not because Humbert "had torn something inside her" (1979, 472). Levine, Toker (1989), and Tamir-Ghez (1979) comment, respectively, on "the stark act" and the "certain discrepancies" without clarifying what they think these actually are. Phelan, who indicates that he believes "life" refers to sex organ, refers to the "certain discrepancies" and the "stark act" without problematizing their meaning, although his interpretation of "life" enables us to infer that he defines them as organ size and intercourse (1981, 164).

22 There is, of course, an important distinction between intercourse and procreation (as we see in Lolita's fate), and perhaps Humbert is referring to Lolita's lack of interest in or preparedness for producing children. However, we would be remiss to discount the association of intercourse with procreation, whether conception occurs during intercourse or not. For my purposes, I will emphasize the first step in procreation, intercourse.

23 Critics offer a range of opinions on whether Humbert experiences true "moral apotheosis" and love or whether his confession is "a virtuoso performance: an artfully contrived *apologia*" (Haegert 1985, 778), although most critics argue that Humbert's claims are genuine. Among those who believe Humbert experiences a true "moral apotheosis" or is no longer a pedophile or both are Alexandrov, Appel (1967), Bader, Bullock, Field, Fowler, Gullette, Levine, Maddox, Morton, Pifer, Tamir-Ghez, Toker, and O'Connor. Butler challenges this view, arguing that "Humbert's expression of love still functions as one of the novel's modulations" (1986, 436 n.22, 434), and Kauffman argues that Humbert is "far from being in love with Lolita," that he is "completely obsessed with the mental image he incessantly projects with random girls and women" (1993, 159), and that what critics usually cite as signs of Humbert's love are "signs not of overpowering love but of domination" typical of father–daughter incest (p. 161).

Part IV

CULTURAL CONTACTS

8

NABOKOV AND THE SIXTIES

D. Barton Johnson

Nabokov in the sixties

The sixties was the Nabokov decade in American literature. The decade was ushered in by *Lolita* which was still on the *New York Times Book Review*'s bestseller list nearly a year and half after its American publication (Boyd 1991, 387). Oddly enough, it was in competition with a novel by another Russian writer, Boris Pasternak, whose *Doctor Zhivago* had just won a Nobel Prize, although its author had been forced to decline (Boyd 1991, 370–373).[1] By January of 1960 *Lolita* had just gone into its first American paperback edition (Juliar 1986, 222). With the release of Stanley Kubrick's film version in June 1962, a wave of *Lolita*-mania swept the country. *Lolita* was that rare cultural phenomenon that left its mark in public consciousness from the most austere member of the intellectual community to sweaty-palmed adolescents in small-town America. Nabokov's face (with actress Sue Lyon's Lolita as a gigantic backdrop) appeared on the cover of *Newsweek* (June 25, 1962).

Nor was *Lolita* the only source of interest in Nabokov. Just prior to *Lolita*'s film premiere, *Pale Fire*, which was to become the most critically acclaimed novel of the sixties, had appeared. Although much less erotic and far more cerebral than *Lolita*, it too soon climbed the bestseller list (Boyd 1991, 467). In a famous essay, Mary McCarthy hailed it as "one of the very great works of art of this century, the modern novel that everyone thought dead and that was only playing possum" (Page 1982, 136).

Capitalizing on his new fame, Nabokov quickly published translations of his Russian work. The starkly modernist *Invitation to a Beheading* (1938), the work most "esteemed" by its author (Nabokov 1973, 92), had already appeared in late 1959 to the considerable mystification of an audience who knew Nabokov only as the author of *Lolita*. *The Gift*, called by one critic "the greatest novel Russian literature has yet produced in this century" (Field 1967, 249), appeared in 1963, quickly followed by *The Defense* (1964), *The Eye* (1965), *Despair* (1966), the play *The Waltz Invention* in 1966, and *King, Queen, Knave* in 1968. Only *Mary, Glory*

139

and most of the short stories were still untranslated by the end of the decade. The pre-*Lolita* English novels were also reissued. *The Real Life of Sebastian Knight* (1941), Nabokov's first English-language novel, was republished in 1964, as was the 1947 *Bend Sinister*. The last, reissued in paperback by a major book club, included an extended foreword by the author that perhaps gave many readers their first inkling of the elegant intricacy that lay beneath the surface of his writings. *Speak, Memory* (1966), the revised and expanded version of Nabokov's 1951 autobiography, was a Book-of-the-Month Club selection. In addition, there was the barrage of short stories and novel excerpts which appeared in mass-circulation journals such as *Playboy* and *Esquire*.

Nabokov also kept his name in public view with some thirty interviews that appeared during the sixties. The dozen-odd that were later collected into *Strong Opinions*, together with the newly written forewords to his translated novels, did much to create the public image of the elitist, strongly opinionated aristocrat who did not suffer fools gladly. It was a persona that, while not without basis, was often at odds with the more genial image Nabokov presented to his few intimates.

Not content with republishing his own work, Nabokov found time in the sixties to see through to press his idiosyncratic translation of Pushkin's *Eugene Onegin* with its three volumes of scholarly commentary (1964). As unlikely as it seems, Nabokov's translation of a long Russian poem barely known to the American reading public led to one of the great intellectual imbroglios of the decade. Edmund Wilson, Nabokov's old friend and the crusty dean of American literary critics, published a long, detailed, and thoroughly negative review of Nabokov's literalist translation – not omitting to take several personal potshots at his former friend. Their feud, for that is what it was, was carried on in the intellectual press over a three-year period and drew in dozens of participants. The elegant acidity of the two main protagonists provided nearly as much entertainment for the intellectual community as Kubrick's film had for the mass audience.

Nabokov's name was everywhere in the sixties. It was rare to pick up any issue of the literary press without seeing his name – a review of a new book, a quotation, Nabokov as a standard of comparison for a new writer, and so on. Samuel Schuman's critical bibliography makes it possible to chart the ubiquity of Nabokov during the period. In pre-*Lolita* 1956, there were no publications about Nabokov. In 1958–1960, there were 112, mostly reviews of *Lolita*. 1962 saw twenty-seven review articles of *Pale Fire*, plus many more of the film version of *Lolita*. The years 1963–1965 brought about sixteen items apiece. The first critical monograph, Page Stegner's *Escape into Aesthetics*, appeared in 1966, and was quickly followed by Andrew Field's *Nabokov: His Life in Art* (1967) and Carl Proffer's *Keys to Lolita* (1968). The first collections of scholarly articles also appeared: *Nabokov: The Man and his Work*, edited by

L. S. Dembo (1967), and *Nabokov: Criticism, Reminiscences, Transla-tions, and Tributes* (1970), edited by Charles Newman and Alfred Appel, one of Nabokov's best early critics. The first doctoral dissertation appeared in 1966 to be followed by a handful of others – often by people who would themselves become writers of fiction. Two notable examples were Susan Fromberg Schaeffer, author of the first Nabokov dissertation, and Bobbie Ann Mason, both of whom went on to become well-known but decidedly un-Nabokovian writers.

If Nabokov's *Lolita* ushered in the literary sixties, *Ada*, his longest novel, brought the decade to a rollicking close. It was immediately on the bestseller list (Boyd 1991, 567) and a Literary Guild book club selection (Juliar 1986, 307), although it seems unlikely many readers made it past the dense opening section – much less the abstract essay on the nature of time and space near the book's end. Nabokov was on the cover of *Time* (May 23, 1969), the world's most widely-read weekly. In the following months over a hundred review articles appeared. Just as the 1969 moon walk culminated the space race and the Woodstock festival marked the high point of the decade's anti-establishment youth counterculture, *Ada* rounded off the literary decade in America.

Nabokov loomed over the literary sixties in a way that no other Ameri-can author has ever dominated a decade. This came about through a set of fortuitous circumstances. *Lolita*, whose sensational subject matter was a far more important source of its popularity than its literary merit, played a central role in the liberation of the arts from the old social strictures. The novel and ensuing film put Nabokov in the public eye, and the publishing industry, the media, and Nabokov himself were all quick to make the most of the situation. Nabokov, even in the days when his literary earnings were minuscule, had (mostly through his wife, Vera) paid close attention to the business side of his writing. Realizing the financial potential of *Lolita*, Nabokov conferred with the high-powered William Morris Agency in New York on his literary affairs (Boyd 1991, 482, 519), and for Hollywood negotiations hired one of the shrewdest and most aggressive agents in the American entertainment industry – Irving "Swifty" Lazar, who was to become a life-long friend. Nabokov found himself in an almost ideal situ-ation (Boyd 1991, 365, 407). Most authors who enjoy a major commercial success are faced with the difficult task of producing new work before public interest fades. Nabokov's position was very different in two ways. Not only was he suddenly famous and a hot commercial property, but he had a thirty-year reservoir of material that was unknown to his new audi-ence. No less important was that unlike many writers of overnight sensa-tions, Nabokov had the admiration of the literary critical community that places a work in the canon and, with luck, assures a long-term readership. Nabokov's situation was unique. How many authors have the opportunity to publish the formidable output of a lifetime in a single decade? Nabokov and his publishers exploited this combination of circumstances to make him the preeminent figure on the American literary scene of the sixties.

Nabokov's regal preeminence was undisputed, but distinctly odd, for he was reigning *in absentia*. The Nabokovs had moved to Europe in late 1959 and, apart from visits in connection with the movie script for *Lolita* and for the film's premiere, never again lived in America (Boyd 1991, 388). During the early sixties Nabokov often spoke of his intention to return (Nabokov 1973, 28), but as the years passed the Nabokov family settled ever more firmly into their quarters at the Palace Hotel in Montreux which soon became a Mecca for the literary world.

Nabokov and the American literary scene of the sixties

Nabokov had made literary history in the sixties, but he was also a part of literary history. What was Nabokov's role on the American literary scene? What was its impact upon him, and, more crucially, his on it? First, the social scene. Nabokov's postwar years in the United States had been a relatively quiet time domestically. But after the calm (some would say "stupor") of the Eisenhower years, came the turbulent sixties. The decade began auspiciously with the election of John Kennedy, the youngest-ever U.S. president. But by the time of Kennedy's assassination three years later, the phenomena that were to overshadow the decade were emerging. It was Kennedy who ordered troops into Birmingham, Alabama, following civil rights protests and the arrest of Martin Luther King, and it was Kennedy who ordered the first U.S. "advisers" to Vietnam. By the end of the decade, the country was polarized over the civil rights issue and the peace movement. The two causes would merge to create a radicalized young generation and a genuine counterculture with its own music and literature. Nor was the shift in social attitudes limited to the counterculture. Sexual attitudes were changing, practically facilitated by the wide-spread use of the contraceptive pill.

The American literary scene of the sixties was also a radical change from the quiescent fifties. "Literary" decades are, of course, artificial constructs that may or may not closely coincide with chronological decades. It can be argued that the American literary sixties actually began in the late fifties – with Nabokov's *Lolita* as one of the trailblazers. Apart from the ephemera that make up most (but not all) of the *New York Times* bestseller list, one can distinguish three broad trends in "serious" American fiction that provided the context for Nabokov's three novels of the period.

There was a mainstream represented by J. D. Salinger, John Updike, Saul Bellow, Joseph Heller, the young Philip Roth, Joyce Carol Oates, and Norman Mailer (who would soon shift literary allegiances, as would Roth a decade later). The mainstream is, of course, a group too diverse to represent under any one label, but "realist" might serve as well as any. Salinger was already near the end of his active literary career. The early sixties saw *Franny and Zooey* and *Raise High the Roof Beam, Carpenter*. John Updike, another writer closely associated with *The New Yorker*, launched his career as Salinger withdrew from the literary scene.

Perhaps the best and most prolific of the mainstream writers, Updike published the first volume of his brilliant *Rabbit* series in 1960 and soon followed it with *The Centaur*. The highly erotic *Couples*, whose publication would have been unthinkable in pre-*Lolita* years, came out in 1968. These novels (and others), together with his many short stories and literary journalism, gave him a sort of sustained public visibility that made him Nabokov's only competitor with the serious reading audience. So far as I know, only Updike, among the mainline writers, has expressed his appreciation of Nabokov at length. He warmly reviewed many of Nabokov's novels for *The New Yorker* and other prestigious journals and offered his estimate of Nabokov as "distinctly ... the best writer of English prose now holding American citizenship" (Page 1982, 154).[2] Joyce Carol Oates was to express her admiration of *Lolita* as "one of our finest American novels," while at the same time voicing a wide-spread sense that *Pale Fire* and *Ada* bespoke a "tragic" Nabokov whose compassion for his characters was limited to those few who shared his own subjectivity (Oates 1973, 37). Norman Mailer offered praise in a characteristically egocentric manner. When rumor reached him in the fall of 1969 that he might get the Nobel Prize, his first thought was, "How could one really look Nabokov in the eye? Or Henry Miller?" (Mailer 1971, 5–6). As Edmund White has remarked, Mailer and Nabokov, both widely imitated writers, constitute admirable antipodes on the American literary scene (1973, 34).

Nabokov, for his part, was generally careful to restrict both his public commendation and condemnation to the dead. Indeed, when reviewing interviews prior to their publication, he often insisted that the interviewers strike out his off-the-cuff remarks about other authors (Nabokov 1989, 395–396; Boyd 1991, 485–486). Exceptions were his words of praise for Salinger and Updike (Nabokov 1973, 57). Saul Bellow, who has described his intent as the rediscovery of the magic of the world under the debris of modern idea, is wary of modernist writers such as Nabokov, who, for his part, shrugged off Bellow's *Herzog* (1964), saying that he found it so boring that he left it unfinished (Boyd 1991, 491). In a personal letter to Carl Proffer about his *Keys to Lolita*, Nabokov wondered whether it was possible to eliminate a blurb for a critical study of Bellow, saying "Saul Bellow, a miserable mediocrity, should never have appeared on the jacket of a book about me" (Nabokov 1989, 434). Heller's black humor novel of World War II, *Catch-22* (1961), Nabokov harshly (and privately) dismissed as "a torrent of trash, dialogical diarrhea, the automatic produce of a prolix typewriter" (Boyd 1991, 422–423). Although Nabokov's thoughts about Norman Mailer remain unrecorded, it seems certain that Mailer's highly politicized works such as *Why We are in Vietnam* (1967) and *Armies of the Night*, a surrealist account of the 1967 anti-Vietnam march on the Pentagon, would not have sat well with Nabokov's views of either art or politics. This is broadly hinted at in two comments. Asked whether he had read and admired Mailer's recent political and social reportage such as *Miami and the Siege of Chicago* (1968), he seemingly ducked the question: "You know, it sounds preposterous, but I was invited to cover that political convention in Chicago ... I did not go, naturally, and still believe it must have been some sort of joke on the part of *Esquire* – inviting *me* who can't tell a Democrat from a Republican and hates crowds and demonstrations" (Nabokov 1973, 125–126). In another interview when asked whether the sexual revolution had peaked, he replied, "Artistically, the dirtier typewriters try to get, the more conventional and corny their products become, e.g., such novels as *Miller's Thumb* and *Tailor's Spasm*" (Nabokov 1973, 133).

Another major figure of the sixties, Philip Roth, would evolve from a more or less traditional chronicler of the American social scene to become the author of *Portnoy's Complaint* which shared a place on the bestseller list with Nabokov's *Ada* at the end of the decade (Boyd 1991, 567). Then there were the "Beats" – those spiritual children of Henry Miller – Kerouac, Ginsburg, William Burroughs, Ken Kesey, and others. Poet Allen Ginsberg's plangent "Howl" (1956) and "Kaddish" (1961) launched the movement which was to be closely identified with San Francisco – in spite of its New York origins. "Howl"'s surrealistic indictment of America ("I saw the best minds of my generation destroyed by madness...") led to one of the landmark obscenity trials that would liberate the literature of the sixties. William S. Burroughs's *Naked Lunch*, a wildly comic and inventive work saturated with drugs, sex, and violence, had, like *Lolita*, originally been published by Olympia Press in Paris. Published in the U.S. in 1961, the same year as Henry Miller's *Tropic of Cancer*, it too triggered an obscenity trial won by its publisher. But perhaps the most influential book of the Beat Generation was Jack Kerouac's *On the Road* (1957), a thinly disguised novelization of the adventures of the author and his friends in their hedonistic search for beatitude. During the sixties, Kerouac was to produce a succession of novelistic chronicles of his peripatetic life. Another "Beat" work that enjoyed great popularity was Ken Kesey's *One Flew Over the Cuckoo's Nest* (1962). Kesey was to be a transitional figure in the Beat Generation as it evolved into the "flower power" generation with its psychedelic visions of a new world – a vision that reached its peak in San Francisco's famed Haight-Ashbury district, circa 1967.

The writers of the Beat Generation have, to my knowledge, left little record of their attitude toward Nabokov; nor he toward their writings. It can be assumed, however, that some of his blanket comments directed toward literary bohemia were aimed at the noisy movement. The "Beats'" interest in Dostoevsky, their uninhibited confessional tone, "spontaneous" prose, and Buddhist inclination were all antithetical to Nabokov's way of thinking and writing.

The rise of the postmodernists – John Barth, William Gass, John Hawkes, Robert Coover, Donald Barthelme, Thomas Pynchon, and Gilbert Sorrentino – coincided almost exactly with the Nabokov decade of the sixties. At the center of the postmodern vision, at least in the sixties, was an all consuming nihilism in which redemption, if such were to be had, lay in obscure artifices seemingly spun by hidden artificers. "Reality" is unknowable, but pattern is where you find it (or make it up). The prototypical figure is Thomas Pynchon, who, oddly enough, was a student in Nabokov's classes at Cornell, although only Vera professes to remember him and that for his eccentric handwriting – an irony that doubtless delights the reclusive Pynchon (Nabokov 1973, 75–76). Pynchon's *V.* (1963) tells of Benny Profane, the human yo-yo, who embraces meaninglessness as a way of life. But he too is caught up in the search for the mysterious "V.," a mythic woman who symbolizes controlling serenity. *The Crying of Lot 49* (1966) is an equally riotous pursuit of seeming pattern in a world of aimlessness. John Barth's elegantly bleak first two novels, *The Floating Opera* and *The End of the Road*, were written during the *Lolita* years, but the *The Sot-Weed Factor* (1960) and *Giles Goat-Boy* (1966) are archetypal postmodern works. Robert Coover, Gilbert Sorrentino, Stanley Elkin, Joseph McElroy, William Gass, and Richard Sukenick all published their first novels during the sixties.

The postmodernist writers, many of them connected with major universities, are a very self-aware group. They tend to be well informed about the history of literature and to have strong theoretical views about literature and their place in it. Nabokov is one of their touchstones. At a 1988 gathering of leading postmodern writers, a French critic offered a humorous ten-point check list for spotting a postmodernist writer (Couturier 1993, 247). The last item was "he admires Nabokov, who, thank goodness, is dead." According to Maurice Couturier who recounts the event (and supplied much of my information on Nabokov and the postmodernists), John Hawkes, one of the group's senior figures, wryly objected that he in fact lamented the death of Nabokov whom he especially admired for his handling of sex and eroticism. More seriously, Hawkes has defined the avant-garde tradition in terms of facing the ugliness of the world with "a savage or saving comic spirit and the saving beauties of language.... A writer who truly sustains us is Nabokov" (Scholes 1967, 59). John Barth has singled out Nabokov, Borges, and Beckett as among the few writers who point to a way out of the "exhaustion" of literature which he and others saw looming in the late sixties (Barth 1967). Postmodernist comment on Nabokov is too abundant to summarize, but *Pale Fire* seems to be a key text for the movement. It is even explicitly mentioned in Sorrentino's irrepressible *Mulligan Stew* (1979) where a Nabokov interview is parodied and the author of *Fire Pail* is ·referred to as Vladimir Papilion. Pynchon incorporates wry allusions to *Lolita* into *The Crying of Lot 49* (Couturier 1993, 249). Nor is it by chance that two of the postmodernists, Barth and Elkin, were invited to contribute to *TriQuarterly*'s *Festschrift* for Nabokov's seventieth birthday (Appel and Newman 1970). Joseph McElroy (1973, 34) perhaps speaks for the group when he says:

> John Barth's *The Sot-Weed Factor* would have happened anyhow
> – but surely one movement of fiction in the Sixties away from
> plainer modes and into parody, labyrinth, and self-conscious con-
> volutions of wit owed something to Nabokov. *Lolita* and *Pale Fire*
> ... made me feel freer to go ahead and slip the regular vein of sen-
> sitive, even-tempered American realism...

Nabokov, who had left America at the beginning of the decade, was not present during the flowering of the postmodern movement. Although he did follow events in America, he did not choose to comment on the young postmodernists, apart from Barth and that only for "the lovely swift speckled imagery" in a short story (Nabokov 1973, 313). Given Nabokov's work load in the sixties, it is more than possible that he did not follow new writing closely. Had he done so, however, he would have seen that it was among the postmodernists that he had left the deepest imprint. Their often obsessive interest in language play, literary allusion, and, most of all, intricate patterning all point to close familiarity with Nabokov's work. There is, however, one essential difference. Postmodernist pattern-ing was detached from any extra-textual reality because, for them, the existence of that reality was more than problematic. For Nabokov, "reality," although infinitely complex, was at some level "out there" and somehow reflected in his art.

Our brief survey of major trends in American writing of the sixties points to one obvious conclusion. Nabokov, however great his prestige, stood apart from all trends. And he would not have wished it otherwise.

Nabokov and the legacy of the sixties

Nabokov presents something of a paradox on the American literary scene of the sixties. Physically absent, he was nonetheless the most visible pre-sence in American literature. Critics as various as George Steiner (1970, 127) and Tony Tanner (1971, 33) viewed him as a seminal figure of the period. Nabokov both was and was not an American writer. Steiner came closest to an accurate appraisal when he labelled him (along with Borges and Beckett) as "extraterritorial," pointing to the phenomenon of the interpenetration of linguistic and cultural traditions that underlay

Nabokov's work. Nabokov, however, clearly considered himself an American writer (Nabokov 1973, 26, 63). Granted this, his removal to Europe, which turned out to be permanent, seems strange. As we have noted, Nabokov initially planned to stay abroad for a relatively short time and in fact repeatedly spoke of his impending return even late in his life. So why did Nabokov, who considered himself an American writer and who asserted that it was in America that he had been happiest, never return (Nabokov 1973, 10)?

The answer perhaps lies in the American sixties, for the country seemed to have changed greatly, and – for a man of Nabokov's generation and background – for the worse. Throughout the sixties, Nabokov in Montreux closely followed events through newspapers, magazines, and conversation with American visitors. There is no denying that America was in the midst of a sea change: the anti-Vietnam demonstrations, the civil rights protests and riots, the psychedelic and sexual revolutions, and so on. Social disruption disturbed him greatly. Perhaps it evoked the Russia of his youth or Germany in the thirties – events that had turned his life (and the world) upside down. And, of course, the media upon which Nabokov relied for most of his information about the United States presented a highly colored version of events – in some cases virtually creating a social climate rather than reporting on it. Nabokov, a most apolitical man in spite of his hatred of totalitarian regimes, undoubtedly had an exaggerated sense of the degree of social chaos in the America of the sixties. His few "political" comments on the scene were largely motivated by his lifelong hatred of Communism and the herd instinct. In foreign policy whatever was bad for Soviet Communism was to be endorsed, and Nabokov strongly supported U.S. government action in Vietnam (Boyd 1991, 503). On the domestic scene the anti-war activities and the social disruption arising from the civil rights movement seemed to Nabokov to reflect a sort of herd mentality that he found abhorrent. At least from Switzerland, America no longer looked like the country that had provided Nabokov shelter and stability for the first time in his adult life. By the late sixties, America, at least in Nabokov's mind, may have become, like the Russia of his youth, another lost paradise to which there was no return.

The Nabokov decade left a double legacy to American letters – one to academic literary theory, the other to readers. The sixties saw the rise of literary theory, and Nabokov, a man who cheerfully despised literary abstractions, became an iconic figure in the literary wars. As the towering literary figure of the period, he, or rather his work of that time, became a focal point in the debate over modernism and postmodernism. The French critic, Maurice Couturier, provides a well-informed survey of the question (1993). Some critics have seen Nabokov as the last avatar of European high modernism. Others, such as Brian McHale, focussing on the English novels of the sixties, find *Pale Fire* to mark the dividing line between a modernist *Lolita* and the postmodern novels that followed. Still other critics, such as Couturier himself, see all of "sixties Nabokov" (including *Lolita*) as postmodern. Whatever the answer to the conundrum (and much hangs on the obscure meaning of the term "postmodern"), one thing remains clear. Nabokov's stature in the sixties was such that his work is considered pivotal in delineating two major literary movements.

Questions of literary theory exercise only academics. Nabokov's work of the sixties left more tangible legacies. *Lolita* was a landmark book in the liberation of literature from censorship both in America and elsewhere. Because of its unusual publication history, it had already (in small but influential circles) been recognized as a classic before its American publication. This, together with the courage and determination of Putnam, the novel's old-line American publisher, did much to facilitate *Lolita*'s American publication in 1958. Much to everyone's surprise, there was no obscenity trial. On the other hand, suits were filed against *Lady Chatterly's Lover* in 1959, and subsequently against Henry Miller's *Tropic of Cancer* and William Burroughs's *Naked Lunch*. All of these were unsuccessful and were, indeed, ludicrous after *Lolita*'s bestsellerdom. Public standards had changed. Only after *Lolita* could Updike publish *Couples*, or Roth *Portnoy's Complaint*. The "Beat" writers and the postmodernists were also major beneficiaries.

Nabokov's prestige on the American literary scene in the sixties was such that one would have expected his work to serve as a springboard for a generation of young writers. By and large, this did not happen. As we have noted, the postmodernists were his most obvious epigones, but the similarities are limited to an attitude toward language and patterning. A writer who can lay claim to closer affinity is David R. Slavitt, whose novels of the early seventies, *Anagrams* and *ABCD*, displayed a witty elegance of style and structure that was distinctly Nabokovian.[3] The reasons for Nabokov's lack of "successors" are not far to seek. No other American writer had Nabokov's acute perception, rich multicultural background, linguistic dexterity, and lush imagination. Nabokov is destined to remain a standard of excellence and comparison, but not of emulation.

Notes

1 *Lolita* was third in national sales in 1958 and eighth in 1959, whereas *Doctor Zhivago* was first in both years (Hackett 1976). Odder yet, in 1957 Russian-born Ayn Rand's *Atlas Shrugged* had been on the list. All three would achieve their greatest sales as paperbacks during the sixties. Like Nabokov, Rand wrote in English but her literary roots were deep in the Russian didactic literary tradition. The trio contributed examples of very different Russian literary traditions to the American reading public: Rand – the social utilitarian à la Chernyshevsky; Pasternak – the philosophical realist novel à la Tolstoy; and Nabokov – the modernist.

2   The Russian Americanist Aleksei Zverev (1995) provides a good survey of
    Updike's views of Nabokov.
3   As a young assistant editor at *Newsweek*, Slavitt had done the unsigned cover
    story on Nabokov at the time of the publication of *Pale Fire* and the release of
    the film *Lolita*. Already a published poet, he soon turned prolific novelist
    mixing "literary" novels with popular entertainments – the latter often under
    the name Henry Sutton.

9

VLADIMIR NABOKOV AND POPULAR CULTURE

Suellen Stringer-Hye

To myself I appear as an idol, a wizard bird-headed, emerald
gloved, dressed in tights made of bright-blue scales.
(Nabokov 1970, 105)

"Icons are symbols and mindmarks," says Marshall Fishwick, author of
The Seven Pillars of Popular Culture: "they tie in with myth, legend,
values, idols and aspirations" (Fishwick 1985, 134). They are external
images to which adhere complex, sometimes paradoxical, but always
potent, projections of psychic realities. In twentieth-century culture, they
are communicated through the mass media and reach a large and popular
audience. Related historically to the fetish, talisman or religious amulet,
icons operate to transform commonplace objects or real people into recep-
tacles of meaning. Inconsistent in its treatment of literary figures, the
mechanism of iconography often leaves writers untouched. John Updike
and Saul Bellow may be very good writers but they do not "conjure an
image" in the same way figures like Mark Twain or Edgar Allan Poe do. It
was only after the publication of *Lolita* in 1955 that the transplanted
Russian author Vladimir Nabokov, together with the novel and its epony-
mous heroine, became popular culture icons. This chapter traces the
history and evolution of these figures through their portrayal in American
newspapers, magazines, and on the Internet, noting the ideological tensions that keep their iconography intact.

The *Reader's Guide to Periodical Literature*, which an anthropologist in
some obscure future may also scan in order to glimpse the stars and inter-
stices of twentieth-century popular culture, picks up Nabokov's faint tracks
soon after his arrival in America in 1941. An article profiling Nabokov
appeared in the late 1940s but at that time there were more articles about
cousin Nicolas Nabokov, the musician, than about the then critically-
acclaimed but popularly unknown writer. By the time the *Reader's Guide*
published its *Cumulative Index to March 1957 through February 1970*,

150

now using the bolder print and sans serif font of those streamlining decades, articles about Vladimir Nabokov were abundant. *Time* and *Newsweek* carried reviews of his works while *Life Magazine* featured biographical articles about the author. By 1971 the furor had died down. A reviewer of Nabokov's essay and interview collection, *Strong Opinions*, found that the book left "a lingering bad taste, since its author, outside his fictional enterprises and butterfly hunting lacked intellect" and that Nabokov was an "anachronism with little to offer serious readers" (Schuman 1975, 170).

In 1967, Nabokov was not an anachronism. To read the selection of *Playboy* interviews collected for book publication is to walk down the halls of a wax museum of 1960s cultural icons: Vladimir Nabokov, Frank Sinatra, Ian Fleming, Malcolm X, Richard Burton, Ayn Rand, and Sartre along with Martin Luther King, Timothy Leary, and the Beatles. Upright among staring fish, as William Gass commented, Nabokov the image, Nabokov the icon, was a powerful presence in what has come to be loosely and imprecisely called the sixties (Gass 1973, 35). Characteristically, Nabokov himself had the best take on his notoriety. "*Lolita* is famous, not I. I am an obscure, doubly obscure poet with an unpronounceable last name" (Nabokov 1973, 107). An anecdote cited by Brian Boyd in *Vladimir Nabokov: The American Years* captures the refracted images of the sixties Nabokov; celebrity and fan, notable yet unknown. Nabokov himself describes his appearance at the opening of Stanley Kubrick's film version of *Lolita*:

Date: June 13, 1962.
Setting: Loew's State, Broadway at Forty-fifth Street.
Scene: Crowds awaiting the limousines that drew up one by one, and there I, too, ride, as eager and innocent as the fans who peer into my car hoping to glimpse James Mason but finding only the placid profile of a stand-in for Hitchcock.

(Boyd 1991, 466)

The comparison with Hitchcock is perhaps more apt than one of physical resemblance and one that I will return to. Both artists stand at the crossroads of modern and postmodern culture – popularly accessible, yet critically acclaimed.

The pages of the *Reader's Guide* grew quiet in the first few years after his death in 1977. Interest was slightly rekindled by the reminiscences of his son Dimitri Nabokov and John Updike, and Vladimir Nabokov again charmed the "American Public" (and I use that term with all the warmth and attachment of a good politician) with the posthumous publication of his Cornell *Lectures on Literature*. Republication of his works as well as the appearance of a *Lolita*-like novelette, translated by Dimitri Nabokov, called *The Enchanter*, helped maintain Nabokov's literary presence, causing one reviewer to pronounce that "even from the grave Nabokov is still the literary event of the season." In the January 5, 1988 *New York Times Book Review*, Erica Jong wrote a tribute to *Lolita* entitled "Time has Been Kind to the Nymphet, *Lolita* 30 Years Later." Nevertheless, in the eighties, the popular press said less and less about Nabokov, even though an impressive body of critical works was accumulating. The publication of Brian Boyd's biography in the early 1990s was just in time for its reviews to be indexed electronically. Its publication marks the transition between the living and the posthumous reputation of Nabokov the man. Discussed regularly on the Internet in reader's forums such as rec.arts.books, rec.arts.literature, and Nabokv-L, Nabokov is now a comfortable inhabitant of cyberspace. Zembla (http//www.libraries.psu.edu/iaoweb/nabokov/nsinfo.htm), a site devoted to both scholarly and popular interest in Nabokov, is now on the World Wide Web. In 1996, Adrian Lyne, director of "Indecent Proposal," "Fatal Attraction," and "9½ Weeks," completed a cinematic remake of Stanley Kubrick's 1962 version of *Lolita* which Lyne says "adheres more closely to the book's narrative, including the stylish wit, humor, intensely lyrical and wildly funny dialogue." The difficulty Lyne had in finding an American film distributor mirrors Nabokov's own difficulty in the 1950s in finding an American publisher for *Lolita*. Nabokov is still remembered, often revered, by a disparate and often rival audience of American artists, poets, writers, musicians, filmmakers, politicians, and critics. Like so many of the supernovae of the sixties, Nabokov's universe has expanded since its explosion and much of this stellar matter is now the household dust of numerous and unforeseen domiciles.

A lingering but perhaps fading image of Nabokov is that of the sterile aesthete. Influenced by early critical works such as Page Stegner's *Escape into Aesthetics*, this perception has persisted especially in some of Nabokov's academic readership. In the interviews collected in *Strong Opinions*, Nabokov said he was attempting to paint a not altogether unpleasing picture of his personality, but as in all works by Nabokov, the reader had to be wary of trap doors and sleights of hand. Those who took him at his word generally did not and still do not like him. His arrogance, the lack of spontaneity, abrupt dismissals of fellow writers, all rubbed would-be admirers the wrong way. In my copy of *Strong Opinions*, borrowed from the library, I see penciled in the margins the notation, "extreme individualism," while Nabokov's disdain "for the earnest case histories of minority groups" elicits a provoked question mark. The annotator's patience is sorely tested by Nabokov's defense of the "earnest and unselfish motives of the US to nations in distress." He or she must have slammed the book shut in disgust because there are no more exclamated "how trues." The perception of Nabokov as a master gamesman, indifferent to questions of morality and human sentiment, continues to evoke either admiration or contempt, depending on one's own sensibility. This bipolar view of Nabokov informed much of the early Nabokov criticism and, in spite of books such as Michael Wood's *The Magician's Doubts*, which attempt to present a more complex vision of Nabokov's art, the potentially sterile maxim, "Art for Art's sake," continues to be a convenient epithet for the Nabokovian outlook.

Nabokov's creation *Lolita* obscures, while at the same time enhancing, the author's image. Like Charlie Chaplin, to whom Nabokov has sometimes been compared, and whose works he is said to have admired, Nabokov after death no longer necessarily seems to belong to the America he helped to create. The Vladimir Nabokov wondering to Alfred Appel about the currency of slang terms such as "square" and "corny" and the sexual overtones in the word "uptight" (Appel 1974, 63), now can appear remote and elevated; a marbled bust for reporters who speak of him as "one of the great writers of the twentieth century." *Lolita*, on the other hand, is still crammed with references to American popular culture from the Marx Brothers to Dick Tracy, so it is appropriate that she should take her place alongside these other icons of popular culture.

Thomas Reed Whissen, in his *Classic Cult Fiction: A Companion to Popular Cult Literature,* includes *Lolita* along with other cult classics such as J. D. Salinger's *Catcher in the Rye* or Jack Kerouac's *On the Road* in his survey of this fictional genre. According to Whissen, cult literature is differentiated from other literary genres mainly by the status bestowed on it by its readers. Cult books are not written intentionally and the fact that *Lolita* became one was perhaps as much a surprise to its author as it was to his previous American audience who were, for the most part, readers of the *New Yorker*. Cult books seem to express and embody the cultural *gestalt* (to use a word from the sixties) of a given period of time. Some cult books lose their appeal when that epoch has passed and others continue to attract a loyal following. There are several reasons, aside from its literary merit, why *Lolita* remains vivid in the American popular imagination.

Lolita is one of the richest, most complex, and elusive of all the "road" novels comprising an unofficial genre of American literature and a theme in popular American art. From the Journals of Lewis and Clark to Walt Whitman's "Song of the Open Road," Americans have expressed their concepts of freedom in visions of the freeway. In the 1960s this metaphor was particularly potent and the highways and byways of Woodie Guthrie's "This Land is Your Land" became Bob Dylan's "Highway 61 Revisited." In film, the highway figured in movies such as "Easy Rider" and on television in dark neon in shows such as "Route 66." It is difficult to conceive of two more dissimilar styles than that of the spontaneous Jack Kerouac, celebrator of the unconscious, and the intricate, intellectual patterning of Vladimir Nabokov, advocate of the glories of the conscious mind. However, one cannot help comparing *On the Road* with *Lolita*, noting that both cult books, important icons of 1960s American popular culture, revolve thematically around images of the road and investigate notions of freedom and disaffection, topics popular in the 1960s and still very much with us.

Whissen also notes the way in which a book achieves cult status by exhibiting a romantic hope and longing, as well as romantic disillusion and melancholy, with indebtedness to the romantic tradition being a fixture of cult status, if not of bestsellerdom. In Robert Pattison's study *The Triumph of Vulgarity: Rock Music in the Mirror of Romanticism*, the influence of the romantic literary tradition on Rock and Roll is also explored. It should be no surprise then that Sting, the lead singer of "The Police," uses Nabokov in the lyrics of the 1988 hit song "Don't Stand So Close To Me." Courtney Love of the band "Hole," outfitted in teen-queen baby-doll dresses, evoked Lolita in the early 1990s fashion statement dubbed the "Kinder-whore" look. That her husband, Kurt Cobain, entitled an album, by the Seattle band Nirvana, *Incesticide*, echoing the insect/incest theme in Nabokov's *Ada*, is no doubt a coincidence. Still, the parallels serve to highlight another of the media arenas in which *Lolita* continues to thrive in the popular imagination.

Many cultured readers condemn, along with Humbert, Lolita's shallowness, her taste for fudge, pop music, and gooey sundaes. Yet it is the eerie vulgarity of her charms that seduces Humbert first, and the reader next, into her enchanted sphere. Who can forget the moment in which the dreary bourgeois posturing of an adult Charlotte gives way to the immediate loveliness and rapture of the garden, the green, and the stern dark spectacles which appear again in the opening pan in Kubrick's movie? Dolly, mimicking stardom, displays a trashy glamour, a sarcastic defiance that singers such as Courtney Love and Madonna use to their advantage. Drew Barrymore, famous for her childhood role in the film *ET: The Extraterrestrial*, in a *People Online* interview, cites both the character Lolita and the actress Sue Lyon, who plays Lolita in Kubrick's film, as "an inspiration" for her later work.

In the essay, "Lolita Unclothed," pop critic Camille Paglia asserts that *Lolita* was a "grenade" tossed into the landscape of 1950s culture, exploding the myth of sexless and saintly children created by Rousseau and Wordsworth at "the birth of Romanticism" (Paglia 1994, 146). In the same article, author Anne Rice is quoted as saying "Lolita has become today ... the image of the seductive young girl who is every man's dream of sensuality" (Paglia 1994, 149). The Lolita Complex (an unhealthy desire for underage girls), and the Lolita Syndrome (the secret longing of middle-aged males for a young girl), are known today both clinically and in the vernacular. In 1994, Amy Fisher, and her resonantly named lover, Joey Buttafuoco, launched a series of headlines and television movies under the title "Long Island Lolita." A group of paedophiles calling themselves the Lolita Society haunts the Internet. Hundreds of adult bars and strip tease artists revel in the image of the pre-pubescent enchantress. Titles such as *A Lot of Lolita* inspire spicy novels and adorn the shelves of adult video stores worldwide. Lolita is the "keyword" of choice for hundreds of pornography sites on the World Wide Web.

Humbert has not failed to convince many readers that his needs were not criminal and his passions were justified. Some women, tired of the exploitation implicit in the Lolita myth, condemn the book. Kim Morrissey who wrote *Poems for Men Who Dream of Lolita* complains that the character Lolita has no voice (Paglia 1994, 157). Paralleling these complaints are the feminists critical of "baby-doll" fashion, seeing in it the infantilization of the female (Smith 1994, 25). These criticisms point to the ambiguous hold that both the character and the novel *Lolita* have on the popular imagination. Is *Lolita* a story about the beauty of Eros or the horror of incest and child abuse? Is Lolita a vixen seductress or the innocent victim of molestation and exploitation? How these questions are answered depends on the reader. The tension between Nabokov's not easily detected intentions and the popular impression of Lolita-as-sex-kitten fuel the debate.

In truth, "Lolita" is Humbert's creation, a mirage engendered by Humbert's obsessions and his reading list. The girl in the book is known to her friends and family as "Dolly." Nabokov allows us to see her through the gaps in Humbert's prose. Describing Lolita as a combination of naiveté and deception, charm and vulgarity, blue sulks and rosy mirth, "Lolita, when she chose to," says Humbert, "could be a most exasperating brat." This portrait, used not unsuccessfully by Humbert in order to win the reader's sympathy, is not only the description of Lolita, the mythological nymphet, but also a portrayal of normal childhood behavior. Dolly, Humbert implies, was warped by the popular culture in which she was steeped, but Nabokov lets us know that she also retained the unclouded perceptions of an intelligent child who could see through the pretense and pedantry Humbert had to offer. Without refinement, she had a child's disdain for the false in the adult world. Like J. D. Salinger's Holden Caulfield, she was bored by the commonplace trivialities to which she was expected to attend. Even before her life turned sordid, she longed for the same magic, romance, and style that Humbert's culture had found expressed in literature, drawing hers from movies, magazines, and pop music. Like Caulfield, she belonged to a generation of children who, while perhaps lacking cultivation, were still hungry for otherworlds. Nabokov's fondness for his work is legendary but his empathetic regard for Lolita is not always apparent. The interplay between Humbert's romantic invention, "Lolita," and the criminality of his actions towards Dolores Haze portrays the competing demands of the aesthetic impulse and the responsibility of the dreamer to differentiate other from self. These complexities are still being negotiated within the culture, provoking debates about gender, fashion, pornography, and art. Wherever these issues arise, the Lolita icon is inevitably brought into the fray.

Stanley Kubrick's "Lolita" echoes Nabokov's "Lolita" in its status as an object of cult veneration. Alfred Appel in his work, *Nabokov's Dark Cinema*, documents the influence of cinematography on Nabokov's novels. The anecdote cited above, in which Nabokov alludes to his physical resemblance to the famed director Alfred Hitchcock, implies a recognition on the part of Nabokov of an affinity between the two artists that he himself was the first to notice. Slavoj Žižek notes that Hitchcock's films from "Rebecca" to "Under Capricorn" are "thematically centered on the perspective of the female heroine, traumatized by an ambiguous (evil, impotent, obscene, broken . . .) paternal figure" (Žižek 1992, 4). *Lolita* too turns on such a theme. It also inverts playfully, if not intentionally, the Hitchcockian theme employed in the films of the 1950s and early 1960s; that of the male hero blocked from "normal" sexual relations by what Žižek, in the language of Freud, terms "the maternal super ego" but whom Humbert, feeling blocked in his access to Lolita, calls "the big cow." A closer comparison of the two artists is beyond the scope of this chapter; it is enough to note the way in which the psychic color of Hitchcock's portrait lends its hue to Nabokov's neighboring profile.

Evidence of *Lolita*'s impact on literary popular culture can be found in a *Lolita* parody written in a sub-genre of science fiction called cyberpunk, which appeared in the electronic journal, *The Holy Temple of Mass Consumption*. Written by Chuck Hammell and entitled, "A New Lo; or Everybody Into the Memo Pool," it is the tale of Charlie Holmes, Lo's first lover who died in Korea. In "A New Lo," Charlie is now a virtual-reality huckster who, after hawking a five-minute "ride" to a rich tourist just arrived from another planet, reminisces about his first love, giving the voice to Lolita that Humbert never does.

> Like, he is just sooo possessive, you know?" she would go on. "I mean, OK, he takes me on cross-country trips, right? And, like, he buys me lotsa nice presents. But, Jeez, he's got all these rules, you know? He doesn't want me dating other guys. I can't smoke, I can't do amateur theater, I can't do this, I can't do that. I mean, honestly, he treats me like a child! I don't need this.

In a stylized parody of one of Humbert's quatrains, Charlie Holmes asks:

> Where are you hiding, Dolores Haze?
> In your silicon circuitry, snoozin'?
> Let me turn on your pixels in sixty-nine ways—
> Your end-user's hot for some usin' . . .

Lolita does not die in Grey Star as she does in Nabokov's novel but is saved by the narrator.

Nabokov is, of course, cited most often by the media in connection with *Lolita*, but this is far from being the only point of reference. *Speak Memory*, *Lectures on Literature* and, increasingly, *Pale Fire* are the Nabokov books most frequently mentioned in those reading lists, common in newspaper columns, that let us know what some intellectual, celebrity, or politico is currently reading. American writers since the publication of *Lolita* have labored under his influence. In the January 1973 *Saturday Review* issue devoted to Nabokov, novelist Joseph McElroy allows that *Lolita* and *Pale Fire* made him "... feel freer to go ahead and slip the regular vein of sensitive, even-tempered American realism and try to write elaborately clued existential mysteries in tones of various voice that might include the arch or absurdly overbearing" (McElroy 1973, 34). Edmund White, in the same issue notes, that without Nabokov, "Americans might have gone on imitating Norman Mailer, cultists of tough-guy sincerity, thinking *ars gratia artis* meant Oscar Wilde; how useful to know it can also mean ardor, grace *Ada*" (White 1973, 34). Twenty years later in a collection of essays entitled the *Burning Library*, White expresses his admiration for Nabokov:

> Nabokov must be ranked, finally not with other writers but with a composer and a choreographer, Stravinsky and Balanchine. All three men were of the same generation, all three were Russians who were clarified by passing through the sieve of French culture but were brought to the boiling point only by the short order cook of American informality. All three experimented with form but none produced avant-garde trash as Nabokov called it, for all three were too keen on recuperating tradition ... as parodists all three artists loved the art they parodied and made modern by placing old gems in new settings.... Most important, all three men had a vision of art as entertainment, not to be sure as a vulgar courting of debased popular taste but as a wooing of shrewder, more restless though always robust sensibilities.
>
> (White 1994, 186)

Other writers also contemplate Nabokov in their musings. Saul Bellow commends Nabokov's sense of aesthetic bliss in a series of essays called *It All Adds Up* (Bellow 1994, 160). John Updike, in several interviews, states that he was attempting to capture the kind of magic Nabokov manages in *The Gift* for his novel *Brazil*. Nabokov's influence on Thomas Pynchon and Martin Amis is well known and often cited, as evidenced at the several World Wide Web sites devoted to these authors.

Nor are writers alone in claiming kinship with Nabokov. David Cronenberg who directed the movies *The Fly, Dead Ringers,* and *Naked Lunch,* remarks that his overwhelming admiration for Nabokov made it impossible for him to write, only finding his voice finally, in cinematography (Johnson 1993). Christopher Plummer, the actor and long-time Nabokov fan, frequently reads from Nabokov's works in his one-man shows and has acted the role of Professor Vladimir Nabokov, lecturing students on Kafka's "Metamorphosis" in the PBS production, *Nabokov in Residence.* Even politicians such as Massachusetts ex-Governor William Weld, whom journalistic profiles often characterize by his love for Nabokov, is quoted as saying, "If God truly resides in the well-chosen word, *Pale Fire* is a work of divine inspiration."

The pages of today's newspapers are crammed with reviews of worthy or not so worthy new novels inevitably "reminiscent of Nabokov." Good or bad, Nabokov is often the yardstick against which the talent of today's authors is measured. An article in *Time* discrediting Freud uses Nabokov's early pronouncements against the "Viennese Quack" to bolster the argument (Gary 1993). A coiner of words such as "nymphet," Nabokov has been cited by the *American Heritage Dictionary* for being the first to use the phrase "politically correct":

> The earliest citation submitted ... is actually "politically incorrect." In 1947 Vladimir Nabokov used that phrase in his novel *Bend Sinister* to describe the hero, a college professor living under a totalitarian regime who tries to avoid political commitments of any kind.
>
> (Marvel 1994)

Language maven, William Safire, credits Nabokov with first using the term "endgame," a political appropriation of chess terminology (Safire 1994, 13). Soccer player, chess player, lepidopterist, insomniac – there is a bit part to play for every aspect of Nabokov's personality.

Icons of popular culture fade or retain potency depending on their continued significance. Like Hitchcock, Nabokov, at least in his relation to *Lolita* and his later works, represents a cultural turn to postmodernism. As described by Žižek, the modernist work of art which through its incomprehensibility resists interpretation is contrasted to the postmodernist *objet d'art* which tends to appeal to a mass audience but renders the commonplace full of meaning (Žižek 1992, 1). Nabokov's own attitudes toward popular culture are problematic. He seems on the one hand to detest its vulgarity while on the other to celebrate its vigor. Readable by the many, exquisitely erudite for the few, Nabokov is, if we need labels, a modernist who in his 1939 Russian poem "Oculus" wonders to himself, "Who can care for a world of omnipotent vision if nothing is monogrammed there?" (Nabokov 1970, 110). Nabokov, that most mandarin of twentieth-century writers, has left a stamp on the popular culture of his era that is little short of remarkable.

WORKS CITED

INTRODUCTION

Appel, Alfred (ed.). 1970. *The Annotated Lolita*. New York: McGraw-Hill.

Bader, Julia. 1972. *The Crystal Land: Artifice in Nabokov's English Novels*. Berkeley: University of California Press.

Bakhtin, Mikhail M. 1981. "Discourse in the Novel." *The Dialogic Imagination: Four Essays by M. M. Bakhtin*. M. Holquist (ed.). Austin: University of Texas Press, 259–422.

Barabtarlo, Gennadi. 1989. *Phantom of Fact: A Guide to Nabokov's Pnin*. Ann Arbor: Ardis.

Barthes, Roland. 1986. "The Death of the Author." Roland Barthes, *The Rustle of Language*. Oxford: Blackwell, 49–55.

Blum, Virginia L. 1995. Hide and Seek: The Child Between Psychoanalysis and Fiction. Urbana: University of Illinois Press.

Carter, Ronald and Paul Simpson (eds). 1989. *Language, Discourse and Literature: An Introductory Reader in Discourse Stylistics*. London: Unwin Hyman.

Eagleton, Terry. 1991. *Ideology: An Introduction*. London: Verso.

Edelstein, Marilyn. 1996. "Ethics and Contemporary American Literature: Revisiting the Controversy over John Gardner's *On Moral Fiction*." *Pacific Coast Philology* 31.1: 40–53.

Foucault, Michel. 1972. *The Archaeology of Knowledge*. Trans. A. M. Sheridan Smith. London: Tavistock.

—— 1978. *The History of Sexuality, Vol. 1. An Introduction*. Trans. Robert Hurley. New York: Vintage.

—— 1981. "The Order of Discourse." *Untying the Text: A Poststructuralist Reader*. Robert Young (ed.). London: RKP.

Fowler, Roger. 1981. *Literature as Social Discourse: The Practice of Linguistic Criticism*. Bloomington and London: University of Indiana Press.

—— 1990. "The Lost Girl: Discourse and Focalization." *Rethinking Lawrence*. Keith Brown (ed.). Milton Keynes and Philadelphia: Open University Press, 53–66.

Halliday, M. A. K. 1978. *Language as Social Semiotic: The Social Interpretation of Language and Meaning*. London: Edward Arnold.

Hamburger, Henry. 1979. *Games as Models of Social Phenomena*. San Francisco: W. H. Freeman.

Hampton, Christopher. 1990. *The Ideology of the Text*. Milton Keynes and Philadelphia: Open University Press.

Hans, James S. 1981. *The Play of the World*. Amherst: University of Massachussets Press.

Hawthorn, Jeremy. 1992. *A Concise Glossary of Contemporary Literary Theory*. London: Edward Arnold.

Huizinga, Johann. 1955. *Homo Ludens: A Study of the Play Element in Culture*. Boston: Beacon Press.

Hutchinson, Peter. 1983. *Games Authors Play*. London and New York: Methuen.

Irwin, W. R. 1976. *The Game of the Impossible: A Rhetoric of Fantasy*. Urbana: University of Illinois Press.

Johnson, D. Barton. 1985. *Worlds in Regression: Some Novels of Vladimir Nabokov*. Ann Arbor: Ardis.

Kauffman, Linda. 1989. "Framing Lolita: Is there a Woman in the Text?" *Refiguring the Father: New Feminist Readings of Patriarchy*. Patricia Yeager and Beth Kowaleski-Wallace (eds). Carbondale: Southern Illinois University Press, 131–152.

Lilly, Mark. 1979. "Nabokov: Homo Ludens." *Vladimir Nabokov: A Tribute*. Peter Quennell (ed.). London: Weidenfeld and Nicolson, 88–102.

Merivale, Patricia. 1967. "The Flaunting of Artifice in Vladimir Nabokov and Jorge Luis Borges." *Wisconsin Studies* 8.2: 294–309.

Miller, David L. 1970. *Gods and Games: Toward a Theology of Play*. New York: World Publishers.

Mills, Sara. 1997. *Discourse*. London and New York: Routledge.

Morrow, Nancy. 1988. *Dreadful Games: The Play of Desire in the Nineteenth-Century Novel*. Kent, OH: Kent State University Press.

Motte, Warren. 1995. *Playtexts: Ludics in Contemporary Literature*. Lincoln and London: University of Nebraska Press.

Packman, David. 1982. *Vladimir Nabokov: The Structure of Literary Desire*. Columbia and London: University of Missouri Press.

Paglia, Camille. 1991. *Sexual Personae: Art and Decadence from Nefertiti to Emily Dickinson*. New York: Vintage.

Pifer, Ellen. 1980. *Nabokov and the Novel*. Cambridge: Harvard University Press.

Proffer, Carl R. 1978. *Keys to Lolita*. Bloomington and London: Indiana University Press.

Rampton, David. 1984. *Vladimir Nabokov: A Critical Study of the Novels*. Cambridge: Cambridge University Press.

Schneiderman, Leo. 1985. "Nabokov: Aestheticism with a Human Face, Half-Averted." *Psychoanalysis and Contemporary Thought* 8.1: 105–130.

1 THE NABOKOV–WILSON DEBATE

Alexandrov, Vladimir (ed.). 1995. *The Garland Companion to Vladimir Nabokov*. New York: Garland.

Alter, Robert. 1984. *Motives for Fiction*. Harvard University Press.

Barabtarlo, Gennady. 1993. *Aerial View*. New York: Peter Lang.

Boyd, Brian. 1991. *Vladimir Nabokov: The American Years*. Princeton University Press.

Groth, Janet. 1989. *Edmund Wilson: A Critic for Our Time.* Ohio University Press.

Nabokov, Vladimir. 1966a. *Lolita.* New York: Berkeley.

—— 1966b. *The Waltz Invention.* New York: Phaedra.

—— 1973. *Strong Opinions.* New York: McGraw-Hill.

—— 1980. *Lectures on Literature.* New York: Harcourt Brace.

—— and Edmund Wilson. 1980. *The Nabokov–Wilson Letters.* Simon Karlinsky (ed.). New York: Harper and Row.

Rorty, Richard. 1989. *Contingency, Irony, and Solidarity.* Cambridge University Press.

Wilson, Edmund. 1956. Preface to Anton Chekhov, *Peasants and Other Stories.* Edmund Wilson (ed.). New York: Doubleday, vii–xi.

—— 1972. *A Window on Russia.* New York: Farrar Straus and Giroux.

—— 1977. *Letters on Literature and Politics: 1912–1972.* Elena Wilson (ed.). New York: Farrar.

Wilson, Rosalind Baker. 1989. *Near the Magician: A Memoir of My Father, Edmund Wilson.* London: Weidenfeld and Nicolson.

2 TWO ORGAN-GRINDERS

Alexandrov, Vladimir E. (ed.). 1995. *The Garland Companion to Vladimir Nabokov.* New York and London: Garland.

Arendt, Hannah. 1979. *The Origins of Totalitarianism.* New York: Harcourt Brace.

Barta, Peter I. 1995. " 'Obscure Peregrinations': A Surreal Journey in Nabokov's 'The Visit to the Museum'." *Studia Slavica* 40: 227–234.

Boyd, Brian. 1991. *Vladimir Nabokov: The American Years.* Princeton: Princeton University Press.

Brecht, Bertolt. 1964. *Brecht on Theater.* New York: Hill and Wang.

Calvino, Italo. 1986. "Definitions of Territories: Comedy." *The Uses of Literature.* New York: Harcourt Brace, 62–64.

Clancy, Laurie. 1984. *The Novels of Vladimir Nabokov.* New York: St. Martin's.

Foster, John Burt, Jr. 1995. "*Bend Sinister.*" In Alexandrov, 25–36.

Gass, William. 1989. "Mirror, Mirror." *Fiction and the Figures of Life.* Boston: David R. Godine, 110–119.

Howe, Irving. 1992. *Politics and the Novel.* New York: Columbia University Press.

Jameson, Fredric. 1981. *The Political Unconscious.* Ithaca, New York: Cornell University Press.

Kermode, Frank. 1962. "Nabokov's *Bend Sinister.*" *Puzzles and Epiphanies.* New York: Chilmark Press, 228–234.

Maddox, Lucy. 1983. *Nabokov's Novels in English.* Athens: University of Georgia Press.

Nabokov, Vladimir. 1980. "Good Readers and Good Writers." *Lectures on Literature.* New York: Harcourt Brace, 1–6.

—— 1981 *Lectures on Russian Literature.* New York: Harcourt Brace.

—— 1989a. *Lolita.* New York: Vintage International.

—— 1989b. *Selected Letters 1940–1977.* Dmitri Nabokov and Matthew J. Bruccoli (eds). New York: Harcourt Brace.

—— 1989c. *Speak, Memory*. New York: Vintage International.

—— 1990a. *Bend Sinister*. New York: Vintage International.

—— 1990b *Strong Opinions*. New York: Vintage International.

Swift, Jonathan. 1973. *The Writings of Jonathan Swift*. Robert A. Greenberg and William B. Piper (eds). New York: W. W. Norton.

Woolf, Virginia. 1970. *The Death of the Moth and Other Essays*. New York: Harcourt Brace.

3 OKRYLYONNYY *SOGLYADATAY* – THE WINGED EAVESDROPPER

Barnstead, John A. 1986. "Nabokov, Kuzmin, Chekhov and Gogol: Systems of Reference in 'Lips to Lips'." *Studies in Russian Literature in Honor of Vsevolod Setchkarev*. Columbus: Slavica Publishers.

Benua, Aleksandr. 1990. *Moi vospominaniya*. Book 5. Moscow: Nauka.

Berberova, Nina. 1996. *Kursiv moy*. Moscow: Soglasiye.

Bethea, David M. 1995. "Nabokov and Blok." *The Garland Companion to Vladimir Nabokov*. V. Alexandrov (ed.). New York: Garland, 374–381.

Blok, Aleksandr. 1931. *O literature*. Moscow: Federatsiya.

Bogomolov, Nikolay. 1995. *Mikhail Kuzmin: Stat'i i materialy*. Moscow: Novoe literaturnoe obozrenie.

—— and Malmstad, John. 1996. *Mikhail Kuzmin: iskusstvo, zhizn', epokha*. Moscow: Novoe literaturnoe obozrenie.

Ellis, Havelock. 1936. *Studies in the Psychology of Sex*. New York: Random House.

Engelstein, Laura. 1994. *The Keys to Happiness*. Ithaca and London: Cornell University Press.

Field, Andrew. 1963. "Notes on a Decadent Prose." *The Russian Review* 20: 300.

—— 1987. *VN: The Life and Art of Vladimir Nabokov*. London: Macdonald Queen Anne Press.

Freud, Sigmund. 1991. "On Narcissism: An Introduction." *Freud's "On Narcissism: An Introduction."* Joseph Sadler, Ethel Spector Person, and Peter Fonagy (eds). New Haven and London: Yale University Press, 3–32.

Gillis, Donald C. 1978. "The Platonic Theme in Kuzmin's *Wings*." *SEEJ* 22: 336–347.

Greene, Thomas M. 1982. *The Light in Troy*. New Haven and London: Yale University Press.

Harer, Klaus. 1992. "*Kryl'ja* M.A. Kuzmina kak primer 'prekrasnoj legkosti'." *Amour et erotisme dans la littérature russe du XXe siecle*. Leonid Heller (ed.). *Slavica Helvetica* 41: 45–56.

Ivanov, Georgiy. 1994. *Sobranie sochineniy v trekh tomakh*. Vol. 3. Moscow: Soglasie.

Johnson, D. Barton. 1985. "The Books Reflected in Nabokov's *Eye*." *SEEJ* 29.4: 393–404.

Khodasevich, V. F. 1937. "O Sirine." *Vozrozhdenie* 13 Feb.: 4065.

—— 1996. "Konets Renaty." *Nekropol'. Literatura I vlast'. Pis'ma B.A. Sadovskomu*. Moscow: SS, 19–29.

Kohut, Heinz. 1978. *The Search for the Self*. Vol. 2. New York: International Universities Press.

Kuzmin, Mikhail. 1980. *Selected Prose and Poetry*. Michael Green (ed. and trans.). Ann Arbor: Ardis.

—— 1986. *The Diary (1905–1906)*. publ. George Cheron. *Wiener Slawistischer Almanach* 17.

—— 1994. *Podzemnyye ruch'i: Romany, povesti, rasskazy*. Sankt-Peterburg: Severo-Zapad.

Malmstad, John E. 1977. "Mixail Kuzmin: A Chronicle of His Life and Times." M. A. Kuzmin, *Sobranie stikhov*. J. Malmstad and Vladimir Markov (eds). München: Wilhelm Fink Verlag, 3: 7–319.

—— 1989. "Letter of M. A. Kuzmin to Ja. N. Blox." *Studies in the Life and Works of Mixail Kuzmin*. John Malmstad (ed.). *Wiener Slawistischer Almanach* 24: 173–185.

Markov, Vladimir. 1977. "Poeziya Mikhaila Kuzmina." M. A. Kuzmin, *Sobranie stikhov*. John Malmstad and Vladimir Markov (eds). München: Wilhelm Fink Verlag, 3: 321–426.

—— 1984. "Beseda o proze Kuzmina." M. A. Kuzmin, *Proza (pervaya kniga rasskazov)*. Vladimir Markov (ed.). Berkeley: Berkeley Slavic Specialities, vii–xviii.

Matich, Olga. 1994. "The Symbolist Meaning of Love: Theory and Practice." *Creating Life. The Aesthetic Utopia of Russian Modernism*. Irina Paperno and Joan Delaney Grossman (eds). Stanford: Stanford University Press, 24–50.

Nabokov, Vladimir. 1966. *The Eye*. London: Weidenfeld and Nicolson.

—— 1973. *Strong Opinions*. New York: McGraw Hill.

—— 1979. *Stikhi*. Ann Arbor: Ardis.

—— 1989. *Pnin*. New York: Vintage.

—— 1991. *The Gift*. New York: Vintage.

Paperno, Irina. 1989. "Dvoynichestvo i lyubovnyy treugol'nik: poeticheskiy mif Kuzmina i ego pushkinskaya proektsiya." *Studies in the Life and Works of Mixail Kuzmin*. John Malmstad (ed.). *Wiener Slawistischer Almanach* 24, 57–83.

Plato. 1993. *The Symposium and The Phaedrus: Plato's Erotic Dialogues*. Trans. with introduction and commentaries by William S. Cobb. Albany: State University of New York Press.

Rank, Otto. 1971. *The Double. A Psychoanalytic Study*. Trans. and edited by Harry Tucker, Jr. Chapel Hill: University of North Carolina Press.

Schindler, Frantz. 1992. "Otrazhenie gomoseksual'nogo opyta v *Kryl'jax* M. Kuzmina." *Amour et erotisme dans la littérature russe du XXe siecle*. Leonid Heller (ed.). Slavica Helvetica 41: 57–63.

Shakhovskaya, Zinaida. 1991. *V poiskakh Nabokova. Otrazheniya*. Moscow: Kniga.

Shmakov, Gennadii. 1972. "Blok i Kuzmin (Novye materialy)." *Blokovskii sbornik* 2. Tartu: Tartuskiy gosudarstvennyy universitet: 341–364.

—— 1982. Foreword "Dva Kaliostro." M. Kuzmin, *Chudesnaya zhizn' Iosifa Bal'zamo grafa Kaliostro*. New York: Russica Publishers.

Sontag, Susan. 1977. *Illness as Metaphor*. New York: Farrar, Straus and Giroux.

Terapiano, Yuriy. 1933. "Chelovek 30–kh godov." *Chisla* 7–8. Paris: Société Nouvelle d'Éditions Franco-Slaves, 210–212.

Timofeyev, A. G. 1993. "M. Kuzmin v polemike s F.M. Dostoevskim i A.P.

Chekhovym (*Kryl'ya*)." *Serebryanyi vek v Rossii*. Vyach. Vs. Ivanov, V. N. Toporov, and T. V. Tsiv'yan (eds). Moscow: Radiks, 211–221.

4 GETTING ONE PAST THE GOALKEEPER

Boyd, Brian. 1990. *Vladimir Nabokov: The Russian Years*. Princeton: Princeton University Press.

Connolly, Julian W. 1992. *Nabokov's Early Fiction: Patterns of Self and Other*. Cambridge: Cambridge University Press.

Diment, Galya. 1995. "Uncollected Critical Writings." *The Garland Companion to Nabokov*. V. Alexandrov (ed.). New York and London: Garland, 733–740.

Elms, Alan C. 1989. "Cloud, castle, claustrum: Nabokov as a Freudian in spite of himself." *Russian Literature and Psychoanalysis*. Daniel Rancour-Laferrière (ed.). Amsterdam: John Benjamins, 358–368.

Field, Andrew. 1967. *Nabokov: His Life in Art*. Boston and Toronto: Little, Brown.

Green, Geoffrey. 1988. *Freud and Nabokov*. Lincoln and London: University of Nebraska Press.

—— 1989. "Splitting of the Ego: Freudian Doubles, Nabokovian Doubles." *Russian Literature and Psychoanalysis*. Daniel Rancour-Laferrière (ed.). Amsterdam: John Benjamins, 369–379.

Hutchinson, Peter. 1983. *Games Authors Play*. London and New York: Methuen.

Hyde, G. M. 1977. *Vladimir Nabokov: America's Russian Novelist*. London: Marion Boyars.

Kimmel, Michael S. 1994. "Masculinity as Homophobia." *Theorizing Masculinities*. Harry Brod and Michael S. Kaufman (eds). London: SAGE, 119–141.

Morrow, Nancy. 1988. *Dreadful Games: The Play of Desire in the Nineteenth-Century Novel*. Kent, OH: Kent State University Press.

Nabokov. Vladimir. 1955. *Lolita*. New York: Putnam's.

—— 1962. *Pale Fire*. New York: Putnam's.

—— 1966a. *Despair*. New York: Putnam's.

—— 1966b. *Speak, Memory*. New York: Putnam's.

—— 1971. "Rowe's Symbols." *New York Review of Books* Oct. 7.

—— 1989a. *King, Queen, Knave*. New York: Vintage.

—— 1989b. *Laughter in the Dark*. New York: Vintage.

—— 1990. *Bend Sinister*. New York: Vintage.

—— 1991. *Glory*. New York: Vintage.

Rowe, William W. 1971. *Nabokov's Deceptive World*. New York: New York University Press.

Sedgwick, Eve Kosofsky. 1988. *Between Men: English Literature and Male Homosocial Desire*. New York: Columbia University Press.

Shute, J. P. 1984. "Nabokov and Freud: The Interplay of Power." *Modern Fiction Studies* 30.4: 637–650.

Toker, Leona. 1989. *Nabokov: The Mystery of Literary Structures*. Ithaca: Cornell University Press.

Welsen, Peter. 1989. "Charles Kinbote's Psychosis – a Key to Vladimir Nabokov's *Pale Fire*." *Russian Literature and Psychoanalysis*. Daniel Rancour-Laferrière (ed.). Amsterdam: John Benjamins, 381–400.

5 THE CREWCUT AS HOMOEROTIC DISCOURSE IN NABOKOV'S *PALE FIRE*

Barthes, Roland. 1957. *Mythologies*. Paris: Seuil.

Coover, Robert. 1982. *Spanking the Maid*. New York: Grove Press.

Edwards, Catherine. 1993. *The Politics of Immorality in Ancient Rome*. Cambridge: Cambridge University Press.

Foucault, Michel. 1978. *The History of Sexuality*. Vol. 1. Trans. Robert Hurley. New York: Vintage.

—— 1985. *The Use of Pleasure*. Vol. 2 of *The History of Sexuality*. Trans. Robert Hurley. New York: Vintage.

Fussel, Samuel Wilson. 1991. *Muscle: Confessions of an Unlikely Bodybuilder*. New York: Avon.

Gass, William. 1978. "Upright Among Staring Fish." *The World Within the Word*. Boston: Nonpareil, 203–207.

Halperin, David. 1990. *One Hundred Years of Homosexuality and Other Essays on Greek Love*. New York: Routledge.

—— 1995. *Saint Foucault: An Essay in Gay Hagiography*. New York: Oxford University Press.

Hyde, G. M. 1977. *Vladimir Nabokov: America's Russian Novelist*. London: Marion Boyars.

Irigaray, Luce. 1985. "Any Theory of the 'Subject' Has Already Been Appropriated by the 'Masculine'." *Speculum of the Other Woman*. Trans. Gillian C. Gill. Ithaca: Cornell University Press, 133–242.

Jameson, Fredric. 1981. *The Political Unconscious: Narrative as a Socially Symbolic Act*. Ithaca: Cornell University Press.

—— 1985. "Baudelaire as Modernist and Postmodernist." *Lyric Poetry: Beyond New Criticism*. Chaviva Hosek and Patricia Parker (eds). Ithaca: Cornell University Press.

Johnson, D. Barton. 1979. "The Index of Refraction in Nabokov's *Pale Fire*." *Russian Literature Triquarterly* 16: 33–49.

Juvenal. 1967. *The Sixteen Satires*. Trans. Peter Green. New York: Penguin.

Lacan, Jacques. 1975. *Encore. Le séminaire de Jacques Lacan*, XX. Jacques-Alain Miller (ed.). Paris: Seuil.

Larmour, David H. J. 1990a. "Nabokov *Philomelus*: The Classical Allusions in *Lolita*." *Classical and Modern Literature* 10: 143–151.

—— 1990b. "The Classical Allusions in *Bend Sinister*." *RLT* 24: 163–172.

Lévi-Strauss, Claude. 1971. *Tristes Tropiques*. Trans. John Russell. New York: Atheneum.

Meyer, Priscilla. 1988. *Find What the Sailor Has Hidden: Vladimir Nabokov's Pale Fire*. Middletown, CN: Wesleyan University Press.

Murgatroyd, Paul. 1991. *Tibullus: Elegies 1*. Bristol: Bristol Classical Press.

Nabokov, Vladimir. 1962. *Pale Fire*. New York: Putnam's.

Petronius. 1959. *Satyricon*. Trans. William Arrowsmith. Ann Arbor: University of Michigan Press.

Platter, Chuck. 1993. "Depilation in Athenian Old Comedy." Foucault's *History of Sexuality*: Revisions and Responses. Lubbock, TX, 24 Apr.

—— 1996. "Longhairs Get the Gnat: *Comica Adespota* 12." *Classical World* 89.3: 207–212.

Sedgwick, Eve Kosofsky. 1990. *Epistemology of the Closet*. Berkeley: University of California Press.

Timbuk 3. 1986. "Hairstyles and Attitudes." *Greetings from Timbuk 3*. International Record Syndicate, 5739.

Walton, Jean. 1994. "Dissenting in an Age of Frenzied Heterosexualism: Kinbote's Transparent Closet in Nabokov's *Pale Fire*." *College Literature* 21.1: 89–104.

6 SEEING THROUGH HUMBERT

Alexandrov, Vladimir E. 1991. "*Lolita*." *Nabokov's Other World*. Princeton: Princeton University Press, 160–186.

Appel, Alfred (ed). 1991. *The Annotated Lolita*. New York: Random House.

Barnes, J. C. M. 1959. "*Lolita* – Technically Pornographic." *Books and Bookmen* 4 Mar.

Barthes, Roland. 1977. "The Death of the Author." *Image-Music-Text*. Trans. Stephen Heath. New York: Hill & Wang, 141–148.

Booth, Wayne C. 1983. *The Rhetoric of Fiction*. Second edn. Chicago: University of Chicago Press.

Donleavy, J. P. 1958. *The Ginger Man*. Paris: Olympia.

Eckley, Grace. 1985. "Game Playing and Playacting." *Children's Lore in Finnegans Wake*. Syracuse: Syracuse University Press, 130–180.

Gennette, Gérard. 1972. "Discours du récit." *Figures III*. Trans. Jane E. Lewin as *Narrative Discourse. An Essay in Method*. Ithaca: Cornell University Press.

Joyce, James. 1939. *Finnegans Wake*. New York: Penguin.

Kauffman, Linda. 1989. "Framing Lolita: Is There A Woman in The Text?" *Refiguring the Father: New Feminist Readings of Patriarchy*. Patricia Yaeger and Beth Kowaleski-Wallace (eds). Carbondale: Southern Illinois University Press, 131–152.

—— 1992. "Framing Lolita: Is There A Woman in The Text?" *Special Delivery: Epistolary Modes in Modern Fiction*. Chicago: University of Chicago Press, 53–79.

MacKinnon, Catharine A. 1983. "Feminism, Marxism, Method, and the State: An Agenda for Theory." *The Signs Reader. Women, Gender and Scholarship*. Elizabeth and Emily K. Abel (eds). Chicago: University of Chicago Press.

—— 1993. *Only Words*. Cambridge: Harvard University Press.

McNeely, Trevor. 1989. "'Lo' and Behold: Solving the *Lolita* Riddle." *Studies in the Novel* 21.2: 182–199.

Morrison, Toni. 1970. *The Bluest Eye*. New York: Washington Square Press.

Nabokov, Vladimir. 1989. *Lolita*. New York: Vintage.

—— and Edmund Wilson. 1980. *The Nabokov–Wilson Letters: Correspondence Between Vladimir Nabokov and Edmund Wilson, 1940–1971*. Simon Karlinsky (ed.). New York: Harper.

Page, Norman (ed). 1982. *Nabokov: The Critical Heritage*. London: Routledge.

Paglia, Camille. 1991. *Sexual Personae. Art and Decadence from Nefertiti to Emily Dickinson*. New York: Vintage.

Porter, Robert. 1985. *The Mackeson Book of Averages*. London: Deutsch.

Proffer, Carl R. 1968. *Keys to Lolita*. Bloomington: Indiana University Press.

Rampton, David. 1984. *Vladimir Nabokov: A Critical Study of the Novels*. Cambridge: Cambridge University Press.

Ricks, Christopher. 1987. "Lies." *The Force of Poetry*. New York: Oxford University Press, 369–391.

Riquelme, John Paul. 1983. *Teller and Tale in Joyce's Fiction. Oscillating Perspectives*. Baltimore: Johns Hopkins University Press.

Roth, Philip. 1967. *Portnoy's Complaint*. New York: Random House.

Schuman, Samuel (ed.). 1979. *Vladimir Nabokov: A Reference Guide*. Boston: G. K. Hall.

Tammi, Pekka. 1985. *Problems of Nabokov's Poetics: A Narratological Analysis*. Helsinki: Suomalainen Tiedeakatemia.

Trilling, Lionel. 1958. "The Last Lover: Vladimir Nabokov's *Lolita*." *Encounter* 11: 9–19.

Updike, John. 1960. *Rabbit, Run*. New York: Knopf.

7 DISCOURSE, IDEOLOGY, AND HEGEMONY

Alexandrov, Vladimir E. 1991. *Nabokov's Otherworld*. Princeton: Princeton University Press.

Appel, Alfred. 1967. "Lolita: The Springboard of Parody." *Nabokov: The Man and His Work*. L. S. Dembo (ed.). Madison: University of Wisconsin Press, 106–143. Rpt. in *Vladimir Nabokov's Lolita: Modern Critical Interpretations*. Harold Bloom (ed.). New York: Chelsea House, 1987, 35–51.

—— 1991. *The Annotated Lolita*. Rev. edn. New York: Vintage.

Bader, Julia. 1972. *Crystal Land: Artifice in Nabokov's English Novels*. Berkeley: University of California Press, 57–81.

Bakhtin, M. M. 1981. "Discourse in the Novel." *The Dialogic Imagination: Four Essays by M. M. Bakhtin*. Trans. Caryl Emerson and Michael Holquist. Michael Holquist (ed.). Austin: University of Texas Press, 259–422.

The Blue Angel. Dir. Josef von Sternberg, 1930.

Booth, Wayne C. 1983. *The Rhetoric of Fiction*. 2nd edn. Chicago: University of Chicago Press.

Brand, Dana. 1987. "The Interaction of Aestheticism and American Consumer Culture in Nabokov's *Lolita*." *Modern Language Studies* 17.2: 14–21.

Bullock, Richard H. 1984. "Humbert the Character, Humbert the Writer: Artifice, Reality, and Art in *Lolita*." *Philological Quarterly* 63.2: 187–204.

Butler, Steven H. 1986. "*Lolita* and the Modern Experience of Beauty." *Studies in the Novel* 18.4: 427–440.

Centerwall, Brandon S. 1990. "Hiding in Plain Sight: Nabokov and Pedophilia." *Texas Studies in Literature and Language* 32.3: 468–484.

Corrigan, Maureen. 1992. *All Things Considered*. National Public Radio. WCBE, Columbus, Ohio. 21 Sept.

Fetterley, Judith. 1978. *The Resisting Reader: A Feminist Approach to American Fiction*. Bloomington: Indiana University Press.

Field, Andrew. 1967. *Nabokov: His Life in Art*. Boston: Little, Brown.

Fowler, Douglas. 1974. *Reading Nabokov*. Ithaca: Cornell University Press.

Frosch, Thomas R. 1982. "Parody and Authenticity in *Lolita*." *Nabokov's Fifth*

Arc. J. E. Rivers and Charles Nicol (eds). Austin: University of Texas Press. Rpt. in *Vladimir Nabokov: Modern Critical Views.* Harold Bloom (ed.). New York: Chelsea House, 1987, 127–143.

Giblett, Rodney. 1989. "Writing Sexuality, Reading Pleasure." *Paragraph* 12.3: 229–238.

Goldner, Virginia. 1991. Introduction to Elsa Jones 1991, vii–x.

Green, Martin. 1966. "Tolstoy and Nabokov: The Morality of *Lolita.*" *Kenyon Review* 28.3: 352–377. Rpt. in *Vladimir Nabokov's Lolita: Modern Critical Interpretations.* Harold Bloom (ed.). New York: Chelsea House, 1987, 13–33.

Gullette, Margaret Morganroth. 1984. "The Exile of Adulthood: Pedophilia in the Midlife Novel." *Novel* 17.3: 215–322.

Haegert, John. 1985. "Artist in Exile: The Americanization of Humbert Humbert." *English Literary History* 52.3: 777–794.

Jones, Elsa. 1991. *Working with Adult Survivors of Child Sexual Abuse.* London: Karnack Books.

Jong, Erica. 1988. "Time Has Been Kind to the Nymphet: *Lolita* 30 Years Later." *New York Times Book Review* 5 June: 3: 46–47.

Kauffman, Linda. 1993. "Framing Lolita: Is There a Woman in the Text?" *Major Literary Characters: Lolita.* Harold Bloom (ed.). New York: Chelsea House, 149–168.

"Lethal Lolita." *People.* October 12, 1992.

Levine, Robert T. 1979. "'My Ultraviolet Darling': The Loss of Lolita's Childhood." *Modern Fiction Studies* 25.3: 471–479.

"Lola." The Kinks. *Lola versus Powerman and the Money-go-round.* Reprise Records, 1970.

Lolita. Dir. Stanley Kubrick. With James Mason, Shelley Winters, Peter Sellers, and Sue Lyon. MGM, 1962.

McNeely, Trevor. 1989. "'Lo' and Behold: Solving the *Lolita* Riddle." *Studies in the Novel* 21.8: 182–199. Rpt. in *Major Literary Characters: Lolita.* Harold Bloom (ed.). Chelsea House: New York, 1993.

Maddox, Lucy B. 1983. *Nabokov's Novels in English.* Athens: University of Georgia Press.

Nabokov, Vladimir. 1977. *Lolita.* New York: Berkeley Books.

O'Connor, Katherine Tiernan. 1989. "Rereading *Lolita*, Reconsidering Nabokov's Relationship with Dostoevskij." *Slavic and Eastern European Journal* 33.1: 64–77.

Packman, David. 1982. *Vladimir Nabokov: The Structure of Literary Desire.* Columbia: University of Missouri Press.

Parker, Dorothy. 1993. "Sex – Without the Asterisks." *Major Literary Characters: Lolita.* Harold Bloom (ed.). Chelsea House: New York, 9–10. Rpt. of same in *Esquire* 50.4 (1958): 103.

Phelan, James. 1981. *Worlds from Words: A Theory of Language in Fiction.* Chicago: University of Chicago Press.

—— 1989. *Reading People, Reading Plots: Character, Progression, and the Interpretation of Narrative.* Chicago: University of Chicago Press.

Pifer, Ellen 1989. "Shades of Love: Nabokov's Intimations of Immortality." *Kenyon Review* ns 11.1: 75–86.

Rabinowitz, Peter J. 1987. *Before Reading: Narrative Conventions and the Politics of Interpretation.* Ithaca: Cornell University Press.

Rampton, David. 1984. "Lolita." *Vladimir Nabokov: A Critical Study of the Novels*. Cambridge: Cambridge University Press, 101–121.

"Stark." *The American Heritage Dictionary of the English Language*. 1992 edn.

—— *Webster's New Collegiate Dictionary*. 1981 edn.

Tamir-Ghez, Nomi. 1979. "The Art of Persuasion in Nabokov's *Lolita*." *Poetics Today* 1.1–2: 65–83.

Toker, Leona. 1989. *Nabokov: The Mystery of Literary Structures*. Ithaca: Cornell University Press.

Trilling, Lionel. 1958. "The Last Lover: Vladimir Nabokov's *Lolita*." *Encounter* 11.4: 9–19.

8 NABOKOV AND THE SIXTIES

Appel, Alfred and Charles Newman (eds). 1970. *Nabokov: Criticism, Reminiscences, Translations, and Tributes*. Evanston: Northwestern University Press.

Barth, John. 1967. "The Literature of Exhaustion." *The Atlantic* August 1967: 29–34.

Boyd, Brian. 1990. *Vladimir Nabokov: The Russian Years*. Princeton: Princeton University Press.

—— 1991. *Vladimir Nabokov: The American Years*. Princeton: Princeton University Press.

Couturier, Maurice. 1993. "Nabokov in Postmodern Land." *Critique* 34.4: 247–260.

Field, Andrew. 1967. *Nabokov: His Life in Art*. Boston: Little, Brown.

Hackett, Alice Payne and James Burke. 1977. *80 Years of Best Sellers, 1895–1975*. New York: R. R. Bowker.

Juliar, Michael. 1986. *Vladimir Nabokov: A Descriptive Bibliography*. New York: Garland.

McCarthy, Mary. 1962. "A Bolt from the Blue." In Page (ed.), 124–136.

McElroy, Joseph. 1973. "The N Factor." *Saturday Review of the Arts* 6 January: 34–35.

Mailer, Norman. 1971. *The Prisoner of Sex*. Boston: Little, Brown.

Nabokov, Vladimir. 1973. *Strong Opinions*. New York: McGraw-Hill.

—— 1989. *Selected Letters 1940–1977*. Dmitri Nabokov and Matthew J. Bruccoli (eds). New York: Harcourt, Brace.

Oates, Joyce Carol. 1973. "A Personal View of Nabokov." *Saturday Review of the Arts* 6 January: 36–37.

Page, Norman (ed.). 1982. *Nabokov: The Critical Heritage*. London: Routledge & Kegan Paul.

Scholes, Robert. 1967. *The Fabulators*. New York: Oxford University Press.

Schuman, Samuel. 1979. *Vladimir Nabokov: A Reference Guide*. Boston: G. K. Hall.

Slavitt, David R. 1962. "Lolita's Creator – Author Nabokov, a 'Cosmic Joker'." *Newsweek* 25 June: 51–54.

Stark, John. 1974. *The Literature of Exhaustion: Borges, Nabokov, Barth*. Durham: Duke University Press.

Steiner, George. 1970. "Extraterritorial." In Appel and Newman (eds), 119–127.

Tanner, Tony. 1971. *City of Words: American Fiction 1950–1970*. London: Jonathan Cape.

White, Edmund. 1973. "The Esthetics of Bliss." *Saturday Review of the Arts* 6 January: 33–34.

Zverev, Aleksei. 1995. "Nabokov, Updike, and American Literature." *The Garland Companion to Vladimir Nabokov*. Vladimir Alexandrov (ed.). New York: Garland.

9 VLADIMIR NABOKOV AND POPULAR CULTURE

Appel, Alfred. 1974. *Nabokov's Dark Cinema*. New York: Oxford University Press.

Bellow, Saul. 1994. *It All Adds Up: From the Dim Past to the Uncertain Future*. New York: Viking.

Boyd, Brian. 1991. *Vladimir Nabokov: The American Years*. Princeton: Princeton University Press.

Fishwick, Marshall W. 1985. *Seven Pillars of Popular Culture*. Westport: Greenwood.

Gary, Paul. 1993. "The Assault on Freud." *Time* November 2: 46–51.

Gass, William H. 1973. "Upright Among Staring Fish." *The Saturday Review of The Arts* January: 35–36.

Hammell, Chuck. 1994. "A New Lo; or Everybody Into the Meme Pool." *Holy Temple of Mass Consumption*, htomc 026.gz http://math.umbc.edu/~gseidman/HToMC

Johnson, Brian D. 1993. "A Director's Obsession." *Maclean's* September 13: 39.

McElroy, Joseph. 1973. "The N Factor." *The Saturday Review of the Arts* January: 34–35.

Marvel, Bill. 1994. "Political Correctness: Battling through the 90's." *Dallas Morning News* April 24.

Nabokov, Vladimir. 1970. *Poems and Problems*. New York: McGraw-Hill.

—— 1973. *Strong Opinions*. New York: McGraw-Hill.

Paglia, Camille. 1994. "Lolita Unclothed." *Vamps & Tramps: New Essays*. New York: Vintage.

Pattison, Robert. 1987. *The Triumph of Vulgarity: Rock Music in the Mirror of Romanticism*. New York: Oxford University Press.

Playboy Interviews. 1967. Chicago: Playboy Press.

Readers' Guide to Periodical Literature. 1901–. New York: H. W. Wilson.

Safire, William. 1994. "On Language: Ragtag Modalities." *New York Times Magazine* October 9: 22.

Schuman, Samuel. 1975. *Nation*. May 31: 665.

Smith, Joan. 1994. *The Guardian*. September 24.

Stegner, Page. 1966. *Escape Into Aesthetics; The Art of Vladimir Nabokov*. New York: Dial.

Whissen, Thomas R. 1992. *Classic Cult Fiction: A Companion to Popular Cult Literature*. New York: Greenwood.

White, Edmund. 1973. "The Esthetics of Bliss." *Saturday Review of the Arts* January: 33–34.

—— 1994. "Nabokov: Beyond Parody." *The Burning Library*. David Bergman (ed.). New York: A. A. Knopf.

Wood, Michael. 1994. *The Magician's Doubts: Nabokov and the Risks of Fiction*. London: Chatto & Windus.

Žižek, Slavoj. 1992. *Everything You Always Wanted To Know About Lacan But Were Afraid to Ask Hitchcock*. London: Verso.

INDEX